GEORGE W. TRUETT LIBRARY

Volume III

SOME VITAL QUESTIONS

THE INSPIRATION OF IDEALS

BAKER BOOK HOUSE
Grand Rapids, Michigan

SOME VITAL QUESTIONS

GEORGE W. TRUETT, D.D., LL.D.

Edited by
Powhatan W. James, Th.D., D.D.

Copyright 1946
by the William B. Eerdmans Publishing House

Reprinted 1980 by Baker Book House
with the permission of the copyright holder

FOUR-VOLUME SET
ISBN: 0-8010-8854-2

PHOTOLITHOPRINTED BY CUSHING - MALLOY, INC.
ANN ARBOR, MICHIGAN, UNITED STATES OF AMERICA

DEDICATION

This and subsequent volumes
of sermons and addresses
by Dr. George W. Truett
are dedicated to
his beloved
First Baptist Church Church, Dallas, Texas
where most of them
were delivered

FOREWORD

DR. GEORGE W. TRUETT rarely ever personally reduced his sermons to manuscript form. As a rule he made an outline of his sermon on the back of an envelope. This outline he studied carefully beforehand but never consulted during delivery of the sermon.

Hundreds of his sermons were voluntarily taken down in shorthand and from the radio, and later typed by various people, who were not always expert at shorthand or at typing. The result was manuscripts which Dr. Truett seldom ever saw.

As a matter of fact, it was an exceedingly difficult matter to report Dr. Truett's sermons. He spoke very rapidly. Repetition, with variations, was his favorite method of emphasis. His major concern was to reach the minds, the hearts, the consciences, and the wills of his auditors with the impact of truth.

The public often wondered why more of Dr. Truett's sermons were not published during his lifetime. The simple reason was that he was such a busy man that he could not take the time to prepare for publication the very imperfect manuscripts of his sermons. He well knew that even a true manuscript of the spoken word usually needs careful editing before it appears on the printed page.

Therefore, by legal document, Dr. Truett, some months before his death, gave exclusive rights to his biographer, Powhatan W. James, and his daughter, Jessie Truett James, to copyright and publish such sermons and addresses as were available. Pursuant to this responsible assignment, the manuscripts of the Truett sermons and addresses are being assembled with a view to their publication in a series of volumes.

Some Vital Questions is Volume I of the Truett Memorial Series. Readers will note that the full setting of the occasion on which the particular message was delivered has been preserved in most instances. Especially has this been true of the messages for New Year, Easter, Stewardship Day, and Christmas.

It is felt by a host of Dr. Truett's friends that more of his sermons should be made available to the world in book form. To meet this desire, and because they produced such blessed spiritual results when they were delivered by him, they are now published with the earnest prayer that they may bless their readers somewhat as they blessed their hearers in the days that are gone.

Appreciation is due to Dr. Louie D. Newton, Pastor of the Druid Hills Baptist Church, Atlanta, Georgia and Honorary Secretary of the Baptist World Alliance, for his biographical sketch, "George W. Truett: Peerless Preacher," which originally appeared in the *Baptist Training Union Magazine*, Nashville, Tennessee, in slightly different form.

POWHATAN W. JAMES

PRESIDENT'S OFFICE
BETHEL WOMAN'S COLLEGE
HOPKINSVILLE, KY.

BIOGRAPHICAL SKETCH

George W. Truett: Peerless Preacher

STANDING one morning at dawn, I got my first view of Mont Blanc, highest peak in the Alps. Never shall I forget that impression — an impression of grandeur and majesty and beauty. Someone asked me to describe my impression of Mont Blanc, and I remember the feeling of utter helplessness and inadequacy which came over me. I had to say that one must see Mont Blanc to understand its meaning.

Similarly, to write about Dr. George W. Truett, I find my heart overcome with a sense of utter inadequacy, and I must say again that one would have to see and hear Dr. Truett to understand the grandeur and majesty and beauty of his life.

A Glance at His Boyhood

Born May 6, 1867, the son of Charles Levi and Mary Kimsey Truett, in the little house on a small farm in Clay County, North Carolina, near the village of Hayesville, George W. Truett was the seventh child in a happy family of eight children. Blessed with a strong body, he increased daily in physical strength, working with his father and brothers on the farm and participating in outdoor sports in that lovely mountain country.

Taught daily by his saintly father and mother from the open Bible and led by them to lift up his eyes unto the hills, whence cometh our strength — unto the Lord who hath made heaven and earth, he also grew in the knowledge of the Lord.

He attended the Haysville Academy, from 1875 to 1885, and then began teaching school at Crooked Creek schoolhouse in

Some Vital Questions

Towns County, Georgia. In this one-roomed schoolhouse he taught two three-month sessions. In his nineteenth year he was converted and joined the church, though Dr. Truett tells in the book by Dr. Powhatan James that at the early age of six years he was deeply convicted and again when he was eleven. But it was not until the meeting in 1886, when J. G. Pulliam was assisting J. G. Mashburn in a meeting at Hayesville and Mr. Pulliam preached from the text, "The just shall live by faith: but if any man draw back, my soul shall have no pleasure in him," that Dr. Truett finally yielded to the Holy Spirit and accepted Jesus Christ as his Saviour and Lord.

Hiawassee

Nestled in the Blue Ridge Mountains, four miles south of the North Carolina state line, is the little Georgia village known as Hiawassee.

Following Dr. Truett's brief term of teaching at Crooked Creek schoolhouse, he was invited by his cousin, Dr. F. C. McConnell, to come to Hiawassee and discuss with the people of that community the idea of establishing a school. The conferences ended with the unanimous purpose to start the school, and in January, 1887, Hiawassee Academy was founded. The first session was conducted in the courthouse at Hiawassee with Dr. Truett as the principal. The school grew rapidly, and by 1889, when he went with his parents to Texas, the enrolment had grown to three hundred. Included in the student body were many aspiring young men, including twenty-three young preachers and fifty-one public school teachers. The atmosphere of that school was distinctly spiritual and it is remembered as one of the shining examples of true Christian education.

The Truetts Turn to Texas

At the Georgia Baptist Convention in 1888, in Marietta, Georgia, Dr. F. C. McConnell, who was making a speech on

BIOGRAPHICAL SKETCH

the work of the Home Mission Board in its mountain school program, called young George Truett from the back seat of the Cobb County courthouse to the platform and coaxed him into making his first public speech. That speech thrilled the Georgia Baptist Convention, and several men arose to offer to pay young Truett's way through Mercer University — the dream of his life. But it was not to be. God had another plan — a plan revealed in the decision of Dr. Truett's parents to move to Texas in 1889.

Arriving in Texas in the summer of 1889, the Truetts settled in Grayson County, near the town of Whitewright, and immediately identified themselves with the church at Whitewright. In the summer of 1890, at the Saturday conference of the church, a deacon arose and moved that George Truett be ordained to the full work of the gospel ministry. Dr. Truett tells in his own words, as quoted by Dr. James, how he struggled through the long hours of Saturday afternoon and evening, at last yielding himself to the call of the Holy Spirit to preach the gospel.

Presently, Dr. B. H. Carroll asked Dr. Truett to join him in the effort to raise $92,000 to pay the debt on Baylor University; it was during that campaign, that young Truett, traveling with the honored and beloved Dr. Carroll, discovered Texas and Texas discovered Truett. The campaign was a great success, and upon its conclusion, young Truett entered Baylor University in 1893, graduating in 1897. Not long after his graduation, he was elected president of Baylor, but he declined, stating that God had given him the shepherd heart, and he could not entertain the thought of leaving the pastorate.

During his student life at Baylor he had accepted the pastorate of the East Waco Baptist Church, and it was Dr. Truett's purpose to devote his life to that pleasant field. He had married Josephine Jenkins, June 28, 1894, and they were very happy in their work with the East Waco Church.

Some Vital Questions

The First Church, Dallas

Within a few days after his graduation from Baylor, a committee from the First Church, Dallas, called on him to ask if he would accept the pastorate of that church. He demurred, declaring his joy in the prospect of devoting his life to the work at the East Waco Church, but the committee would not be denied. They asked him to pray, even as they promised that they would continue to pray, and in September, 1897, Dr. and Mrs. Truett entered upon their ministry in Dallas.

He had many invitations to other pastorates in this and foreign countries, but he never once gave them serious consideration. He knew that he was in God's will, and he would not entertain the suggestion of human judgment as against the will of God.

The church grew Sunday by Sunday, becoming the largest Baptist church in the world both in membership and in gifts. Its influence has reached the farthermost rim of the earth. Steadily expanding the physical equipment until it now covers a solid block in downtown Dallas, Dr. Truett held the church to the lofty ideal of giving as much to missions as was used for local expenses. Often the church gave far more to denominational causes than for local expenses.

Dr. Truett devoted at least one Sunday each month throughout all his years at Dallas in service to other churches and to the denomination at large. He held several evangelistic meetings in other churches each year, and he nearly always conducted his own meetings usually in the month of April.

His ministry at First Church, Dallas, continued unbroken from September, 1897 to his death, July 7, 1944.

Peerless Preacher

I say without hesitation that Dr. Truett was the most effective preacher I ever heard and the most inspiring Christian I ever knew.

I heard him preach on the steps of the national capitol in 1920. I heard him later in London, in Stockholm, in Paris, in Berlin, in Jerusalem, in Toronto, in Dallas, in Atlanta, and in numerous other world centers. He was always the peerless preacher. I like to think of Dr. Truett in terms of the quatrain he so often quoted:

> Happy if with my latest breath
> I may but speak his name;
> Preach Him to all, and gasp in death,
> "Behold, behold, the Lamb!"
> — CHARLES WESLEY.

He was the peerless preacher because he preached Christ crucified. Blessed beyond measure with voice and personality and charm of expression, Dr. Truett held faithfully to the central theme of Christ crucified, the power of God, and the wisdom of God.

It seems to me that the explanation of Dr. Truett's life is found in four short but mighty words: "Thy will be done." From my earliest knowledge of him, I recall how he invariably chose these four words as the basis of his approach to every situation. He wanted to be a lawyer, but when the Holy Spirit laid it upon his heart to preach the gospel, he said: "Thy will be done." Regardless of what the question was in all the many decisions he made, the one touch-stone for him was this saying of Jesus, "Thy will be done."

LOUIE D. NEWTON

PASTOR'S STUDY
DRUID HILLS BAPTIST CHURCH
ATLANTA, GEORGIA

CONTENTS

                                                                                     page

Biographical Sketch of Dr. George W. Truett 9
    By Louie D. Newton, D.D.

1. What Is Your Life? 17
   A New Year's Message

2. What Keeps You From Christ? 29

3. Whom Say Ye That I Am? 47
   An Easter Message

4. What Does Salvation Involve? 63

5. What Are You Living For? 77
   A Commencement Message

6. Why Be Discouraged? 87

7. What Think Ye of Christ? 97
   An Anniversary Message

8. Am I My Brother's Keeper? 111

9. Despise Ye the Church of God? 125
   A Stewardship Message

10. Who Is My Neighbor? 139

11. How May We Know Christ Better? 149
    A Message to College Students

12. Who Knoweth What Is Good for Man in This Life? 157

13. What Is Your Attitude Toward Life? 167

14. What If Christ Had Not Come? 179
    A Christmas Message

QUESTION I

What Is Your Life?
A New Year's Message

QUESTION I

What Is Your Life?
A New Year's Message

~~~~~~

What is your life?
JAMES 4:14

JAMES asks a question in the epistle of which he is the author, which question, it seems to me, is exceedingly pertinent for our consideration: "What is your life?" He gives the answer to it, immediately following the question: "It is even a vapor, that appeareth for a little time, and then vanisheth away." And preceding the question he gives a picture of this busy life of ours:

> Go to now, ye that say, Today or tomorrow we will go into such a city, and continue there a year, and buy and sell, and get gain:
> Whereas ye know not what shall be on the morrow. For what is your life? It is even a vapor, that appeareth for a little time, and then vanisheth away.
> For that ye ought to say, If the Lord will, we shall live, and do this, or that.

Could we have a more appropriate question this first Lord's Day of a new year, into whose early moments we are entering, than this question of James? It suggests the brevity of human life, and certainly that thought needs again and again to be laid faithfully to heart by us, one and all. It is very difficult to realize how soon the earthly life is spent. If this morning and this evening we have had in this church auditorium two thousand people, as a conservative estimate, then, based on the well-known laws of mortality, sixty-six of these people within this church building shall pass into eternity this year, and in ten years almost six hundred of these

Some Vital Questions

two thousand people within these walls today will have passed into eternity; and in fifty years, out of these two thousand people far less than one hundred will be left to tell the story of human life. Oh, if we could realize how soon the earthly life is spent, how fast it speeds into the great eternity! It was Augustine who said that he did not know whether to call this earthly life of ours a dying life or a living death. It is both. Each person before me in this auditorium is hurrying along the road that leads to physical death. There is some part in your body this minute decaying, and every beat of that pulse means that you have one less for the earthly existence. Augustine was right when he said that this experience here called human life is a dying life and is a living death, from the cradle to the grave. From the hour of our birth change sets up in these bodies, until the hour of our death, and works its way in human life.

Oh, if we could realize how soon the earthly life is spent — if we could realize it! And yet, if we look around us and see how easy it is for one to pass from time into eternity, we might realize it. The slightest thing, and one is carried away. Do you not recall that Justinian, the emperor of old, went into a newly painted room, and the odor of the paint cost him his life without delay? Do you not remember that one of the popes, Adrian by name, was strangled to death by a fly? Do you not remember that one of the chief consuls lightly struck his foot against furniture in his own house and, despite all the skill of all the mighty physicians who could be brought to his bed, he passed away?

Oh, there are a thousand gates to death! The easiest thing in the world is for you and me to pass from this life into the great beyond. A falling building, a burning house while we sleep, the crash of a mighty aeroplane, a fast-flying train coming into collision with another, a sinking boat on the river or in mid-ocean, a runaway horse, an accidental discharge from a gun — how many the ways to hurry us away from earth into eternity! Is there a more appropriate theme for us, as we

What Is Your Life?

start upon another year, than the theme, Life so soon is spent? Let us lay that great fact as we ought to our heart.

Now, James seeks here to impress practical men of old, and practical men of the present time as well, with the brevity of life. He exhorts them to be wise with reference to the supreme thing, and he asks his question, and answers it: "What is your life? It is even a vapor, that appeareth for a little time and then vanisheth away." Many definitions have been given by men through the centuries concerning life. The moralist has tried his hand at answering the question, "What is your life?" And the scientist has tried his hand, and the prophet of God has tried his hand, and the poet has tried his hand, and all classes of men have tried their hands at answering the question, "What is your life?" Shakespeare called it a drama. Sir Walter Raleigh called it a journey. Another great writer called human life a storm at sea in which the vessel sinks. Burke, that mighty orator said: "What shadows we are, and what shadows we pursue!" These moralists and prophets and scientists and literary men and women through the centuries have been giving us their definitions of human life. Now, when we turn to the Bible, we find many definitions of human life. Here is one stated for us in our text by James: "What is your life? It is even a vapor, that appeareth for a little time and then vanisheth away."

Haven't you fixed your eyes on the cloud in the early morning, and dwelt upon it, and beheld its changes, and even as you looked the cloud was dissolved and you saw the cloud no more at all? James is saying that human life is like that. Many are the illustrations and the figures employed in Holy Scripture to set forth the brevity of human life. You will have an interesting study if you will take your pencil and, from first to last in the Bible, mark the statements therein that set forth the brevity of human life. In one place it is compared to foam on the water. How expressive! In another place it is compared to the grass growing up in the morning and flourishing, but cut down in the evening and withered

Some Vital Questions

when the nightfall comes. In one place it is compared to an eagle in the swiftness of his flight as he hasteth to his prey. In one place in the Bible human life is compared to a swift ship at sea. Yonder it is, in sight. It is passing, fast passing, faster, faster — a tiny speck — it cannot be seen now. That is human life. These are all Bible figures. Your days, says the Bible, are but as a handbreadth. They are gone in a moment. They are swifter than a post, the man in the olden time who carried the message from king or other important dignitary, carried it fast from this post to that one. Swifter than the post is human life. You hear the clatter of the horse's hoofs, as down the road he comes, bearing the message from one king to another. He passes before you, you see him for a moment, and then he is lost, and the echo itself is lost. He is hurrying to his destination. That is human life. Oh, the brevity of human life! Where will this audience be fifty years from now? By the well-known laws of mortality, not a dozen of you will be here, nor a half dozen. Where will this audience be ten years from now? By the well-known laws of mortality a large percentage of you, will be in eternity. Oh, if you and I could only realize the uncertainty of life! God, help us, that we may be wise men!

In another place you hear God Himself, turning preacher and exhorting humanity with all the pathos of a prophet, as He says: "Oh, that men and women would consider their latter end, that they might be wise!"

Now, these figures, these mighty arguments, these passing illustrations, these great statements in the Bible concerning human life are therein revealed that you and I may lay to heart as we ought the lessons touching human life and its brevity. What effect ought this teaching of the Bible concerning the brevity of human life to have upon us all? A gloomy effect? Not at all, not at all. It is not meant for it to have that effect. In the Bible God utterly forbids any such attitude toward life. What effect should the knowledge of the brevity of life. the uncertainty of life, the ease with which

What Is Your Life?

life's little, invisible thread is snapped in sunder — what effect should that doctrine have on you and me and on our fellows around us? Not a gloomy effect, not a depressing effect, not a pessimistic effect, not a morose effect, at all; but there should be wrought within us the most cheerful acquiescence to it all. And, now, why?

First of all, because this earthly scene is not intended as the immortal abode of men and women. When God brought you and me into being, and gave us bodies and minds and souls, He never intended that this earth should be our dwelling place perpetually. Not at all. That is not the great, divine intention in our creation. The earthly scene does not provide an adequate range for the spirit of man. Earth is entirely too little for any human being that God has ever made to stay here forever. Oh, no! God never intended that this world and human life in it should be all there is for us. He meant something far larger and grander than that. If you and I are to live and to suffer and to bleed and to dream and to hope and to aspire, and then to die and fill six feet of earth there in the grave and that be all, O Life, thou dost mock us and the game is not worth the candle! There is too much of suffering and of sorrow and of heartbreak in human life. If these years, forty or sixty or seventy or thirty or twenty, are to be lived by us, and then we are to have but six feet in the earth and no more, the game is not worth the candle. God never intended that this life should be all.

The brevity of life should not at all depress us because we should lay to heart the fact that life's machinery is constantly wearing out. There are men before me who were strong when I first knew them, nearly a score of years ago. They are tottering now. I looked at them this morning, and had a clutch at my heart as I beheld them — and women, too. They were in life's prime when first I began to preach in this city. Strong they were, like strong men to run a race, and there was about their step an elasticity and a strength that made you think of the giant, and there was about their eye the eagle flash, the lightning impression, that made your soul quiver when the eye looked into your eye. It is not so now. Age is telling, with all its wearing power, on these men and women. Life's machinery wears out. It is true with every part of our machinery. This body of ours is destined to decay, and even now, as I remarked a moment ago, decay and change are doing their work in each of our bodies. Somewhere in every body the work of death even now has its plowers out, turning its furrows and marking its desolation. The body wears out. Read the twelfth chapter of Ecclesiastes and see how God's Book pictures the human body as it wears out. See the picture there of the old man, with his teeth gone, and his vision bad, and his shoulders stooped, and his heart timid, afraid of everything that is high, afraid of the grasshopper.

I had an interview of some length with one soon to be eighty and five years of age — eyesight gone, led about by loved ones. In the other years his endurance and strength were very great. Now he is led about by grandchildren and great-grandchildren; eyesight gone, little children read to him, and the people wait on him, as though he were some helpless babe, as, indeed, he is. That is the picture of life for you and me when we are eighty and five, or even less. Life's machinery wears out.

And not only that, but the mind, that regal thing that sits on the throne in the human body, itself is often deteriorated by the eroding waves of time. Not many old men and women are alert in mind. There are some very rare exceptions. The usual thing is that as age comes on and the body is enfeebled and enervated by waste and decay, the mind likewise tumbles and totters from its high dominion and weakens along with the body. It is the rarest thing that the man of seventy-five or eighty can stand forth alert and strong and masterful in mental achievement and in mental assertiveness — a rare thing, indeed! Second childhood generally arrives when such age is reached. The man who before could stand, at life's middle time, at fifty or sixty or sixty-five, a giant and a leader and commander of his fellows, now at seventy-five and eighty talks about the past, dwells in the far gone years. Childhood the second time is his experience. The machinery wears out.

And not only that, but the human affections are beaten upon by the encroaching waves of Time as age advances. Let the man of eighty look around for his friends, for his intimate friends. Where are they? Back yonder, years agone, he stood as one of many, like the great trees in a thickly studded forest. Then, wherever he turned his eyes, there were his friends to salute him, and to wave him glad words of greeting and friendly cheer. Now, at eighty, he looks about him. Where are his friends? The sightless old man with whom I talked said, "Where are my friends, those intimates, those associates, those who were to me as David was to Jonathan, where are they?" And then, after a pause, he said, "Every intimate friend in all the world is gone, and I wait, like the old tree, riven by the lightning of Time." The machinery is worn out.

Oh, you and I were not made to stay here. That is not God's design for us, and we should accept cheerfully His plan about it. Then, too, we should accept the fact of the brevity of life cheerfully, without repining because God has prepared and is preparing for us the true home, the real abiding place, for all His friends. This life here is but a little probationary period. God never meant, I repeat, that it should be perpetual, that it should be final here. A little probationary period is allowed us here, but the real home, the real dwelling place where the conditions are adapted and designed for us in all their fulness and glory by the Master of life Himself, such dwelling place is not here at all, but yonder. "I go to prepare a place for you. And if I go and prepare a place for you, I will come again, and receive you unto myself; that where I am, there ye may be also." Do you object to that? I do not. Oh, thanks be unto God, this world is not all! Thanks be unto God, a perfect land is being prepared by the Master of life for His friends!

What effect then should all this doctrine of the brevity of life have on us? Why, we should just meet life here like it ought to be met — as a great privilege, a great trust, a great opportunity. God put us here, in time and on earth, for a few years at the most. He put us here for some wise and beneficent purpose. Then let us relate ourselves to life like we ought. Let us do with life what we ought. Let us accept this great dower from God, this mighty trust from our Maker, and use it, not abuse it. That is the way for us to look at life.

If in this life we honestly seek to fulfill God's purposes for us, then when the time comes for us to embark from time into eternity we can serenely put forth for the farther shore, which is the Land of Light and Life and Love, the land where the rainbow never fades, where tears never flow, the land from which ignorance and hate and sin and death are forever banished. There we shall be greeted by those whom we have loved long since and lost awhile. There we shall be welcomed by Him who redeemed us with His own precious blood. There our very souls will be ravished by the music of heaven's perfect harmonies.

God has that country for His people, for His friends. I want to go there, when He has finished His program with me here. But, wait. I shall not go there unless I am rightly related to the Lord Jesus Christ. I shall not go to that land unless I am rightly related to Jesus Christ. Neither will you go there unless you are rightly related to Jesus, unless you can truly say: "The Lord's will I accept as the program for my life." Whoever humbly and honestly accepts the Lord's will as the program for his life shall go there, blessed be His name! And when the little earthly day is done, beyond the sunset and the night, we shall live with Him forever.

Oh, the destiny, the eternal destiny, that is being determined now by you and for you! And you are determining it. You are determining it. If your heart says, "Lord Jesus, Light of the world, Saviour of sinners, rightful Master of mankind, the one Mediator between God and sinners, Lord Jesus, I take Thee to be my Saviour, my refuge, my righteousness, my Master, my Redeemer and my Guide," then indeed you will win. You will sing the triumph song. You will walk the streets of gold. You will be crowned with the fadeless crown of life.

What then will you do with Jesus? Will you choose Him as the Lord and Master of your life? On this first day, as we start another year, won't you do that greatest thing possible for a human being — say "Yes," in truth, from your deepest heart to the call of Jesus? Listen to Him now. "Boast not thyself of tomorrow; for thou knowest not what a day may bring forth." Listen to Him now. "If ye hear His voice, harden not your heart." Listen to Him now. "Commit thy way unto the Lord; trust also in Him; and He shall bring it to pass."

Are you ready and willing tonight to make the highest choice any human being can make — the choice of Jesus to be the Master of your life, the forgiving Saviour, who will put away your sins and make your standing safe and right in the sight of God? Will you thus decide for Jesus? Won't you thus decide for Jesus? Based on the well-known laws of mortality, out of the estimate — two thousand people who have passed within these walls today, sixty-six will have died before next New Year's Day. Will you be one of those sixty-six? Will you, young man, be one of those sixty-six? And, gentle girl, to whom life is so fair and sweet, will you be one of those sixty-six? And, man with the gray about your temples, will you be one of the sixty-six? Greetings and congratulations, hearty and heaven high, if you, being one of those sixty-six, are rightly related to God; for then you will enter before the rest of your comrades into the land where conditions are perfect, and happiness is absolutely and eternally satisfied. Are you ready tonight to say: "I pray the prayer of the publican, 'God, be merciful to me, a sinner'?" Are you ready tonight to say: "I cast myself, by a definite and deliberate choice, on Jesus, who says, 'He that cometh to Me I will in no wise cast out'?" Here is a brother's hand to greet you, and a brother's heart to bid you Godspeed if you take that supreme step. The angels of God will rejoice. The Son of God who died for you will be made glad, and you will be able to answer back to the author of our text and say: "My life is no longer a vapor but it is an eternal possession which I have committed unto Christ who will keep it — and perfect it against that Great Day."

What, then, will you do with your life? The answer is with you.

QUESTION II

What Keeps You From Christ?

QUESTION II

What Keeps You From Christ?

*Then Jesus . . . said unto him,
One thing thou lackest.*

MARK 10:21

THE STORY of the rich young ruler, as given in the tenth chapter of Mark, is one of the most intensely interesting and tragically sorrowful stories to be found in all this Book of incomparable records. It is one of the most familiar stories in all the Bible; yet I wish to read it again, and perchance we may see this story with something of a new setting this evening:

> And when he [Jesus] was gone forth into the way, there came one running, and kneeled to him, and asked him, Good Master, what shall I do that I may inherit eternal life?
> And Jesus said unto him, Why callest thou me good? there is none good but one, that is, God.

That is the only time Jesus ever made an answer like that, concerning which we have any record, and the answer is perfectly plain. "Do you understand to whom you talk? I claim to be God. There is but one who is good, and that is God. Do you understand, therefore, to whom you are making your appeal? Why callest thou Me good? There is none good but one, that is, God."

> Thou knowest the commandments, Do not commit adultery, Do not kill, Do not steal, Do not bear false witness, Defraud not, Honour thy father and mother.
> And he answered and said unto him, Master, all these have I observed from my youth.
> Then Jesus beholding him loved him, and said unto him, One thing thou lackest: go thy way, sell whatsoever thou hast, and give

> to the poor, and thou shalt have treasure in heaven: and come, take up the cross, and follow me.
> And he was sad at that saying, and went away grieved: (or, as Matthew puts it, he turned sorrowfully away): for he had great possessions.
> And Jesus looked around about, and saith unto his disciples, How hardly shall they that have riches enter into the kingdom of God!
> And the disciples were astonished at his words. But Jesus answereth again, and saith unto them, Children, how hard is it for them that trust in riches to enter into the kingdom of God!
> It is easier for a camel to go through the eye of a needle, than for a rich man to enter into the kingdom of God.
> And they were astonished out of measure, saying among themselves, Who then can be saved?
> And Jesus looking upon them saith, With men it is impossible, but not with God: for with God all things are possible.

Do you wonder that this story enchains the attention of men? You cannot read it, no matter how many the times, except with deep moving of heart. Sometimes the commentators speaks of it as "The Great Refusal." Dante speaks of it as "The Great Decision." It might be just as appropriate, or more appropriate, to speak of it as "The Great Inquiry." Here is a young man of high position and of wealth; these two things would give him prominence anywhere, and at any time.

Jesus was leaving Perea, where He had been ministering for a season. But the time of His ministry there was at an end, and He had to go elsewhere. As He was leaving, this young man of position, of family, of distinction, of wealth — an outstanding man in all the country — came hurriedly to Jesus, and asked Him a most momentous question: "What shall I do that I may inherit eternal life?" To see a young man serious on any religious question is a sight to stir within us deep emotions. When we behold a young man give himself to any worthy task, and then dedicate his powers to that task and to the living of the right kind of a life, we have great hope for his future. Good men applaud him and cheer him.

This young man came to Jesus running, revealing his interest, his great seriousness, his earnestness of heart; and then,

What Keeps You From Christ?

when he reached Jesus, he knelt before Him, betokening his humility and his reverence. He asked Jesus the question, "Good Master, what shall I do that I may inherit eternal life?" And Jesus replied by asking him a question of very solemn implications, "Do you understand that there is only one who is good, and that one is God? Do you understand that you are talking to God manifest in the flesh? My claim forever is that I am the equal of the Eternal Father, and I came forth from Him to reveal Him. I and the Father are one. There is only one that is good, and that is God."

And then Jesus probed his heart with another question, "Thou knowest the commandments; what about them?" And the young man made answer without delay, "Why, I have kept them." Outwardly perhaps he had, after a fashion. "What lack I yet?" said the young man, and there the record tells us that Jesus looked upon him and loved him.

Evidently this young man was not the type of young man, sometimes seen, who has sinned to the flesh and of the flesh will reap corruption, and then go on in the whirlwind of destruction and ruin. Oh, what a pity for a young man to imagine that he must sow his wild oats! What a pity it is for him to conclude that it is a part of life's program for him to be unchaste and debauched and to cheapen the highest and finest things in human life! What a tragedy!

Here is a young man whose life has been clean. "Master, all these commandments which you have quoted I have kept from my youth. What lack I yet?" No wonder Jesus loved him. Then Jesus put to him the test, toward which He had drawn closer and closer as that conservation had developed. "If you would have eternal life, if you would make sure of the highest things, then I have one observation to make to you and one solemn request to make of you: One thing thou lackest; go thy way, sell whatsoever thou hast, and give to the poor, and thou shalt have treasure in heaven; and come, take up the cross and follow me." And there the curtain fell. There the interview was terminated. At that saying the young man's countenance fell and his heart was sad. From that moment the young man, in that crisis of his life, "turned sorrowfully away, for he had great possessions." Oh, that test, that test! And he did not meet it.

We shall do well to look at two or three truths that stand out in this story which constitutes one of the ominous and fearful warnings in all the Bible. I think, indeed, that it is a threefold warning, and I should like to speak of it as such.

First of all, this young man's case is a warning against the peril of money, against the peril of earthly property. Jesus said: "How hard it is for them that have riches to enter into the kingdom of God." And why did Jesus make a statement like that? Is it not because the tendency of riches is to fill one with a sense of self-sufficiency and turn that one away from simple, humble trust in God? Wealth is a form of power which tends to give one a sense of independence of both God and men. It is so easy for one to rely on his wealth because money can buy so many things which men crave. It can buy position and honors, and services and preferments and all manner of material things which human beings so highly prize. But there are some things which money cannot buy. Among these are eternal life and the kingdom of God and abiding happiness of the heart.

There comes to mind the story of the rich farmer about whom Jesus tells us in the twelfth chapter of Luke. His crops were abundant, but his old barns were inadequate to hold them. So he reasoned with himself, saying, "I will pull down my old barns, and I will build greater, and in these greater barns I will bestow my fruits and my goods soon to be harvested; and then, rain or shine, drought or what not, I will say to my soul: 'Soul, thou hast much goods laid up for many years. Take thine ease. Eat, drink, and be merry.'" That is life with all its self-sufficiency and self-confidence. But God said unto him, "Thou fool, this night thy soul shall be required of thee; then whose shall these things be?" Any man is a fool who thinks his soul can be satisfied with things, mere things.

What Keeps You From Christ?

I would pause to say that money as a master is man's worst master. Money as a servant is one of man's most valuable servants. If only man can be the master of his wealth, and hold it as a trust to be used for God's causes and for humanity, then his property shall prove a great asset.

But in the case of the rich young ruler, his great possessions became a stumbling block, a millstone about his neck, dragging him down and causing him to miss the supreme chance of a lifetime. Sad of countenance and heart, he chose his wealth rather than Christ, his earthly treasures rather than treasure in heaven, his creature comforts rather than eternal life. Verily, his was "The Great Refusal," and it fills our hearts with sadness as we see him go away in sorrow. Then it was that Jesus said, "How hardly shall they that have riches enter into the kingdom of God!"

So the disciples said: "Master, who then can be saved?" And He said, "How hard it is for those who trust in their riches to enter into the kingdom of God." The danger is that they will trust in their riches, that their confidence shall be in human equipment and power, that they shall forget the arm supreme and everlasting, and pass by the hope most worthy.

First of all, then, there is this peril in money. And, young man making money, let me beseech you, make it never at the expense of your soul, in any fashion, to any degree. Take no short cuts at any time to make a point and to gain a dollar, or many dollars. Go with a conscience clear in the sight of men and of God, and what you do get, if it be but a little, get it with gladness and humility and gratitude. Never cut a corner, never betray a trust, never debauch conscience, to get a dollar that you ought not to have. That means that every form of gambling and reckless speculation is a thing to which no man, young or old, ought ever to put his hand, any more than he would put his hand on the coiled serpent.

Some Vital Questions

Beware of the peril which is in money. The man who has but a little money may have the peril as well as the man of great wealth. The love of money is the root of every kind of evil on the earth. The Bible declares it. Do not imagine that you must get well-fixed, and have a home, and have it splendidly appointed, before you will heed the call of the highest. There is the peril of money. There is the deadening power of money. There is its corrosive touch. There is its blight, its menace, its deadly spell of death. Beware of the peril of money, and see in this man's case what the dangers are.

Then there is another warning in this story of the rich young man; and that is, we are to see to it that we do not trust in human goodness to be saved. Every man must watch that point, and not trust in human goodness to be saved. All the human goodness on this earth won't save a soul. We are not to trust in human goodness to save. This young man came, wrapping his cloak about him, quite conscious of his righteous life, as he said, "Why, all these commandments I have kept from my youth. What lack I yet? I have not stolen. I have not debauched virtue. I have not defrauded. I have not dishonored my parents. I have kept these commandments from my youth. What lack I yet?" And all the while there was within him a self-sufficiency and a self-preference which, left to itself, would dethrone God and turn the moral universe topsy-turvy.

Oh, how defective, how frail, how unworthy, how fallen, how sinful, is every human soul, and how impossible of recovery within itself! Do not think to get to heaven by your own goodness. You can climb to heaven on a spider's web as easily as you can save yourself, ignoring God's remedy for a sinner. Let no soul be betrayed at this point. It is every way better for a young man not to sow his wild oats, not to drift and go with the tides which are darksome and undoing and shaming and blasting. Let no man suppose that his morality, worm-eaten as it is, or his goodness, shot to pieces with ten thousand deceptions, can get him home to God. If you go now and shut yourself up in a room, and tarry there a thousand years, and think by that to fix the robe of self-righteousness about you, how abashed you will be when you look into the face of Christ! Heaven is not won by man's goodness, else Jesus would never have come, else God would never have sent Him, else the Bible never would have been given, else the Holy Spirit would never have been sent to exercise His regenerating power. Salvation is through the riches of the grace of a Person, whose name is Jesus. Do not be mistaken then at this point. If you have said, "Now I will turn a new leaf, and, thereby be saved," without linking your trust, putting your all, into the hands of the one being in this universe, who was appointed to save you, you shall come short of eternal life. If you have said, "I will be baptized and come into the church," forgetting that all that is missing the mark if you have not first put your trust in Christ; then you will be deceived by the thought that somehow, by human righteousness, you will be saved. Vain hope! Delusive snare! "Not by the works of righteousness which we have done," declares this Book, "but according to God's mercy doth He save us by the washing of regeneration and by the renewing of the Holy Ghost." And again it declares, "By grace are we saved through faith; and that not of ourselves; it is the gift of God; not of works, lest any man should boast. For we are his workmanship, created in Christ Jesus unto good works." And again, "The gift of God is eternal life, through Jesus Christ our Lord." O man or woman, think not to be saved now by any work of human righteousness which you can do! All of our works are as filthy rags in the sight of an infinite God. Do not be mistaken at that point, for the test comes to you and to me just as it came to that young man.

When the young man said to Jesus, "Now, if it is a question of keeping the commandments, I am all right," Jesus, who ever insists on being given first place in our love and loyalty, then said in effect to the young man, "You say you wish to have eternal life. Then, in your case, I urge that you go and part with your property. Make the best disposition of it you can. Bring the money back. Put the money on the altar to help the poor. Take up your cross and follow me, and then will it be well with you." What a center shot was that! There was the Ithuriel spear to discover to the young man what the situation with him really was. At that saying his countenance fell. At that saying he "turned sorrowfully away." His decision was, "I cannot part with my property, even to please Christ, even to take care of my soul. Even to get to heaven, I cannot; I will put my possessions first." What of his goodness now? His money is his god. Some men make gods out of their bodies. This man's god was his money. The thing that dominates a man becomes his master. That is why Jesus insists, "I must be first. I must be first." But the young man gave his possessions first place. He failed the test.

There is a third warning in the story. It is an awful warning against presumption concerning our religious privileges. The young man came, it would seem, right up to the gate of the heavenly kingdom. There he stood and heard the call. He saw the open door and heard the invitation to enter. But he retreated. He retraced his steps. He went back to the old life. "He turned sorrowfully away." O presumption, presumption, how many souls thou dost slay! Almost within, and yet he turned sorrowfully away. Not far from the kingdom of God, and yet he turned sorrowfully away. Presumption! Presumption! O young man, a moment ago, when you came running, and knelt before Jesus, and said, "What shall I do that I may inherit eternal life?" we thought that in a few moments more, when the truth was explained and the way pointed for you, that you would accept the truth and walk in the way, and go on, a glorious disciple of Jesus.

And what a glorious one he would have made! His position, his fame, his property, his distinction, his outsanding place — oh, what a disciple he would have made! How he

What Keeps You From Christ?

was needed! — needed by Jesus in carrying forward His great work. But he turned sorrowfully away. "I cannot face it. I won't conform to it. I am sorry. My heart troubles me. But I turn back to my own way!"

He soon had to die, and he soon had to stand before the judgment bar of God, and he soon had to meet his destiny in heaven or hell. And yet he went back. Oh, presumptuous trifling with privileges that God gives us!

Again and again, in these long years in Dallas, I have seen people turn away sorrowfully as did the young ruler. I think I have told you before of one of the most splendid of our businessmen. I shall be as careful as I can be not to identify him, for I have no respect for a minister who takes advantage of men by dealing in personalities. One morning, years ago, he was in this congregation. Sometimes he came, maybe twice a year — and I changed my subject immediately when I saw him as I entered the pulpit, for I said, "I may never get him again, and all this that I have in mind seems ill adapted for that one citizen." Many a time the preacher makes a change like that when he comes in to the pulpit and sees some one present, for whose presence he has prayed, as I had in the case of this man. I put away the theme I had chosen and took another, and that day I preached to one man.

And when the service was done and the call was given, he came not — but some others came, thank God! The color came and went in his face — white like the snow, almost, and red like crimson — and there was a battle that betokened the emotions that seethed within him, like some mighty furnace. And when the people were dismissed, I went hurriedly to the outer door, and I held his hand as I pulled him a little to one side, and I said, "How is my friend?" His face blanched, and he essayed a smile as he said, "I never was as healthy as I am now." I said, "I know, that is not it, and you know it is not it. How is my friend today?" And then he looked at me with an expression of pathos too deep to put into words, "Mr. Truett, I was never as solemn in the world as I have been in the past hour." I said, "I can well understand that, for every word I said was backed by the most fervent prayer I could pray that God would direct it into your heart by the power of the divine Spirit. What are you going to do about it?" Still I held his hand. He looked at the floor a minute, and then at me as I said again, "What are you going to do about it? The years are going by. What are you going to do about it? The call is the highest call. What are you going to do about it?" Then he named three businesses, which I shall not mention because many of you would then know his name at once. "This one demands me, and this one absorbs me, and this one engages me, and any one of them is enough for any man." I said, "I know, but is this business, or this business, or that business, any one of them, or all three of them, more important than your right adjustment with Christ? What are you going to do about it?" He said plaintively, "You let me off, and I solemnly promise you when I get a little further along I will give heed to this great question." I said, "Why, my friend, it is not for me to let you off. I am a poor fellow sinner like yourself, saved by the grace of God, in which grace I have joy too deep for words. I am but a witness for Christ. It is not for me to grant you any reprieve at all. Your issue is with God's Son, who died for you, and today He calls. The call is clear, and the call is urgent. What will you do about it?" He looked at me so piteously! His nervousness was very apparent. He said, "Why, I cannot fix it up now. I cannot now. I will later." And then he was gone. Sadly I listened to his retreating footsteps, as down the street he went, never to come back again, never to come back again. A few weeks later, I went to the East for an engagement of two or three weeks, and when I returned late one night, my home people said, "You have been called daily for a week. This case is serious beyond words. This man is in the grip of a great affliction, and you have been called for constantly. They have been

WHAT KEEPS YOU FROM CHRIST?

told that you were away, but you are to be called for tonight if they need you."

I went away to my sleep at midnight, but about four o'clock in the morning, the telephone rang. And when I put the receiver to my ear, that man's wife said, "You are back home? You will come at once? They have told you all? In his wild delirium for days he has spoken your name hundreds of times. I am not sure that he will know you, but we want you here. I know that he has called for you constantly hour after hour, and often in his wild flights he calls your name and none other." I said, "I will be there, as quickly as possible." When I reached his bedside five physicians were there, but unable to help him at all. They said, "He will know you in a minute," and they placed a chair beside his bed. I took his hand, and in a moment more he was conscious, and recognized me. He said, "Oh, my friend, you have come! I never wanted to see anyone like I wanted to see you. You will teach me how to die? Teach me quickly, for you must know what the danger is." I said, "Listen to me, my friend," and I bent low beside his face, as a mother would do to soothe her child. I sought to fix his attention vitally on the subject, but in half a minute he was talking about the first business, and then about that second, and then about that third. Oh, how baffled I was! I waited a moment and he was conscious again. He clutched at me most nervously and said, "Don't you understand? Haven't they told you? I must die, and I am not ready! Sir, oh, teach me how! Teach me how!" I said, "I will. You listen to me now." And I bent beside him again, but in half a minute it was the first business, and then the second, and then the third. I waited beside him until the grey of the early morning came, and until the great sun came up to light the earth, but his spirit went out talking about those three businesses.

Oh my people, a human soul ought not to presume until that late date. A human soul ought not to wait until that perilous hour.

Some Vital Questions

I am thinking of a young man who was here a while ago, just a few brief years, who, when the congregation had gone, tarried with me and sobbed his broken-heartedness over his pitiful plight in the sight of God. I showed him that there was salvation only through Christ, and that though his sins were as scarlet, as he declared them to be, he would have forgiveness and recovery and salvation, assuredly, once for all, eternally, if he would surrender utterly to Christ. Christ or nothing! Christ and all! Which would he choose? He said, "I will fix it later. I will do that later. I will pursue that course later." Sometimes he came again after that, but that great hour was never his again; that great moment was never his again; and when awhile ago I saw him, he said, "I have reached a strange state of mind and heart. I am no longer responsive. My soul no longer is bestirred. I seem desensitized in spirit. I am dead in conscience. I have gone so far on the wrong way. I have sinned so against light, I have so misused the truth, which I knew I ought to follow, that I am now seemingly impervious to all religious impressions."

Oh, tragedy of tragedies, to presume upon spiritual privileges! Oh, tragedy of tragedies, if, when your heart was touched and you were stirred deeply by the gospel appeals, you turned away from the Saviour's call, saying to yourself: "I know I ought, and I will . . . but not just yet." By so doing and so saying you played into the hands of the great deceiver of souls, the great despoiler of souls, the great enemy of souls. You played into his hands. This text is an awful warning against presuming on your spiritual privileges and opportunities. A man may come up to the very gates of the kingdom of God, where he can hear the voice of the Spirit plainly calling, but turn away into the hopeless wilderness wanderings of indecision and procrastination with the result that he will never enter the kingdom.

> "Almost persuaded," now to believe;
> "Almost persuaded," Christ to receive;
> Seems now some soul to say,

What Keeps You From Christ?

> "Go, Spirit, go thy way,
> Some more convenient day
> On Thee I'll call."

That word about the convenient day is a word born in the pit of destruction. It is Satan's deadly opiate to be-drug the conscience and turn people back from hope and light and salvation. That is the warning against presumption.

Well, the young man had his test. His answer was, "My choice is my property. I won't give it up. Though God asks it, though the Eternal Jehovah asks it, though my Maker asks it, though the One who died for sinners asks it, I will not give it up. I will join the issue with Him. I will lift up my voice, my tiny, little voice, in the face of the Eternal One, and I will mock Him, and I will dispute Him." You know the rest. You know the outcome. It could not be otherwise.

A man said to me the other day, "I do not like your Saviour." "Why?" I said. He said, "Because He sends men to hell." I said, "I have never heard of His sending anyone there. Men send themselves there." "I would, but ye would not." "As I live, I have no pleasure in the death of the wicked." "I would that ye all would turn unto me and live." And yonder Jesus is weeping over doomed Jerusalem, "Jerusalem, O Jerusalem, how often would I have gathered thy children together, as a hen doth gather her brood under her wings. I would, but ye would not. Your house is left unto you desolate." Jesus was never at fault because a soul went to hell. Never! Never! No soul confronting Jesus in that great day of days at the judgment bar of God will ever presume to say, "I am lost through your fault." None will say that to Him.

Oh, soul, what is your test? Is it fear of men? Is it the thought that they will shrug their shoulders at you when you go back to the old circles? Let them shrug! Let them taunt! Let them mock! But mind you this: You have an obligation for every one of those souls. If, by changing about fundamentally in your life, you can arouse their attention, and by example can help them at all, and you fail to do that, you have added to your condemnation in the sight of all that is good and high and holy, in time and eternity.

What is the thing that keeps you from Christ? Is it the fear of men? Is it the thought that your position will be jeopardized? Is it the thought that your life may be restricted and impoverished? Oh, do not misjudge Jesus like that. He is the One who gives the abundant life. The stars in their courses, the stones in the field, God and His mighty hosts of power, are pledged to any soul in the world that is in league with Jesus. You need not be terrified. Though all the world should come against you God is greater than them all. He can and will save you, and cleanse you, and keep you, and help you every step of the way if you will accept and confess and trust His Son Jesus Christ as your Redeemer and Master.

What keeps you from Christ? Oh, this delay! This presumption! This procrastination! I beseech you, give up that fearful course. For, mind you, the day's delay makes your difficulties worse. The day's delay makes your obstacles greater. The day's delay makes your probabilities of salvation fewer and smaller. Every day that a soul puts the truth and light and counsel and mercy and call of Jesus away that soul is piling up trouble for itself, and making its difficulties larger and more formidable, and its hopes fewer and dimmer. Let Jesus be your Saviour. Let Him now. I can never get way from the awful solemnity of those lines of Addison:

> There is a time, I know not when,
> A place, I know not where,
> Which marks the destiny of men,
> To heaven or despair.
>
> There is a line, by us not seen,
> Which crosses every path;
> The hidden boundary between
> God's patience and God's wrath.
>
> To cross that limit is to die,
> To die as if by stealth.
> It may not pale the beaming eye,
> Nor quench the glowing health.

What Keeps You From Christ?

The conscience may be still at ease,
The spirit light and gay.
That which is pleasing still may please,
And care be thrust away.

But on that forehead God hath set
Indelibly a mark,
By man unseen, for man as yet
Is blind and in the dark.

And still the doomed man's path below
May bloom as Eden bloomed.
He did not, does not, will not know,
Nor feel, that he is doomed.

He feels, he says, that all is well,
His every fear is calmed.
He lives, he dies, he wakes in hell,
Not only doomed, but damned.

Oh, where is that mysterious bourne
By which each path is crossed?
Beyond which God Himself hath sworn
That he who goes is lost?

How long may man go on in sin,
How long will God forbear?
Where does hope end, and where begin
The confines of despair?

One answer from the skies is sent:
Ye who from God depart.
While it is yet today, repent,
And harden not your heart.

Oh, have you heard God's call at all? Is there something within you which says, "Oh, I need to heed the word of Jesus"? Then He answers today, "If you hear My voice, do not harden your heart." And He answers again, "Though your sins be as scarlet, come with them to Me, and yield yourself utterly to Me, and I will make those sins as white as the snow." He answers again, "Him that cometh unto Me, I will in no wise cast out." Will you come to Him now? Will you yield your heart and your will to Him now?

QUESTION III

Whom Say Ye That I Am?
An Easter Message

QUESTION III

Whom Say Ye That I Am?
An Easter Message

> *Whom say ye that I am?*
> MATTHEW 16:15

THE right views of Christ are necessary. Right relations toward Him and the right service for Him are necessary. The question, therefore, that Christ asked His disciples, when He was here in the flesh nineteen hundred years ago, is the supreme question to be faced by every rational human being. This is His question: "Whom say ye that I am?" His previous question to these same disciples a moment before was, "Whom say the people that I am?" And they said, "Some say thou art John the Baptist; some say Elijah; some say Jeremiah, or one of the prophets." And then quickly he put to them the probing question, "Whom say ye that I am?" And one of the men, Simon Peter, made answer and it was an inspired reply. He said, "Thou art the Christ, the Son of the living God." To which Jesus replied: "Blessed art thou, Simon Barjona, for flesh and blood hath not revealed it unto thee, but my Father who is in Heaven."

That same question, "Whom say ye that I am?" comes echoing its way all down the centuries. And the question will not be downed, for Christ crosses the threshold of every rational life, and puts to every one the probing inquiry, "Whom say ye that I am?" And the sincere, the serious, and the earnest seeker after the truth will at last come to say what Simon here said: "Thou art the Christ, the Son of the living God."

Some Vital Questions

Let us make this question the theme for our meditation this morning hour. Who is Christ Jesus? Whom do you say that He is? "Whom say ye that I am?" is the probing question of Jesus. This question relates directly to the person of Christ. Christianity stands or falls with the person of Christ. Historic, apostolic, supernatural Christianity stands or falls with the person of Christ.

There have been three views in this world about Christ: one that He was wicked; another that He was good, but mistaken about His claims; and the other that He was God — God manifest in the flesh — the Redeemer who came to save a needy world which was estranged from God and lost in sin.

Concerning this first view, one would go a long way before hearing any derisive word concerning Jesus. In all my life time, I have had only one bad letter, deriding Jesus; the writer using ephithets which I shall not quote. I wonder if the man was not crazy. Thoughtful and candid men, whatever may be their unbelief, look at Jesus and say, "He is the fairest among ten thousand, and the one altogether lovely." Many who do not accept the higher claims concerning Him do not hesitate to say that Jesus was the best man who ever lived.

Another view concerning Christ was that He was good, but mistaken in His claims: that He was earth's highest and best but mistaken in His own claims and assumptions. Some clever men have held this view. Edward Everett Hale held this view. Some clever men hold that view today. One wonders how on earth they can believe that Jesus, who made such astounding claims concerning Himself, could be good, wise or sane, if He was nothing more than man. They well know that nothing short of deity can satisfy the claims which Jesus made for Himself.

The theory that Christ was only a man reduces Him to a mere physical being. And this theory, no matter how beautiful, is lacking in that dynamic needed to lift men out of the mire. Men need a power above themselves. Every man needs a power to come into his life, above himself. Mere ethics will not do. Beautiful theories will not do and dainty, perfumed philosophies will not do. If Christ be only a man, He cannot lift men out of the quagmire of sin, guilt and death.

The other view is the one held by you and me. That is the New Testament view that Jesus was just what He claimed to be: God manifest in the flesh. I stake my all on it. I have not the remotest semblance of a question in my mind concerning this other view — that Christ was more than man; that Christ was God and man in one personality — the Godman. That hyphen both joins and divides. That hyphen marks a distinction as though He were God and not man at all, and as though He were man and not God at all.

John describes Jesus in five little words: "The Word was made flesh." Paul, speaking of Jesus, said: "Great is the mystery of godliness: God was manifest in the flesh, justified in the Spirit, seen of angels, preached unto the Gentiles, believed on in the world, received up into glory." That is Paul's majestic description of the person and worth of Christ. Victor Hugo states the case — the universal verdict, almost — when he said that Jesus was the "ultimate in all life"; and even Lord Byron rose up and said, "If ever man was God, and if ever God was man, this Jesus Christ is both." And Browning said, "The acceptance of God in Christ solves for us all problems in this world and the next."

Charles Lamb once said that he was at a luncheon with a group of brilliant men and women and their subject that evening was: "The Person I Would Like Best to Have Seen." A great array of brilliant personages was passed in review that evening. One said he would like to have seen Chaucer; another said John Milton; another said John Bunyan; another said Shakespeare. On and on they talked. Presently, Charles Lamb said: "If Shakespeare were to come into this room, we would all rise and bow to him; but I am thinking of One other whose name has not been called. If HE were to come into this room now, all of us here would fall down on our knees and cry out with Thomas of old, 'My Lord and my God'."

Christ stands forth, unapproached and unapproachable, incomparable. Indeed, never was there another person like unto Him in all the annals of time and never will there be another like Him — Christ, the divine Son of God. Born, nineteen hundred years ago in a stable, and laid in a manger because there was no room for the mother in the inn, in that crisis hour of her life. Born in a stable, and yet about that humble place there gathers more interest than about all the other treasure-houses of the great, from the first man until the last. His name is the most potent, the most inspiring, the most majestic in all the world. His is the name which is above every name. "Thou shalt call his name Jesus; for He shall save His people from their sins." He is the One who stirs our hearts, who shares our sorrows, and gives us life and love and peace and joy.

We unwaveringly subscribe to the declaration made by Simon Peter, when he said to Jesus: "Thou art the Christ, the Son of the living God." Without hesitation or any semblance of doubt I declare my belief that Christ is the divine Son of God; that He is unlike any other being the universe has ever known, or ever shall know; that He is the Way, the Truth, the Life, the Pilot, the older Brother, the Guide who came to bring be-darkened, sinning men and women home to God. I believe Him to be the one Mediator between God and man; the One by whom alone we can gain access to the Father and receive His forgiving and unfailing love.

Now, why do we hold unwaveringly to this higher view of Christ? The reasons are varied, but I think they are valid. Let us hurriedly look at some of them. The life of Christ is the answer to all contentions as to Himself. He flings out the challenge, "Who of you can convict Me of sin?" We can convict all others of sin. We can find defects in any other who ever walked the paths of earth. The founders of great religions, like Mohammed and Buddha, were wretchedly wrong in their own lives in many respects, which fact they did not disguise or deny. But Christ flings out the challenge to the whole world: "Which of you can convict Me of sin?" Is there one ill-advised word that He ever spoke? Is there one selfish deed that He ever did? Who of all the world can convict Him of sin? There He stands against the horizon: "THE Son of Man" – not *a son of man*, but THE Son of Man – for all humanity is summed up in Him. THE Son of Man, yet the sinless Son of Man!

If you look for the highest example of meekness that the world has ever known, you will not turn to Moses, called the "meekest man," but you turn to Christ, unprecedently meek and lowly in heart. If you look for the highest example of patience, you do not turn to Job, called the "most patient man," but to Christ who, when He was reviled, reviled not again. If you ask for the highest example of wisdom, you do not turn to Solomon, called "the wisest man," but to Christ, "who spake as never man spake." For the highest example of zeal, you do not turn to Paul but to Christ, concerning whom it is written: "The zeal of thine house hath eaten me up." For the highest example of love, you do not turn to John, gentle John, but to Christ who so loved us that He left His Father's house and came down to earth, and lived His life of unselfishness, and climbed His cross and died thereon, out of pure love for you and me, and for all our broken, sinning fellow-humanity.

The life of Christ is the answer to His own divine claim. Not even Pilate could find fault in Him. The searchlight of criticism, both from His friends and His foes, has been focused on Jesus for over nineteen hundred years, and yet, there He stands, flawless, spotless, sinless! You cannot say that about anyone else. You can find faults with Moses, and with Abram, and with Job and with Isaiah and with David, and with Paul and with Barnabas. You can put your finger

Some Vital Questions

on the defects of men up and down the world, without any exception; but Christ alone stands, flawless, spotless, and without sin. You cannot say that about any other life. His life attests His divine claims.

May we look at his teachings? Christ is the One universal Teacher. You see, sometimes, a picture on the wall, and no matter where you are, those eyes look right at you. You may change your place wherever you will, and those eyes follow you no matter where you go. So it is with the teachings of Christ. They find universal humanity. He is the universal Teacher and His words are equally adapted to men of all races and all countries and all centuries; to the white man, the black man, the brown man, the red man, every man of every color. His teachings are for all men.

He is the one we want to hear about. Jesus, born in the first century, belongs to the twentieth century even as He did to the first. Born a Jew, He belongs to all races. Born in the little country of Palestine, He is now the universal Teacher of all men. The wise and the ignorant, the high and the low are probed alike by His questions and by His teachings. They find universal humanity.

Shakespeare, the very flower of the Elizabethan era, was marvelous in the eyes of the English people, but not so in the eyes of the French people. Victor Hugo was marvelous as a literary leader with the French people, but not so with the English people. And Napoleon, that military genius, swayed France in an amazing way; and yet he was altogether undesirable and repellent in the eyes of the English people. Oliver Cromwell deeply impressed England, but he was abhorred and abominated by France.

But Jesus belongs to all people. He spoke His first words and His last words, recorded in the New Testament, over nineteen centuries ago, and these words are not out of date today. Was there ever another lullaby sung by a mother to her child so haunting and so sweet as those words from the lips of Jesus: "Come unto me, all ye that labor and are heavy

WHOM SAY YE THAT I AM?

laden, and I will give you rest. Take my yoke upon you, and learn of me; for I am meek and lowly in heart: and ye shall find rest unto your souls. For my yoke is easy and my burden is light." Take these invitations from Christ and they are as honey out of the Rock of God. And He comes closer and closer, and more vitally, into relation with us every hour we live. That saying of Jesus, "Render unto Caesar the things that are Caesar's, and unto God the things that are God's," ushered in the sunrise of a new day. That was Christ's announcement of a principle designed for universal application. That saying of Jesus is the true Magna Carta of the doctrine of the separation of church and state, which doctrine some day, please God, will be embraced by all the nations of earth.

Christ is the only person who can answer the big question that comes to us, "How can I make my peace with God, though I am broken by sin'?" He said, "I am the Way, the Truth and the Life. No man cometh unto the Father but by me." How shall I treat my fellow-man? What are to be the relations of my race toward the other races of men? Jesus said, "Do unto others as you would have others do unto you." Jesus answered that by giving the Parable of the Good Samaritan, showing that the man of a hated race was neighbor to the Jew in need.

"Then, who is my neighbor?" we ask. Jesus tells us: Your neighbor is anybody on the face of the earth who needs you. Maybe he lives in Dallas; maybe he lives in the wilds of Africa and is the most ignorant creature walking the earth today. Very well. Wherever, under the whole heavens, there is a human being who needs you, he or she is your neighbor. Hasten to him and help him in every possible way.

In South America, North America, in Europe, in Asia, in Africa, people have heard the divine teachings of Jesus and have bowed before those teachings. Unparalleled among the religions of the earth are the words of Jesus, for Christ the Son of God "taught as never man taught."

Some Vital Questions

Christ stands at the open grave, in the presence of darksome bereavement, telling us that death is not all. He cries, "I am the resurrection, and the life: he that believeth in me, though he were dead, yet shall he live: and whosoever liveth and believeth in me shall never die." "Because I live, ye shall live also." Be not afraid of this last and greatest enemy called Death, if your trust is in Christ.

What else? Not only does the life of Christ attest His divine claims, and not only does His teaching give added attestation, but His death on the Cross attests His divine claims. The centurion, standing at the foot of that Cross, seeing Jesus die and hearing Him as He prayed for His murderers, properly made the explanation when it was all over: "Truly, this was the Son of God."

The death of Christ was unique, substitutionary, redemptive. Wherever the facts concerning Christ's life and death are told throughout the world, men's hearts and consciences are stirred and they begin to ask, "What must we do to be saved?" And why? Jesus tells us: "And I, if I be lifted up from the earth, will draw all men unto me. This he said, signifying by what death he should die." The death of Christ was more than a dramatic example. It was a dynamic, sacrificial, substitutionary atonement for human sins. Verily He was the sacrificial Lamb of God which taketh away the sin of the world. The scriptures tell us that He bore our sins in His own body on the tree; and that His blood cleanseth us from all sin.

John Newton was a notorious sinner — one of the world's most outstanding sinners, we are told; but when he had a full view of Christ dying on the Cross, his heart was utterly broken and he made his surrender to Christ, and in the glow of that great surrender, he penned a hymn we often sing:

> In evil long I took delight,
> Unawed by shame or fear,
> 'Till a new object struck my sight
> And stopped my wild career.

Whom Say Ye That I Am?

> I saw One hanging on a tree,
>   In agony and blood —
> Who fixed His languid eyes on me,
>   As near the cross I stood.
>
> Sure, never 'til my latest breath,
>   Can I forget that look.
> It seemed to charge me with His death,
>   'Though not a word He spoke.
>
> My conscience felt and owned the guilt,
>   It plunged me in despair;
> I knew my sins His blood had spilt,
>   And helped to nail Him there.
>
> A second look He gave, which said
>   "I freely all forgive;
> This blood is for thy ransom paid:
>   I die that thou mayest live."

This is the way home. The death of Christ attests His divine claims. No wonder it wins over legalism, over Judaism, over paganism. "For every knee shall bow and every tongue shall confess that Jesus Christ is Lord, to the glory of God the Father."

Socrates died like a philosopher. Jesus died like a God. He was God. He died, "the just for the unjust, that he might bring us to God."

Then again, let us look at the resurrection of Christ. Millions are thinking about that on this Sunday called Easter. They are thinking about it around the globe. They are thinking about it on the great ships in mid-ocean; they are thinking about it in churches, in hospitals; they are thinking about it in homes where life is about to be snuffed out by some fatal illness; they are thinking about it as they bend over the bodies of their dear, departed dead; they are thinking about it the world around. What shall I say about the fact of Christ's resurrection? Christ is not in the grave! He is risen! "Come, see the place where the Lord lay!" He is risen! He is alive from the dead! He is alive forevermore!

If your eyes and mine were not holden, we would see Him in this great throng. He is bringing to bear the resources of

Some Vital Questions

wisdom and mercy and power and love on us. Christ is alive from the dead! The grave was empty of its contents. That body carried to the grave, came forth from the grave. Even now Christ is reigning yonder on high! And some day, He is coming again to judge the world in truth and righteousness. And we believe that He will come with the same body that was put to death on the Cross. We shall see that body glorified with the glorification which God will give to the redeemed in Christ who shall rise first to meet Him in the air on the resurrection morning.

Greenleaf, our greatest authority on evidence says: "The best attested fact of all history is the fact that Jesus rose from the dead."

The Holy Scripture tells us that Jesus was seen five times on the resurrection day. He was seen of Mary; He was seen of the women; He was seen of Simon Peter; He was seen by two disciples on the road to Emmaus; He was seen by the apostles as they sat at meat. Later, He was seen by seven apostles by the sea, and by above five hundred at another time. He was seen by James, and last of all, He was seen by Paul, earth's chiefest apostle. The evidences external and internal that Christ rose from the grave are overwhelming. That is our hope in the face of broken humanity; that is our hope in the face of life; that is our hope in the face of death.

Christ went down into the grave and came up out of the grave, and He says to you and to me through His teachings: "You can trust Me and when your time comes to die — no matter where, nor when, nor how — I will be there to pilot you through the dark waters, and to take you home on the other side, victorious, white robed, and eternal conqueror over death and the grave."

What else? His influence is world-wide . Christ is cutting His way through all history, and His purposes are ripening with the rising and setting of every sun. We are in no losing battle. The hands of Christ's clock never turn back. The wheels of God's chariot never cease rolling. Here is His own

Whom Say Ye That I Am?

great promise in the Bible: "HE MUST REIGN, till he hath put all enemies under his feet." It is a predestinated necessity. Christ MUST reign — not *may* reign — but HE MUST REIGN. Some day, "from the River unto the ends of the earth," Christ will be Lord of all, and even death shall be under his feet.

Behold! Christ comes to you and to me saying, "If you will put your trust in me, I will show you the way. If you will decide for me, cleave to me, follow after me, I will bring you out of the darkness; I will heal your broken heart; I will give you the joy of forgiveness; I will give you the sense of freedom; I will give you the spirit of triumph; I will put within you the power to overcome the temptations that assail you, and I will bring you out more than conqueror, when you come down to death, if you will put your trust in me." Here is the crowning promise: "I will never leave you nor forsake you."

Christ puts Himself to the test by demonstration: "Come and see!" "Come and trust me. Come and give up to me. Come with your doubts! Come! I will dissolve them for you! Come with your fears! I will drive them back and dissipate them. Come with all your sins! Though you be marred and stained by sin; though your sins be red like crimson, come, yield to me! With my own life, with my own atoning death, I will forgive you and I will set you free!" Will you come?

Here is the real proof and demonstration, which should satisfy all science and all philosophy — a demonstration of experience. A young man once asked an outstanding scientist what was his greatest discovery. The scientist waited a moment and then replied: "Young man, my greatest discovery of all is my discovery that Jesus Christ is my personal Saviour! I have trusted Him; He has saved me and I know it!" Ah, here is the true test — the test of personal experience. "Therefore being justified by faith we have peace with God, through our Lord Jesus Christ," because our trust is in Him.

Some Vital Questions

I saw a little boy awhile ago trying to comfort his father. The father had lost his wife; the boy had lost his mother. The ten-year-old little fellow was a Christian. The big brawny man held the little, sobbing boy against his own heart. The lad put his arms around his father's neck and said: "Daddy, it will not be long until we go home. You won't cry like that anymore, will you? You and I love Jesus like Mama did and it will not be long until we go home, too. You won't cry anymore, will you, Daddy?" The big man straightened up and said: "My boy, you have said the right word. Certainly not. We will think of the time when we will all go home." Take all your bereavements, woes, looses, shadows, and every kind of grief to that wonderful Saviour.

> 'Tis the Saviour that can give,
> Sweetest pleasures while we live.
> 'Tis the Saviour must supply,
> Solid comfort when we die.
> After death my joy shall be,
> Lasting as eternity.
> Be that Living Christ my friend,
> Then my joys shall never end.

Oh, my men and women, heavy-burdened men and women; needy men and women; busy, suffering, sinning men and women! Oh, men and women making one quick passage through time into eternity! What have you done with Christ? Do you say, "Sir, I trust Him. I am leaning on Him. Other refuge have I none, nor do I want any other"? Can you say, "I know whom I have believed and am persuaded that he is able to keep that which I have committed unto him against that day"? Does your heart say that? Then, go your way rejoicing!

But what of you who are not saved, dear men and women, boys and girls? You have heard about Jesus today. Will you not turn squarely and face Him as you hear Him ask, "Whom say ye that I am?" Is He what He claims to be? Is He the one Saviour for all mankind? Is He the Arbitrator, the Mediator, the Pilot, the Guide, the Redeeming Saviour to bring

Whom Say Ye That I Am?

you victoriously home? Is He? And does your heart say, "Yes"? Then, give yourself to Him. Will you yield to Him? Will you decide for Him? Will you decide for Him NOW? Will you decide for Him before the sermon is over? Before the day is out? Before the dark night comes? Before the door of hope closes? Before the gate of opportunity slowly swings shut for the last time? Will you come now with a definite surrender to Christ? Why should you wait, since He saves, since He does it all; since waiting has in it all of peril? He asks for you in spite of your sins, your difficulties, your sorrows and your fears. And since He is the Saviour, and since He does it all, and since His time is now, will you let Him save you now?

Surely there are men and women, fathers and mothers, husbands and wives, young men and maidens, sons and daughters, happy boys and girls who will say to Jesus, "Today I bow to Thee, Lord; today I decide for thee; today I respond to Thy call; today I say 'Yes'." Since Jesus does all the saving — all of it — and His time is now, your time is now too! Won't you take Him now?

> Oh Happy Day that fixed my choice,
> On Thee my Saviour and my God.
> Well may this glowing heart rejoice,
> And tell its raptures all abroad.

QUESTION IV

What Does Salvation Involve?

QUESTION IV

What Does Salvation Involve?

> *If the righteous scarcely be saved where shall the ungodly and the sinner appear?* I PETER 4:18

IN THE first epistle of Peter, the fourth chapter and eighteenth verse, there are found the very solemn words of the text.

It is not easy to be saved. Jesus never one time said it was easy. How candid, how faithful He was, as He pointed out to men the way of salvation! He said: "Wide is the gate, and broad is the way that leadeth to destruction and many there be which go in thereat: but strait is the gate, and narrow is the way which leadeth unto life." Listen to His exhortation: "Agonize ye to enter in at the strait gate." The old word here is "strive," but the proper word, is "agonize." The whole nature is required. "Agonize ye to enter in at the strait gate: for I say unto you that many shall seek to enter in" — half-heartedly seek, somewhat seek, partially seek, superficially seek — but such seeking will be in vain. They shall never be able to enter in. How candid Jesus is about the heavenly way, about what walking in it means!

When we read the solemn words of Peter in our text, we are forced to inquire as to their meaning: "If the righteous scarcely be saved, where shall the ungodly and the sinner appear?" Does He mean to indicate here that the righteous are not going to be saved? No! He means to say that salvation as to its *process* is very difficult, but as to its issue, as to its outcome, is certain. He means what Paul meant when he said to some of the converts on his first missionary tour:

Some Vital Questions

"We must through much tribulation enter into the kingdom of God." (Acts 14:22) He and Paul both knew from experience that this was true. Yes, they both knew that salvation as to its process is unspeakably difficult, but as to its reality and its final issue it is gloriously certain. Were it not for the blessed assurance that God will complete the good work of salvation begun in us, we should likely despair amid the tribulations of the processes of the heavenly way. Let us note some of those assurances.

"My sheep hear my voice, and I know them, and they follow me: And I give unto them eternal life; and they shall never perish, neither shall any man pluck them out of my hand. My Father, which gave them me, is greater than all; and no man is able to pluck them out of my Father's hand." "I and my Father are one." We must hear language like that, in the midst of a text confronting us like this, to be certain, to be reassured.

Listen again: "We are begotten again unto an inheritance incorruptible, and undefiled, and that fadeth not away, reserved in heaven for you, who are kept by the power of God through faith unto salvation ready to be revealed in the last time." And again: "Because I live, ye shall live also." We must be fortified with these great assurances from God's own book, from Christ's own lips, to be strong in the face of a solemn text like this: "If the righteous scarcely be saved, where shall the ungodly and the sinner appear?"

The tragic fact confronts us at every turn of life's road that professed Christians can live very shabbily. We can follow Christ afar off. We can know Him only a little, and grow only a little, and do only a little in the Christian life. Or we can live it grandly. We can go from one mountain summit to another. We can grow in grace and in the knowledge of Christ continually. We can come to the stature of strong men, and quit ourselves like men in the kingdom of Christ, or we can dawdle and trifle and be babes in the Christian life from its beginning even down to the grave.

What Does Salvation Involve?

Why is it difficult for the righteous to be saved? "If the righteous scarcely be saved!" Is it because Jesus is weak? Nay! Nay! The government is on His shoulders. He is called the Mighty One. He has all power given into His hands, in heaven yonder, on earth here. With Him are the mighty issues of power. He is not weak. He does not lack in might. Why, then is it difficult for the righteous to be saved? It is not because Jesus is weak — keep that in mind — nor because He lacks in strength. We are told, "Wherefore he is able also to save them to the uttermost that come unto God by him." He is able to save them unto the uttermost, all of them; unto the uttermost of guilt, the uttermost of age, the uttermost of race, the uttermost of sin, the uttermost of besmirched character, the uttermost of doubt, the uttermost of unbelief. "He is able to save unto the uttermost of all that come unto God by him."

Again, we are told by Paul, "This is a faithful saying, and worthy of all acceptation, that Christ Jesus came into the world to save sinners; of whom I am chief." Oh, the power in His hands! If this world, all the adults in it, would turn to Jesus honestly, in one second, before my sentence is done, the world would be saved. If this audience, having in it complicated cases, every heart with its own story, every soul with its own sin, every spirit with its own burden, if Jesus were honestly trusted by those who are away from Him, in one short breath the angels would start their music, because sinners here would be saved.

Oh, it is not with Jesus that the difficulty lies. "Whosoever will, let him take the water of life freely." Like that He calls to men. "Ho, every one that thirsteth" — and every human being thirsts — "Ho, every one that thirsteth, come ye to the waters." "He that hath no money, let him come without money and without price." A life-giving fountain has been opened and whosoever will drink of that fountain shall live forevermore, with sins left behind. The word divine is: "Though your sins be as scarlet, they shall be as white as snow. Though your sins be red like crimson, they shall be as wool." "I will put your sins behind your back." "I will mention them to you no more." "I will put them from you as far as the east is from the west, if you will come to me." Oh, what a Saviour is Jesus!

What then is the meaning of this language: "If the righteous scarcely be saved"? What does it mean? Why is it difficult for them to be saved? There are three reasons, and they are right at hand.

First, there is the deceitfulness of our old nature. Were you like I was when you were changed? I went for years seeking Christ. From a lad I sought Him. I was definitely called when I was eleven years old. As vividly as though it were yesterday I can remember my burden, my pain, my loneliness, my fear. I was shrinking. I was timid. I could not venture to speak to anybody. Oh, if somebody could have divined my situation and have taught me! I knew I was wrong. I knew I was a sinner. I knew I was lost in my old nature. I had the sense of alienation from the holy God and of condemnation on my own head and heart, because of personal sin. I knew it all, but I could not see the way. I groped in the darkness. Then, after years and years, when young manhood came on, in a quiet church house *like this,* one Sunday, a man threw out the lifeline and said to me, "Lay hold on eternal life," and I laid hold.

From that little church, I went down the country road wondering if I would ever have another battle again. The skies were beautfiul beyond words. The very stars seemed to be one great galaxy of mighty choirs praising God, and all about me nature seemed in unison with the divine will. I thought I would never, never, never know what it was to step aside, to stray, to blunder, to err again. And yet the very next day every dog out of the pit seemed at my heels. Doubts came, darts pierced, temptations smote, and clouds enshrouded. Oh, how little I knew about what the Christian life means! For you see, when we are born again we are not yet sanctified,

What Does Salvation Involve?

we are not yet perfected. It is the spirit that is born again, but it has to live in a house which is terribly exposed. Those dear friends who tell us that down here in the flesh they are as good as God, are woefully mistaken. They have widely missed the truth. There are no perfect people down here in the flesh. The mightiest prophet God has in the earth, three score and ten years of age, is not a perfect man at all. If you will read the autobiography of Martin Luther, you will find that clear on down to his grave he bewailed the weaknesses in his old flesh. If you will read the story of John Knox, in that autobiography where he put on paper again and again the thoughts and emotions and struggles and conflicts in his heart, you will find that great old John Knox, who made Queen Mary tremble as she did not tremble before a great field of armed men, was filled with distress because he was not a better man. It is the weakness of the flesh. You see, this body is not born again yet. This body will be born again when we are raised from the dead. The body will be redeemed and glorified when the trump of Christ shall sound and the sleeping dust shall come to life at the call of infinite power. You can put a well man in a bad physical environment and he will soon be sick. His environment will affect him. A saved man still lives in the old house of clay which has a thousand difficulties about it, and his old nature, this unregenerated body is to the last degree deceitful. Now, that explains somewhat why the righteous are saved, as to the process, with great difficulty.

And next, the righteous are saved, as to the process, with great difficulty, because of the weakness of the new nature. When a man is born into the kingdom of Christ he is very weak and undeveloped. When a little, tiny babe comes into our home, oh, what a weak thing it is! How helpless it is, as it lies there on its mother's heart! How dependent, that tiny little bit of humanity! Even so when you and I were born again, born by the power of God, born by the Spirit, born from above, taken out of the kingdom of darkness and

Some Vital Questions

put into the kingdom of light, changed to the very center of our being by divine power, when that happened we were babes in Christ — just babes, not strong men. Oh, what nurture, what watching, what reinforcement that little babe needs! And every little Christian ought to have a great cordon of defenders and reinforcements around him. And every little Christian, because of the weakness of the new nature, must "grow in grace," as God's Book puts it. Grow. Eat the right food. Take the right exercise. As Christians. grow! Work where you ought to work. Live as you ought to live. Eat what you ought to eat, and grow in grace and in the knowledge of Christ. The new nature is very weak when we begin. But by battling and struggling and fighting and praying and resisting and triumphing, we shall come, after a while, to be men in the kingdom of God. But it is a great battle!

Then, again, the saving of the righteous is attended with very great difficulty because of the power of that great evil giant in the earth, whose name is Satan! And there is a great, evil giant, my friends, an evil personality, in this world of ours, deceiving, enticing, corrupting, seducing, darkening, deadening, seeking to drag us down to doom, just as really as there is a great, good, holy personality, summoning us to the upward way.

Every one has to come into close quarters with Satan, the temptations he suggests, the doubts that he brings, the meshes that he fixes for our feet, the enticements that he plans to catch us in our unwary, unguarded moments. Every man has to watch against the power of Satan. If we do not watch against the evil, powerful agent, whose name is Satan, we shall surely trip and fall, we shall shame our profession as Christians and give occasion to the enemies of God to blaspheme. It was Satan who sifted Simon Peter. Satan made Simon Peter lie concerning Jesus, and swear to his falsehood. Paul said: "I was hindered by Satan." Job said: "Satan from the very pit came before me and accused me." Yes, Satan

What Does Salvation Involve?

deceives. Satan resists. Satan entices. Satan accuses. Satan bewitches. In many ways Satan uses his arts to keep us from walking in the right path. The person who forgets that is in terrible danger.

Christian experience confirms what I am saying; namely, that the matter of salvation as to its process is very difficult. Not as to its outcome, not as to its goal, not as to its harvest, but as to its process, it is very difficult. Christian experience confirms that. I could put every Christian in this house on the witness stand and by their testimony quickly show that the Christian has to wage a battle all the time down here in the flesh. For you see, the spirit redeemed — the spirit begotten, born again, the spirit changed — lives in a bad environment, lives in an unregenerated house of flesh. Paul describes it in the seventh chapter of Romans. He says, "When I would do good, evil is present with me." He says, "For the good that I would I do not; but the evil which I would not, that I do. When I would do good, evil is present with me. . . .O wretched man that I am! who shall deliver me from the body of this death?" Who shall deliver me from this dead body? I am tied to a dead body. Who shall deliver me? It is the battle the Christian fights.

And that is not all. Oft times the Christian is painfully apprized of his weakness by his surprising defeats. He began well, but he was bewitched. He is now following Christ afar off. He is cold as ice. He is prayerless, and his religion has become perfunctory and mechanical and passionless. It has lost the glow and the passion with which it began. His defeats teach him that he is in the midst of a terrible battle. Simon Peter, presumptuous man! The Lord and Master looked on him and said, "Before the cock shall crow, thou shalt deny me thrice." You remember how he denied Christ, and then to his denial added profanity. There it is. There it is. O men, the very day and hour that you are careless in your Christian life, that day and hour you will be victimized by Satan. You will come short of duty, you will compromise the truth, and you will give the enemies of Christ occasion to mock and to blaspheme. Even David, that glorious poet-king, that man "after God's own heart," that mighty man of valor, that sweet singer of Israel, that glorious leader; even David, that magnanimous, chivalrous soul — even David went into the depths of darkest sin in the unwary, unguarded hour.

The Bible just tells the plain truth about men. When David blackened his name with a blackness that all time won't wash off, the Bible set it down. When Moses came short, as he led Israel, the Bible reported his dereliction. When Abraham, the father of the faithful and the friend of God, went wrong, the Bible recorded it. When Paul and Barnabas, those messengers of peace and good will to the world, came into a sharp contention and quarreled about a kinsman of Barnabas, and went their separate ways, the Bible was not silent about it. This Book does not gloss over anybody's character. It states the facts as they are. The Bible makes it very plain that God's servants fall into all manner of trouble and disgrace and shame and evil ways, through carelessness and prayerlessness and selfishness and lack of watchfulness.

A man's sins are forgiven; but, let me tell you, gentlemen, the consequences persist. David's awful, double sin of adultery and murder was forgiven. Nevertheless, God said, "I will forgive your sins, but the consequences will be there in your family. The sword will not go out of your house." And so it was. The daughter went to ruin. Handsome, rebellious Absalom broke his father's heart. Ah, me! The consequence of sin is a bloodhound on a man's track. It is a Nemesis that will not quit. "Whatsoever a man soweth, that shall he also reap." He will reap it. He will reap it. God will forgive him. If he repents, God will put his sin from him.

What Does Salvation Involve?

But the sword is there. The consequences are there. Whatsoever a man sows, that shall he reap. If a Christian man presumes, if he goes where he ought not to go, if he is careless and presumptuous, like David, or Moses, or Solomon, or Paul, or Simon, he will shame his Lord by grievous sinning. He will set the tongues of blasphemers to blaspheming against God. How serious it all is!

And then, added to that, the chastenings of love are to correct us. Chastisements come to you and me. What spoiled people we would all be, but for God's chastening rod. "Whom the Lord loveth He chasteneth, and scourgeth every son whom he receiveth . . . . If ye be without chastisement, then are ye bastards, and not sons. Furthermore, our fathers in the flesh corrected us when we were children, and we gave them reverence. Shall we not much rather be in subjection unto the Father of spirits, and live?"

Oh soul, passing under the rod——Christian soul with afflicted body, with afflicted family, with the death angel going through your home, with a grave yonder and flowers on it, now beginning to wither, with your plans intercepted, with your gates shut in your face — One mightier than man is before you, is behind you, is restraining, is constraining, to get the best out of you. That is what it means. Divine chastening for our good!

Now we see it, don't we? Being saved, as to the process, is inutterably difficult. The outcome is sure. "He which hath begun a good work in you will perform it until the day of Jesus Christ." That is His promise. I would despair tonight but for that. I tell you, if I thought tonight that my getting to heaven from this night on depended only on myself, I would be in despair. Christ calls to me, saying, "I will shepherd you and I will keep you. Trust me, and I will forgive you. I will forgive you seventy times seven. I will forgive you fully, if you will turn to me." Oh, the wonder of the forgiving grace of God!

Some Vital Questions

It is a marvelous thing to be the right kind of Christian; to be a stalwart, robust, consistent, conquering Christian; to be a Christian such that the people, when they shall see you, shall take knowledge that you have been with Jesus; it is a great thing to be a Christian after the order of Christ!

Now, "if the righteous scarcely be saved," what follows? Here it is: "Where shall the ungodly and the sinner appear?" If a man who says "yes" to Christ, as I have been indicating, if a man yields his life, scarred and maimed and crippled by sin, to the great Saviour of sinners, Jesus the Lord — if for the man who does that the process is difficult, what do you think of the man who does not do that at all? What do you think of the man who says he will risk it without any of that, who looks at that cross on which the Lord of Glory died and says in his heart: "He can die as much as He will for aught I care, I will not have Him to reign over me," — what do you think of that man's chance?

Oh, that meek and gentle and loving One calls to us and tells us what his chance is! "You shall die in your sins, and whither I go you cannot come." You ask me if I believe in the two places, heaven and hell? Assuredly, I do! "As a man soweth, so shall he reap." As a man lives here in his relation to Christ, so shall he pass out in that little break called death, and either he will be yonder in heaven with Christ, because he loves Him beyond all else, or he will be in the land of waste and death where Christ is not. Which shall it be with you? Which shall it be?

Oh, limping and marred and halting and hesitant, struggling and battling, often swept by doubts and weaknesses, often the heavens seeming like brass above me when I try to pray, yet, oh **Christ**:

> Nothing in my hand I bring.
> Simply to Thy cross I cling.
> Naked, come to Thee for dress;
> Helpless, look to Thee for grace.
> Vile, I to the fountain fly.
> **Wash me, Saviour, or I die.**

What Does Salvation Involve?

Are you trusting Christ? Can you answer with an unequivocal "yes"? Then I urge that you watch, in order that the Christian life be grandly lived. Watch that Satan does not entrap you and destroy your influence for good over others. Watch that you do not in your own life give some lost sinner occasion to blaspheme the Christian religion and say with scorn: "If that is religion, I want none of it." Oh, watch, because a critical world looks on and watches your every step. Strive to be a Christian above reproach. Keep close to Christ and you will be victorious.

"Where shall the ungodly and the sinner appear?" Christ answers: "Where I am, they shall never come who do not trust and love me." Hear His heart-broken lament: "O Jerusalem, Jerusalem, how often would I have gathered thy children together, as a hen doth gather her brood under her wings, and ye would not." I would. Ye would not. "Behold, now your house is left unto you desolate." You have missed the way. You have not chosen the highest. You have lost heaven. You would not come to me that you might have life. Because I wished humanity to be saved, I made atonement for men. I offered myself. I destroy not their wills. I appeal to their wills. I summon their consciences. I call to their wills, the initial spring of human actions, and they must say "Yes" or "No."

I beseech you to say "yes" to Christ even now! Let your honest confession and prayer be something like this: "Lord, a helpless creature am I. I cannot by myself meet life here like it ought to be met. I need Thee now and I shall need Thee as I go down into the Valley of the Shadow. Nor would I go alone out yonder to meet the issues that await every man beyond the grave, where I shall be judged before the Prince of Life. I cannot face that great assize, left to myself. Oh, how I need Thee all the way, Lord Jesus! Be merciful to me, the sinner. I yield to Thee!"

> Just as I am, without one plea
> But that thy blood was shed for me,
> And that thou bidd'st me come to thee,
> O Lamb of God, I come! I come!

If thus you will come, your heart can rest with blessed assurance on His sure promise: "He that cometh to me, I will in no wise cast out." He will receive you. He will forgive you. He will save you, and save you now.

QUESTION V

What Are You Living For?
A Commencement Message

QUESTION V

What Are You Living For?
A Commencement Message

~~~~~~~~~~~~~~~~~~~~

> *I have meat to eat that ye know not of.* JOHN 4:32

WE come once again to the midyear commencement of the Forest Avenue High School of our city. We are glad to have the pupils of this graduation class, together with their teachers and friends, with us this morning and we offer to them our most cordial felicitations. Your achievement in coming successfully to your graduation hour marks a distinct epoch in your life, and such achievement indicates patience and persistence on your part, through the recent years. You will allow me, an older fellow-student of yours, to urge you to go on if possible with still further studies and necessary preparation for the days ahead.

Education was once considered a luxury for just the few. It may now be considered a stern necessity for the many. The old saying that knowledge is power holds true, everywhere. The man who knows has the advantage over the man who does not know. The sure foundations of state are laid, not in ignorance, but in knowledge. You will allow me to adjure you to remember that the fear of the Lord is the beginning of wisdom. Culture that leaves out God has in it untold dangers. The world is suffering now because knowledge too often has been divorced from any recognition of the will of God.

I bid you Godspeed. Remember the saying of the old Troy general to the young man who waited on him and asked him what was the secret of his always winning victories in his campaigns. The wise old general made the laconic reply, "The secret of any and every victory, young man, is in getting a good ready." Get a good ready, my dear young friends, for the big battles of life ahead of you, for the inexpressibly weighty demands that shall be made upon you. The Lord of Hosts be with you everyone and lead you on and have you in His keeping forevermore.

And now, turning away from these personal words, let us think together at this hour about the hidden reinforcements of life. The thought is suggested to us by a sentence used by Jesus. "I have meat to eat that ye know not of."

You will recall the occasion when Jesus used this sentence. I read it to you from the fourth chapter of John's Gospel earlier in this hour of service. Weary and hungry, Jesus sat on the ledge of Jacob's ancient well in the heat of the noonday sun. While He thus rested, His disciples went into the nearby town to buy necessary food. Then it was that a woman came from one of the Samaritan villages to draw water from that famous well. The Master had an opportunity to make an approach to that woman for her higher welfare.

Jesus opened the conversation with her by saying, "Give me to drink." The woman showed surprise, for Jews were not supposed to have dealings with the Samaritans. "How is it that thou, being a Jew, asketh drink of me which am a woman of Samaria?" she inquired. Then Jesus answered, "If thou knewest the gift of God, and who it is that saith to thee 'give me to drink,' thou wouldest have asked of him and he would have given thee living water." "Sir," she said, "give me this water that I thirst not, neither come here to draw."

Then, to discover to the woman her dreadful situation, Jesus faithfully but ruthlessly brought to light the guilty secrets of her immoral life. He probed her conscience. He forced her to see herself as she really was. Then he skillfully led her to a realization that He was the long-promised Messiah.

What Are You Living For?

In the meantime, the disciples came back with food which they urged Jesus to eat. They knew that He had gone a long while without food. Now they said, "Master, eat." But Jesus answered, "I have meat to eat that ye know not of." And when He saw that they were perplexed by that saying, He explained, "My meat is to do the will of him that sent me and to finish his work."

This saying of Jesus, "I have meat to eat that ye know not of," points our meditation today and suggests several vital truths for us. One is that we have spiritual natures which must be fed on spiritual food, just as we have physical natures which must be fed on physical food. That spirit or soul relates us to God and the eternal. That body relates us to the seen and temporal. The big question of life, therefore, is: What am I living for? What is my dominant purpose in life? What spurs me on? Do I live to eat or eat to live? There is a great difference between those two things. What is the meaning of life, with all of its accessories and equipment and reinforcements? What does it all mean? Everyone should ask the question with all possible earnestness: *What am I living for?*

Jesus said, "My meat is to do the will of him that sent me and to finish his work." And yours and mine is to do the same thing, if we are to carry out God's plan for our lives. Have we faced that truth? Do we understand it? If so, are we resolutely, whole-heartedly seeking to conform our lives and our wills to the will of Him, whose we are and whom we live to serve? Certain it is that the things of earth cannot fully satisfy us. Man descends to the level of a mere animal if he lives primarily on the physical plane. Think of the life lived by the debauchee, by the drunkard, by the sensualist, by the mere glutton. Such do not truly live at all. They merely exist like animals. That kind of existence cannot satisfy. The end of it is doom.

Some Vital Questions

> This world can never give
> The bliss for which we sigh;
> It's not the whole of life to live,
> Nor all of death to die.

Augustine was right when he said, "Man, every man and every woman, was made for God and can never rest until he rests trustfully and obediently on the heart of God." The world cannot satisfy. One recalls Napoleon's efforts to cross the desert with his troops on a great expedition. The hot sun was fairly consuming them as they cried out in their agony for water. Their thirst was overwhelming. As they looked ahead they cried, "Lo! yonder is a lake!" They rushed to what they thought was a lake, but it was not a lake at all. It was only a mirage in the desert. Life without God is like that, a mirage in the desert, a fantasm, a delusion. No wonder that brilliant Lord Byron wrote, while he was yet a young man as he debauched his life most terribly and perverted it and prostituted it, no wonder that he wrote:

> My days are in the yellow leaf;
> The flowers and fruits of love are gone;
> The worm, the canker, and the grief
> Are mine alone!

This world cannot satisfy. We are made for a higher destiny than that. Almighty God has a nobler mission for men than gathering together money or land or securing temporal prestige and honor. God has something greater than that for mankind.

Now another truth, suggested by Jesus' words, is that the battle of life is to keep the soul in the ascendancy over the body. That is a hard battle. Paul tells us that the flesh battles against the spirit and the spirit against the flesh and these are contrary one to the other. That is the battle.

Oh, I wish you could see what is given me to see again and again and again, the pitiful cry of some man who has burnt his life out with strong drink! He sits in my office and recounts the downward drift of his life and how hopeless he is in his inability to recover himself and to overcome his passion for strong drink. To gain and keep control over the body and its appetites is a constant battle we need to fight. The conflict between the spiritual and the physical is the hardest battle we have to fight in this life. Shall the soul dominate our lives or shall the body dominate? That is the issue.

Fortunately, there are certain hidden reinforcements upon which our souls may draw in this conflict between the soul and the body. "I have meat to eat that ye know not of," said Jesus. And you and I can say the same thing. There are certain inner resources that each of us has. What are some of these hidden reinforcements?

First of all, we can fall back on conscience and every man is to look well to his conscience. The education most of all needed in this land and every other land is the education of conscience. Paul said, "I also exercise myself to have a conscience void of offense toward God and men always." Every man is to look well to the education of his conscience. We are hearing a great deal these days about crises. I'll tell you the greatest crisis in all the world. It's the crisis of character. If a man trifles with his conscience so that he is willing to tell a lie for any amount of money in the world; so that he is willing to turn a sharp corner, marked by trickery and fraud; that is a crisis — yes, a tragedy — in the realm of character. We are to see that we do not have deadened, desensitized, benumbed, paralyzed consciences.

Everyone is to ask all the time, "What is right?" He must *know* that and *do* that, though the heavens fall. A man is to keep his conscience intact. He is to see that his conscience is not utterly diverted and diseased and doomed. Conscience must be kept as sensitive to the right as the needle of the compass is to the magnetic pole, so that one can safely follow the dictates of his own conscience. The big question is not what is pleasant or expedient or customary or even what is profitable, but what is right.

Some Vital Questions

> For right is right, since God is God,
> And right the day must win.
> To doubt would be disloyalty,
> To falter would be sin.

Think of men breaking covenanted engagements and laughing at them and calling them "scraps of paper." Nations are now staggering and reeling like drunken men because character has been assaulted, character has been despised, character has been debauched, character has been corrupted on a world-wide scale. That spells tragedy for the nations.

There is another reinforcement that we can turn to, and that is a worthy ambition in life which we can keep before us all the time. What are you living for? Are you carrying out your mission in life? Are your steps leading toward the goal that is set before you and that you ought to approximate if it is within your power? We are to keep before us all the time a worthy ambition. George Eliot said, "What makes life dreary is utter want of motive." That is a great statement, but you can make it very much stronger by adding one word. "What makes life dreary is utter want of *right* motive." Now we are to see, all the time, that we are animated by the right motive and keep before us the true goal in life.

Then there is another hidden reinforcement, and that is our unfaltering faith in the final and absolute triumph of righteousness. A man can endure in the flesh a thousand ills if he has an unfaltering faith in the final and absolute triumph of righteousness. We are not in a losing battle when we are trying to do right. We are not in a losing battle when we say: "Whatever the cost, I must do right. If I haven't a friend left, I must do right. If I haven't a bite of food for myself or my family, I must do right; for it is better to starve than to do wrong."

Unfaltering faith in the final triumph of righteousness is a glorious reinforcement to animate us and challenge us as we go on. In *Les Miserables* Victor Hugo described that battle at Waterloo between Napoleon and Wellington; and,

WHAT ARE YOU LIVING FOR?

in his own biting English, Victor Hugo asked, "Was it possible for Napoleon to win at Waterloo?" He answered with great vigor, "No!" And why? Because of Wellington? No! Because of the coming of an allied army? No! Then why? Victor Hugo's answer was, "Because of God." Napoleon had impeached God and had said that right and righteousness do not matter. God accepted the impeachment and overturned him; God brought him to defeat and doom.

That is the fate which, bye and bye, will befall certain men of our day. In the meantime many hearts will be broken and many lives will be crushed. But, "because of God," those ruthless men shall utterly fail just as Napoleon failed. God is ever the champion of the right. In His own time and way He will vindicate and establish the right. That is why we are justified in having an unfaltering faith in the triumph of righteousness. "Christ must reign until He has put all enemies under his feet." One day, every form of disobedience and sin will be under the feet of Christ and death itself shall be destroyed. That is my faith. Is it yours? I haven't a question about the final outcome of righteousness.

There is one more hidden reinforcement. I have named three. A fourth is the conscious companionship of the heart with Jesus, the Divine Saviour and Lord. Jesus, on one occasion, said to His disciples around Him: "Ye shall be scattered, every man to his own, and shall leave me alone: and yet I am not alone, because the Father is with me." And so can we say, "All may fail and flee and yet we are not left alone." Christ's pledge is, "Lo! I am with you alway, even unto the end of the world." "I'll be with you in the sixth trouble and I will not forsake you in the seventh; I will never leave you nor forsake you." These statements guarantee the presence of Christ with His friends. By faith they can see and feel Him standing within the shadows, keeping watch above His own. The presence of Christ with His friends is a reality.

Some Vital Questions

Fanny Crosby, the great hymn writer, wrote many of her greatest hymns after she was blind. She wrote her hymn, *Blessed Assurance,* when she was totally blind.

> Blessed assurance, Jesus is mine!
> Oh, what a foretaste of glory divine!
> Heir of salvation, purchase of God,
> Born of His Spirit, washed in His blood.
>
> This is my story, this is my song,
> Praising my Saviour all the day long;
> This is my story, this is my song,
> Praising my Saviour all the day long.

Fanny Crosby was radiant and triumphant even with her pitiful limitation of blindness.

And full many a time we are to face life like Martin Luther did in his stormiest days, when all the clouds were hanging low about him and when the combination of forces seemed unbreakable. It was then that he said to his associates, "Come, let us sing together Psalm 46; God is our refuge and strength, a very present help in trouble." Do you have an unfaltering faith in the certain and final triumph of righteousness? Do you have the right ambition, the right motive, the right goal in life? Do you know what it is to have blessed fellowship and companionship with Jesus Christ?

To whom do you turn in the dark and cloudy day? Where do you look when the Black Friday comes? To whom do you go when the assaults of life are fiery and awful and when the questions of life are acutely poignant and terrible? Do you say with Simon Peter: "Lord, to whom shall we go? thou hast the words of eternal life"? Christ is the one source, adequate and all sufficient. Hear Him say: "I am the light of the world." Hear Him say: Bring your questions to Me and let Me answer them for you. Bring your difficulties to Me and let Me dissolve them for you in My wisdom and strength. Bring your anxieties and tears to Me and let Me dispose of them in the way best for you and for all concerned. Oh, how glorious it is trustfully and obediently to take Christ at His word and follow where He leads!

QUESTION VI

Why Be Discouraged?

QUESTION VI

Why Be Discouraged?

~~~~~~

> *Why are thou cast down, O my soul? and why art thou disquieted within me?* PSALM 43:5

THE question for our meditation today is a question concerning life's hours of discouragement. One can readily believe that all people at one time or another are visited with their hours of discouragement, of depression, of despondency. All of us at one time or another sail that sea, certainly for a season. Indeed, the contrast of feeling in men's lives today and then again tomorrow is sometimes quite amazing.

Take, for example, Elijah, confronting the false prophets on Mount Carmel, hundreds of them, one lone man against hundreds of the prophets of Baal. Elijah withstands them and with sarcasm, marvelous for its pungency, puts them to rout. The very next day this same brave man flees far into the wilderness before the threat of a wicked woman. Take the case of John the Baptist, standing before Herod and the woman consorting by his side, and mark his marvelous moral courage. A little later, when this same brave man languished in prison and he was cast down in spirit, he sent men to ask Jesus: "Art thou he that should come or do we look for another?" Take the case of Simon Peter, mighty apostle for Christ, who stood on the day of Pentecost and so preached the wonderful gospel of Christ that thousands believed and were added unto the church. Yet that same man on other occasions was a craven, a poltroon, a coward. "The best of men are but men at best." So says the old adage wisely.

Some Vital Questions

Take the case of King David, about whose question we are to meditate this hour. "Why art thou cast down, O, my soul, and why art thou disquieted within me? Hope thou in God, for I shall yet praise him who is the health of my countenance, and my God." One day this brave king — this glorious singer, David — shouted his cry: "The Lord is my light and my salvation. Whom shall I fear? The Lord is the strength of my life. Of whom shall I be afraid?" And the next day there issued from his lips this wailing cry: "I shall one day perish by the hand of Saul."

All of us at one time or another sail this sea, the sea of discouragement. Let us ponder for a little while David's question. "Why art thou cast down?" Why this period of discouragement, of depression, of despondency? You will notice here in this psalm that David quotes this expression three times. "Why art thou cast down, O, my soul?" Three times! The dreary monotony of it. Notice how he rings the changes on it — notice how he rolls it under his tongue — as if it were some sweet morsel! Scientists tell us that the eye of a fly has many facets, little faces, so that it will magnify one thing into a vast number. Now, certainly our eyes are like that at times for we will pick up one occasion of discouragement and with our magnifying glasses make that to be many times larger than it is. Sensitive and earnest people are especially subject to hours of discouragement. Those of you who have taken the pains to read the inner life stories of Shakespeare and Raphael have been impressed by the fact that there came terrible hours in the lives of those great geniuses — hours of depression beyond human speech. All sensitive people, all very earnest people are likely to have their reactions, their painful contrasts, their fearful reverses, in feeling.

We should not pass judgment upon a great issue or upon people when the hour of depression and discouragement is upon us. That old expression, which says "Let me sleep over it and I will answer you tomorrow," has great wisdom in it.

Why Be Discouraged?

For a man in the hour of discouragement is likely to be quite unfair, quite unjust and he will miss the mark sadly, if he be not careful.

We should be on our guard against the hour of discouragement, for discouragement is neither good nor wise nor Christian. And certainly we should not parade our discouragement before people. To do so is harmful, even sinful. A distinguished author begs everyone of us to present an air of positive kindness and good cheer wherever we go, because people around us are probably fighting hard battles and need from us reinforcement rather than discouragement.

We are to search constantly for the causes of discouragement. How shall we search for them? Valiant King David points one way when he says: "Why art thou cast down, O, my soul, and why art thou disquieted within me?" We are to question ourselves. We are to probe ourselves. We are rigidly to examine ourselves to find the cause of our discouragement. We are to be merciless with ourselves in the hour of discouragement, morbidness and depression and to find out and know what is back of and beneath all this gloomy spirit. That kind of self-examination, rigid and thoroughgoing, will lead us to self-control — and self-control is one of life's best assets. How pitiful for a man to be lacking in self-control! "Better he that ruleth his own spirit than he that taketh a city!" Many clever men and otherwise strong men, when they get to the crucial hour, break and their self-control goes to the wind. You have seen them, with their strength and fine points; but right at the crucial hour, when they should have themselves in hand, times without count, they explode and everybody is embarrassed by them and for them. A man's self-control is part of his endowment. Every man should watch himself and check himself and gird himself lest he be lacking in self-control!

The causes of life's hours of discouragement may be many. Frequently the cause is purely physical. The physician knows that better than anybody else. The body is the citadel of life, and ofttimes the body marvelously reacts on the spirit. Everybody should have a care all the time for the right care of the body. The body influences the mind and spirit very, very much. Jesus, when He was in the flesh, understood that perfectly; and one day, right in the midst of a great campaign, He said to a group of tired apostles: "Come ye apart to the desert place and rest awhile." Often a man's battle with discouragement is due to the fact that his body is below par — that he is down physically. Especially is that true of our brave and gentle women whose burdens in life frequently are more exacting than the burdens of men.

Another cause of discouragement is life's monotony. They tell us "variety is the spice of life." So it is. Men and women with little horizon in life, with all their condition circumscribed and narrow, are apt to have hours of discouragement. One of the great nerve specialists of the country told us a little while ago that the vast majority of people in our insane asylums are women from the farms where life is monotonous, where drudgeries are endless, and where routine wears these poor women to the breaking point. Life's monotony may explain why discouragement comes.

Or, it may be due to bitter disappointment. I wonder if you have read Wordsworth's pathetic story, "After the French Revolution." It is one of the most interesting chapters Wordsworth ever penned. He tells us that he thought the outcome of the French Revolution would be *brotherhood* and that all the finest qualities of human life would be extolled and glorified, as the earth had never seen it before. But, "Lo," he said, "a little after the last gun had ceased its echo, men went back to the old scramble of selfishness and bitterness and warfare and unseemly strife." Wordsworth's heart experienced bitter disappointment. The same thing happened following World War One. During and immediately following that war many said: "Now we may look for a long era of peace and good will, of law and order, of righteousness and justice." But alas! We find ourselves in the same battle,

Why Be Discouraged?

the same scramble, the same selfishness, the same lawlessness and disobedience. Now, we must alertly guard ourselves lest we be filled with despair about the moral welfare of the world and allow the days of biting fear and discouragement to benumb us.

Sometimes discouragement is due to personal egotism. The man possessed of great personal egotism is to be pitied — and always he is a man with whom it is difficult for others to deal. Elijah, who fled from wicked Jezebel and lay under the juniper tree, in his awful hour of discouragement, cried out: "I am no better than my fathers." Why, certainly he was not any better than his fathers. Whoever said he was? Why did he think he was? He said: "I have failed. I am no better than my fathers." Any man who is possessed of a great measure of personal vanity is riding for a hard fall. Of all the inexcusable things in man vanity, self-conceit, too high an opinion of one's self are the most inexcusable characteristics. With these tendencies, the hour of discouragement is certain to come to any man.

The cause for discouragement may be due to a false view of the facts of life. This man, Elijah, had a false view of the facts of life. He said, in the hour of discouragement: "I am the only one left. Why should I stay? I am fighting a losing battle. I have held out the best I could for righteousness, for God and for true holiness, but I am the only one left. Why should I keep on with the battle?" And God came with His comforting word and said: "Why, Elijah, I have seven thousand men who have never bowed their knees to Baal. You are not the only one left."

We find the same false views of the facts of life in the case of the young servant of Elisha. He was discouraged and feared in his heart when Elisha was withstanding great hosts of enemies who came with mighty pomp and parade. Elisha prayed: "Lord, open the eyes of this young man that he may see; Lord, open his eyes." And when his eyes were opened, he saw the mountains round about filled with the horses and chariots of God. If you and I could have our eyes opened to the true facts of life, we would understand that there is a plan, a program divine, going forward from victory to victory and that Christ must reign until He puts all enemies under His feet.

How then shall we cure discouragement? Sometimes, it is indicated by the right care of the body. I said to one yesterday, fighting the hard battle with ill health and discouragement and depression to the last degree appalling: "Perhaps the right care of your body will help — some good physician can probably tell you better than your minister. The right care of the body is, perhaps, the cure in your case for the standing mountain of discouragement that afflicts you day and night."

Still again, our discouragement may be entirely eliminated by joining ourselves to other brave souls and magnifying them in their relationship to us. Human companionship with the right kind of people is one of the most vital and helpful things in all human life.

Still again, our discouragement may be cured — full many a time is cured — by comparing ourselves with somebody else. I can take you from this building in twenty minutes to men and women fighting the awful battle with ill health and poverty; and, while fighting, they are singing songs that will send you away distinctly fortified for your own battle! Sometimes by comparing ourselves with somebody else our discouragement will be shamed away, and we will find out what little basis there is for any discouragement at all on our part.

One night sometime ago a little family in this city — the husband and father a devoted friend to God — sang the song:

> Be not dismayed whate'er betide
> God will take care of you.

And then they came down to the last verse:

> No matter what may be the test
> God will take care of you.

Why Be Discouraged?

And the wife looked up at him when they had finished that last stanza and said: "Husband, do we really believe that — 'No matter what may be the test, God will take care of you'? Do we really believe it? Do we really accept it?" And they talked late and long that night and they said: "We do believe it and we do accept it and no matter what shall come God will take care of us." And the next day the same little wife and mother had a terrific hemorrhage from the lungs and, when at last she was quiet, she looked up at the white face of the anxious, stricken husband and he gently bent over and kissed her forehead and she whispered softly to him, "Remember what we sang — 'No matter what may be the test, God will take care of you.'" And with a sob he said: "We will hold to it in this, our deepest trial." And today she is fighting out in the West, and he is fighting here with the babies in Dallas; and God is enabling them both to sing through their tears! Is your battle comparable to that?

Sometimes our discouragement can be cured by work. The most miserable men and women in the world are the men and women who do not work. God's great panacea for a thousand of life's woes is work. Work is honorable in all and idleness is dishonorable and disgraceful and sinful. Many a time work clarifies one's whole moral sky and he goes back to the warfare victorious.

But now the last word and the supreme word of all. Faith in God is the unfailing cure for life's hours of discouragement. David kept battling and kept questioning until he got to the foundation of the matter. "Why — why art thou cast down, O, my soul, and why art thou disquieted within me? Hope thou in God for I shall yet praise him who is the health of my countenance." Oh, soul, tried and beaten and fettered, put your trust in God! We can come out of our depressions and discouragements and vexations and trials and storms, and out of the blackest night and go on our way singing, if we will only stay ourselves on God!

Some Vital Questions

Have you learned the secret of peace? It is to stay yourself on God — absolutely to submit to God! Henry Van Dyke, great Christian, great diplomat, great scholar, stated it in his poem on "Peace":

> With eager heart and will on fire
> I sought to win my great desire.
> "Peace shall be mine!" I said
> But life grew bitter in endless strife.
>
> My soul was weary; my pride wounded deep.
> To Heaven I cried: "God give me peace,
> Or I must die."
> The dumb stars glittered no reply.
>
> Broken at last I bowed my head,
> Forgetting all myself and said:
> "Whatever comes, God's will be done!"
> And in that moment Peace was won.

It is Victory! It is victory for any of you in this great throng who will come to God with all your battles, doubts and sins and struggles and defeats and losses and failures! It is Victory! It is victory if you will stay yourself on God!

QUESTION VII

What Think Ye of Christ?
An Anniversary Message

QUESTION VII

What Think Ye of Christ?
An Anniversary Message

> *What think ye of Christ?*
> MATTHEW 22:42

TODAY, as the congregation and pastor of the First Baptist Church in Dallas begin their forty-third year together, emotions too deep for words stir our hearts. There is the emotion of gratitude, immeasurable and inexpressible. There is the emotion of thankfulness; there is the emotion of hope, as we look upon the untrodden future. Surely all of us wish to pause and raise our Ebenezer today, singing from our deepest hearts, "Hitherto hath the Lord helped us." The pastor cannot express at all in any terms known to him the measure of his gratitude, to God first of all, and then to you, my fellow-workers, as we have companied together through the fast passing years. My heart today freshly adopts Paul's great expression when he said, "I thank Christ Jesus our Lord, who hath enabled me, for that he counted me faithful, putting me into the ministry."

Some of you who know something of my early life know that I had no thought of being a preacher. All my plans and ambitions and hopes were in another direction, but when the clear consciousness came to my heart that it was the Saviour's plan for my life to be linked with Him in witness and testimony and service for His gospel and kingdom, I have never from that moment to this failed to say with Paul, "I thank Christ Jesus, our Lord, who hath enabled me, for that he counted me faithful, putting me into the ministry." If

SOME VITAL QUESTIONS

Christ would multiply my life into a thousand lives this noonday, and if He should say to me, "You wanted during your first life to be a lawyer but I wanted you to be a plain gospel preacher; now, you may do what you will with the thousand extra lives which I give you," I would not hesitate for as long as one second to say, "Master, if thou wilt, let every one of these added thousand lives preach Christ to the end of the earthly day."

It is fitting that I should have heeded Christ's call to be his minister, for my grandfather — whom I do not remember — was a glorious old country preacher in the mountains of North Carolina. When the doctor said to him, "Your hour has come, Brother Kimsey, you are down to the hour of death," he said, "Call in the neighbors as quickly as you can." He wanted to preach to them once more; and the grand old man, with his latest breath, preached Jesus to his neighbors. How glorious to go like that. I thank God for the heritage I received from him!

I hope you will forgive these personal references. Let us now turn away from them and think together on the central question of Christianity, stated for us in five little words: "What think ye of Christ?"

It is always interesting to observe what the people are thinking and saying upon various questions of the day; pressing questions, such as those concerned with the proper relation between capital and labor, or questions of taxation and finance, or questions of state, national and international legislation, or the poignant questions as to the cause and the cure of war — inhuman, atrocious, life-destroying war.

All these are questions that challenge the attention of serious men and women everywhere, but there is another question that takes precedence over all these questions or of any other question that might be propounded: "What think ye of Christ?" Jesus himself asked this question. He asked it at a time when men were plying Him with questions about matters of secondary importance, such as taxation or the marriage relation in the world to come. These critical men who were plying Jesus with questions were not prepared for His question: "What think ye of Christ?"

We do well to mark the emphasis of that question. He did not ask these men what they thought of the church, important as the church may be, nor did he ask what they thought of the ordinances of the church, impressive as they might be; nor of some ceremony or form; nor did he ask them what they thought of this or that creed. He asked, "What think ye of Christ?"

Salvation is not by a church, no matter what church it may be, nor by an ordinance, no matter how impressive its symbolism may be, nor by a sacrament, nor by a ceremony, nor by a ritual nor by a form, nor by a creed, no matter how sound the creed may seem to be. Salvation is by a person, whose name is Jesus Christ. "What think ye of Christ?" This question brings us face to face with the solemn obligation of every Christian to witness for Christ.

How shall we answer this direct question? Sometimes, the best way to answer any question is to ask subsidiary questions. Let us approach this central question that way. Let us ask three subsidiary questions. What think ye of Christ in His own person? What think ye of Christ in His gospel? What think ye of Christ in human experience? Let these three questions form our meditation today, and may the Holy Spirit guide our meditation for our highest good and for the glory of God.

First of all, what think ye of Christ in His own person? Christianity stands or falls with the person of Christ. Historic, apostolic, supernatural Christianity stands or falls with the person of Christ. Fearlessly we take our stand and declare that human nature did not and could not produce Christ. If mere human nature could produce one Christ, pray why has it not in all its amazing progress produced another one in these two thousand years since Christ first came? The answer is that the task is too stupendous for poor human nature to accomplish; for Christ was both God and man in one personality, the God-man in one personality. Never in all the world does the hyphen mean elsewhere what it means here. It both joins and divides; it marks distinction and yet unity. Christ was as really man as though He were not God and He was as really God as though He were not man, the God-man in one personality. Here we come to the glorious doctrine of the incarnation of God in Christ. Paul speaks of it in his first letter to Timothy in these words: "Without controversy great is the mystery of godliness: God was manifest in the flesh, justified in the Spirit, seen of angels, preached unto the Gentiles, believed on in the world, received up in glory."

From whatever viewpoint we may approach Christ, His superhuman character stands out sublimely attested. Look at Christ's words. Never spake a man like He spoke. Take any of His words. He uttered the ultimate word on every subject upon which He spoke. Hear Him as He said: "I am the way, the truth and the life: No man cometh unto the Father, but by me." "Come unto me, all ye that labor and are heavy-laden, and I will give you rest." Put those words on any other lips that you will, and you turn away feeling that a sacrilege has been committed. Put those words on the lips of Washington, revered father of our country; put them on the lips of Lee, the immortal Southener, or on Lincoln, that national and dramatic figure; put them on the lips of Gladstone, or on any other lips in the world, and we shake our heads ominously and turn away; but these words on the lips of Jesus, are as honey from the very rock of God. "Come unto me, all ye that labor and are heavy laden and I will give you rest. Take my yoke upon you, and learn of me; for I am meek and lowly in heart: and ye shall find rest unto your soul." Then, that other great expression of Jesus: "I am the light of the world." What does that mean? Exactly what He is saying: "I am the light of the world." Christ is the supreme light, for all humanity, upon the questions which are supreme above all other questions.

There are certain great universal questions that are asked by interested unbelievers around the world. Men have kept me up late at night, in mystical India and in age-old China and in Burma and in alert Japan, and have plied me with questions concerning God and the great verities of Christianity. People here at home ask the same universal question: "What kind of a God is your God?" To all I say: "Look at Jesus! He was God manifest in the flesh, God uncovered, God revealed in human form, so that poor, needy humanity could come to Him and trust Him and love Him and follow Him. As Jesus went about doing good, comforting the sorrowing, healing the sick, speaking soothingly to the heart-broken, we see God's great heart uncovered for us." That is what Jesus meant when he said: "I am in the Father and the Father in me"; "I and the Father are one"; "he that hath seen me hath seen the Father." If you would know what God the Father is like, then look at God the Son, even Jesus, who is called the Christ.

Then there is another great universal question: "How shall one, conscious of his own moral lapse and weakness, how can he ever get right with One so high and holy and perfect as is God the Father?" Christ the Son came for that very purpose. There is one mediator between God and you, and Christ is that mediator. You cannot make yourself right. You cannot save yourself. You are already sold into slavery on account of sin. You are already condemned by the holy law of God which says, "The soul that sinneth, it shall die," for you have sinned, even as all have sinned. "There is no difference: for all have sinned, and come short of the glory of God." You are broken and defeated; you are condemned and helpless. In your terrible bankruptcy of soul, Christ came to be your helper. There is only one mediator between God and you, and He is Christ. And if you will let Him be your mediator, your umpire, your arbitrator, your physician, your lawyer, He will take care of you. He is a friend who will stick closer than any brother. Even if your own parents have discarded you, He will take you up out of the deepest gutter of sin. He is the one who will get you into right relations with God. It was out of infinite love that the Father sent the Son on this great mission, and out of infinite love the Son came on such mission. Oh, what a gospel we Christians have! What a gospel!

And there is another great universal question which men are asking: "How shall a man relate himself to his fellowmen — in Dallas, in Texas, throughout America, throughout the whole world?" Then comes the Golden Rule: "Do unto others as ye would that they should do unto you." Christ gave us the parable of the Good Samaritan. Do you want to know who your neighbor is? Anybody who needs you is your neighbor. He may live next door to you, or across your state or your nation; he may live in the wilds of Africa, or in mystical India. He may never have heard of your country, nor of you. But wherever in the world he may be, if he really needs you, he is your neighbor. We are all to be world citizens. To follow Christ is to be a world citizen for Christ. Push back all the limits of your boundaries! In other words, "Go ye into all the world and preach the gospel to every creature." Whatever it costs, go! Whatever the sufferings, endure them! Whatever the lonely vigils, complain not, but go on! Christ tells us how to relate ourselves to our fellowmen. Oh, it will be glorious when we get past that time when men resort to tooth and claw and instead, have mercy and compassion toward all the children of man. How horrible! How atrocious! How ghastly! How unpardonable is war!

> When wilt thou save the people —
> O God of Mercy, when?
> Not kings and lords but nations —
> Not thrones and crowns, but men?
> God save the people!

That is our prayer. That is our prayer and it must be our effort, our witness day and night, "God save the people."

What Think Ye of Christ?

Men are being treated like dumb driven cattle by ruthless, merciless dictators, seeking to carry out their own fiendish ends. God save the people! It behooves every man, in times like these, to set himself diligently to the conservation of human life. One human life, a little waif in the street, half-naked today and hungry, is worth more than all the gold in all the mines of the world. Christ's mission here on earth, Christ's gospel, Christ's atoning death all combine to give us some faint conception of the worth of one human being.

Here is another universal question; namely, "If a man die, shall he live again?" "Does death end all?" "Is that grave out there the final chapter?" No traveler can come back to tell us what he found out there, what is beyond. Plato and Socrates, wise men of their day, stood in the presence of death, and their faces were covered with confusion and care as they said,"If there be anything beyond we do not know, we cannot say." Caesar, the great soldier, stood up in the Roman senate and said of a dead senator, "If there is anything more for him we cannot tell." But Christ stands in the market place of life, where the sick and the suffering die, where our loved ones breathe their last and are gone, and He touches us on the shoulder and whispers in our ear: "I am the resurrection and the life: he that believeth in me, though he were dead, yet shall he live: and whosoever liveth and believeth in me shall never die." "Be not afraid," he says to the little mother putting away her precious child, "You will see your darling again in the fair morning beyond." Oh do not be afraid; do not be afraid. Jesus has the keys. He has the keys to death and the grave and eternity; trust Him and go on without fear.

I spoke to several hundred college men in Calcutta, India, one night, and they were set with their keen wits to trap the visiting minister of the gospel of Christ. The man with me, a great Indian and a great Christian said: "Don't allow them to get you angry. If they can get your face red, your words sharp-toned, they will laugh in your face." He said, "They will ask you questions that are very embarrassing"; and I said, "I am sure they could. What will they ask?" And he replied: "They will ask you, 'What do you think about a Christian country like yours burning human beings in retaliation for some grievous thing they have done? What do you think about your cities being the worst controlled cities in the world, with more deaths there, more murders there, more horrible things there?'"

Having been warned, I came before those students and said: "If you have the impression that my country is a Christian land, you are mistaken. It is not a Christian land. There are a great number of Christians there, thank God, and various Christian groups; but ours is not a Christian land. We have wicked, congested cities; and sometimes our men, unrestrained by any thought of mercy or compassion, leap upon a fellow-man and take his life like some simple beast; but we are trying to make a Christian country out of our country. If all of our people would follow Christ and His teachings, we would have a Christian country."

Christ manifests His own deity by His works. Shall we look at His works? A tree is known by its fruit. Here is the true test. "By their fruit ye shall know them." Christ said, "If you will not believe me for my words, then believe me for my works' sake." From His cradle to His grave, there were outflashings of His deity.

The shepherds left their flocks that night and, later, the Magi brought their gifts and bowed down before the child Jesus, and worshipped Him. Years passed, and the lad of twelve went up to the temple where the learned doctors of the law plied Him with questions: and His answers amazed them. Then He turned, this lad of twelve, and asked these learned doctors of the law questions that astonished and baffled them. Time passed on. Then came the three short years of Christ's public ministry. Wherever He worked, sin and demons and death obeyed His voice. He said to the tempestuous waves, "Peace, be still," and they were quiet. He said to the man who was sick, "Take up thy bed and walk," and the man obeyed. He said to one in death, "Arise," and Death, like some frightened animal, departed. Thus the Master's own works attest His claim.

Look at His character. He challenged, "Which of you convicteth me of sin?" and the answer of Pilate must be universal humanity's answer; namely: "I find no fault in him." We can find fault in anybody else. Moses lost his temper and shattered the Tables of the Law. Paul and Barnabas, the apostles of peace and good-will, had a quarrel and separated. You can find fault in anybody else, but you can find no fault in Jesus. Holy, harmless, undefiled, sinless, there He is! Christ is God's way to man; Christ is man's way to God. Christ is the true Jacob's ladder. By Him the penitent sinner, the believing soul, the redeemed child of God may come unto the Father and enter into the house of many mansions.

Again, what do you think of Christ in His gospel? It is enough to say that wherever the facts about Christ are faithfully declared — His supernatural birth, His supernatural life, His supernatural death, His supernatural resurrection — wherever the facts of Christ are faithfully preached, men are overwhelmed by these facts. Many leave their idols and come penitently confessing their sins and accepting Him as their Saviour. In South India alone there are two hundred and forty thousand members of our Baptist churches, who were of the untouchable class. They were born again. They were lifted out of the miry clay, out of ignorance and shame. Among them are now found scholars and preachers and schools and churches and hospitals. That is what Christ's gospel has done in south India. Wherever Christ is faithfully proclaimed men turn to Him and are saved by Him. We need no new religion with which to win the world. "And I, if I be lifted up from the earth, will draw all men unto me." I have seen them all over the world, men and women of every type and temperament under heaven. I have asked them whence their victory came and they with united breath ascribed their victory to the Lamb and His death.

Some Vital Questions

There is one other question. I have asked you two. What do you think of Christ in His own person? What do you think of Christ in His gospel? I have one other: What do you think of Christ in personal experience? Here, we come to the basis of all science and philosophy — personal experience. What do you think of Christ in personal experience? Does He make good? Does He really help? Does He do something with us and to us and for us which no one else can do? What do you think of Christ in human experience? Here is the final test. Sir James Simpson, the great scientist, was waited upon by a group of young scientists who revered and honored him, and they said to him: "We have come to ask you what you count as the greatest discovery you have ever made." Tears were in his eyes for a second as he looked up and said: "Young men, the greatest discovery I have ever made is that Jesus Christ is my personal Saviour; that is the greatest discovery of all."

Oh, I have been with you a long time as your pastor. I have been with you long enough to find out that Christ is our absolute support and our absolute requirement. I see enough in one week in Dallas to come back to my pulpit greatly inspired to preach Jesus and to preach Him to the end of the day. I have seen our men with their money, and then I have seen them behave as Christians ought to behave in their poverty. I have seen men and women lose their wealth and yet go on grandly without murmur or complaint.

Before I went away a few weeks ago for my summer engagements, I went to see one of our blind women. She lived in a lonely little place with surroundings of poverty, and I wondered as I went up to the door, what I could say to her. I heard her singing. So I paused on the doorstep to hear the blind woman sing:

> "Just when I need Him, Jesus is near;
> Just when I falter; just when I fear —
> Ready to help me; ready to cheer,
> Just when I need Him most."

And I went in and said, "You mean that, do you not?" And she said, "Oh, it gets sweeter every day. He is here with me after I am left alone by the others as they go to their work. He is with me."

I have seen men and women in their poverty go bravely on. I have seen them with their health gone, and yet radiant and trustful through it all, they go bravely on, saying, "He doeth all things well."

We buried a mother a short while ago, and the small daughter could not understand it so she came to me saying, "Where is Mama? Is she out there in the cold grave where they took her?" I replied, "No, she is not there!" And she said: "Well then, where is she?" I said: "She is yonder in heaven with Christ, in the house of Life, and there shall be no death there, no sorrow there, no dying, no tears there. All is joy there; all is life there." And the dear child was comforted.

Christ meets every test. Christ meets the test of life and it is a severe test. Christ meets the test of death. Oh, what a test is that! "Fear not; I have the keys; trust me and put away all fear." Christ meets the test of eternity. He has the whole invisible world under His dominion.

Oh, men and women! Who would not live for Jesus? Who would not give Him his all? Had I a thousand lives to give, Lord, they should all be thine. David Livingstone, that grand old man in Africa, wrote: "Today I rededicated myself, my life, my all to Jesus who gave His all for me."

I may have told you before, I think I did, but it will do to tell again. When Livingstone came back to Oxford to receive the honor that Old England confers upon her brave sons, others had received their degrees and when he came out to receive his degree, he said: "Would you men and women like to know what sustained me in Africa, when the natives were cruel and threatened to kill me and the smoke went up from a thousand villages hard by, and darkness, deep and terrible, hung as a black night over Africa; would you like

SOME VITAL QUESTIONS

to know what sustained me?" Then he opened his New Testament and read the blessed promise of Jesus: "Lo, I am with you always even unto the end of the world." And he told that large congregation of world scholars that that was what sustained him. Here is our sustaining help. Christ will support us when we come to pass into the great beyond; Christ is out there to light our way forevermore. Oh, who would not trust Him and serve Him and follow Him to the end of the day?

My heart aches for men and women in Dallas, and it has ached for years past, and some of those are respectfully looking up into my face right now! How I wish you would come to Christ! How I wish you would trust Christ and go with us! He wants us all in His great army, the army of the living God. Have you not waited long enough? Are you not glad you are not cut off, doomed and beyond recovery and hope? Oh, today take Him at His word! "Him that cometh to me, I will in no wise cast out." You who are within sound of my voice, say to Him: "Here, Lord, am I; poor and needy, with sins many and dark. I give up to the Saviour whose death on the cross was an atonement for all human sins. I give up and surrender to Him and receive Him to be my Saviour in His own sovereign way; today I make the glad choice":

> Oh happy day that fixed my choice,
>   On Thee my Saviour and my God.
> Well may this glowing heart rejoice,
>   And tell its raptures all abroad.
> 'Tis done, the great transaction's done,
>   I am my Lord's and He is mine.
> He drew me and I followed on,
>   Charmed to confess His voice Divine.

QUESTION VIII

Am I My Brother's Keeper?

QUESTION VIII

Am I My Brother's Keeper?

Am I my brother's keeper?
GENESIS 4:9

OUR very familiar text of five brief words is the first question ever asked by one member of human society concerning his relation to another: which question was, "Am I my brother's keeper?" You will recall that just before this question was asked, God asked the question, "Where is Abel thy brother?" The man answered, "I know not; am I my brother's keeper?"

This question directs our attention to the first earthly home. In that home were two brothers, Cain and Abel. Those brothers brought offerings before God as expressions of their worship. Abel's offerings were accepted of God. Cain's offering was rejected. The effect upon Cain was immediately very down-dragging. God asked Cain, "Why art thou wroth? And why is thy countenance fallen?" The earthly passion of envy seized upon him, and from that hour Cain plotted against Abel, his brother.

What can be said of envy? The Bible itself asks, "Who shall stand before envy?" It is the weapon of little, petty, mean men. Envy is a consuming evil. The envious person wants something that belongs to someone else. Envy is as a bad infection in one's bones. The Bible shows it to be such.

What has man to be envious about in his relations to other men? If the Lord gives one man five talents, another two and gives you and me one, who are we to be disturbed or concerned in the matter, save that we shall use that one talent that he has given us and not bury it and let it go to

113

waste? We are to use it as wisely and worthily as we can. Leave the other men with the two talents or the five to do the same thing in the sight of God.

In this story of Cain and Abel we see how one sin leads to another. Envy led on and on until cold-blooded murder was its final outcome. Sin is frightfully prolific. It begets other sins. It multiplies itself many fold. It never lives alone and it drags down whatever it touches. Sin has many forms and expressions. In Cain's case, envy of his brother dominated his thinking until his brother Abel lay dead by the hand of Cain. One can visualize the deed. What can Cain be thinking about now? The red blood of his brother — the children of the same mother, the same father — the red blood of one brother stains the earth, at the cruel hand of the other brother. What is Cain thinking about now? Perhaps he says to himself, "This man shall not out-strip me any further. He is out of the way. He is dead."

But God is not dead. That is the solemn fact that men and women can easily forget. God is not dead. He came to Cain in that crucial hour and asked him, "Where is Abel thy brother?" And Cain perjured himself by saying, "I know not. Am I my brother's keeper?" And God reminded him: "The voice of thy brother's blood crieth unto me from the ground." Cain thought that he could creep away, but God knew. The blood had cried from the earth and Cain was doomed from then on to become a vagabond in the earth. God is not dead.

> Careless seems the great avenger —
> History's pages but record —
> One death grapple in the darkness,
> 'Twixt false systems and the Word.
> Truth forever on the scaffold —
> Wrong forever on the throne —
> But that scaffold sways the future,
> And behind the dim unknown,
> Standeth God within the shadows,
> Keeping watch above His own.

"Be not deceived; God is not mocked." Never, in a single case. "Whatsoever a man soweth, that shall he also reap."

AM I MY BROTHER'S KEEPER?

How terrible is sin! My brother, my sister, "Be sure your sin will find you out." The Bible says: "The stone shall cry out of the wall." Yes, at the crucial hour, it will cry out and reveal that awful secret of sin.

Now, in this old-time story there are vivid and awful lessons for us all. Let us look again at some of them today. First of all for us is this lesson: the significance of Cain's question, "Am I my brother's keeper?" The significance of Cain's question is the attempt to evade all responsibility for his brother's whereabouts; but he failed in the attempt. The fact of human responsibility is everywhere assumed in the Bible in very much the same way as the existence of God is assumed in the Bible. The whole Bible is fixed in its purpose and has as its message the reminder of our inescapable responsibility to God and of His proffered mercy to us, if we will come to Him in the right way. Likewise, the fact of human responsibility, the responsibility of one human being for another, is everywhere assumed in the Bible.

We are bound together in this matter of life. We must not ignore our relations to our fellow-man. Oh, there are consequences, direful beyond words, if we attempt to ignore our relations to our fellow-men. We are bound together "in the bundle of life." No member of human society can dare say to another member of human society, nor can one race dare say to another race, nor can one country dare say to some other country: "I have no relation to you and I go on my way ignoring you." The Bible everywhere assumes the inescapable fact of human responsibility.

I *am* my brother's keeper! We are learning that more and more. If you go to foreign countries and try to land at any port, you will be asked for your doctor's certificate, saying you have been completely inoculated against smallpox and typhoid fever. If you cannot show the certificate, you cannot get off the boat, but you will be kept on the boat and turned homeward. We are bound up in the bundle of life.

Some Vital Questions

In the olden days, as today, houses in Palestine had flat roofs, and people sat on those roofs to get the fresher air and the fairer view. The law required home-owners to build battlements around those roofs, lest someone fall off, especially the unthinking child. This law was for the protection of the people.

In the Old Testament times, it was the law that the reapers in the harvest field should leave stray heads of wheat in the fields so that poor people could gather up these stray heads of wheat for their own use. That was why Ruth was able to glean in the field of Boaz. The well-to-do must think of the ill-to-do. The strong must think of the weak. We *are* our brother's keeper.

Here the Parable of the Good Samaritan comes to mind. One man, a priest, passed a man, bruised and bleeding on the roadside and went on his way. Another man, a Levite, came and looked and hurried away. A third man, a Samaritan, came and looked at the injured man and had compassion on him. Having dressed the victim's bleeding wounds, the Good Samaritan then put him on his own beast, took him to the inn, sat with him through the night, and next morning said to the inn-keeper: "I will pay his bill now and whatever more is necessary, I will pay when I come again. He has nothing; he was beaten and robbed. I will pay his bill." "Which of these three, thinkest thou," said Jesus, "was his neighbor?" "The one who looked after the needy man," was answered. "Yes," said Jesus, "go thou and do likewise." The third man felt that he was his brother's keeper. That is the law of God everywhere in the moral government of God. We may not, must not, dare not, be indifferent to any human being anywhere in all the world.

Now, the question arises about why we are to practice this neighborliness. Well, common humanity demands it; just common humanity. If there was no religion anywhere, no accounting to God by and by, common humanity demands that if you find a man on the roadside, bruised and beaten and helpless, you are to help him, and not "pass by on the other side" and get away as quickly as you can. If people are too sick to care for themselves, or too poor to care for themselves, care must be provided. If there are men and women beaten, under-privileged, over-borne, distraught, then we are not to ignore that situation. Care for humanity is to be in all our hearts.

We have the example, the precept, the word and the deed of Jesus to help us at this great point. A few Scriptures give us the picture of Him when He was here: "Jesus went about doing good." "The Son of Man came not to be ministered unto, but to minister and to give his life, a ransom for many." "As my father hath sent me into the world," said Jesus, "even so send I you." They said, wagging their cynical heads and tongues at Jesus as He was dying on the cross: "He saved others, Himself He cannot save." If He had saved Himself, He would not have been adequate to save you and me. We would have no atoning, sin-bearing, mediative redeemer. The example of Jesus everywhere pictures the unceasing and careful concern He had for needy humanity.

And then we ought to remember that great principle which governed Paul. It is for you and me just the same as it was for Paul. He said: "I am debtor, both to the Greeks and to the Barbarians." I am debtor to all men, to the last limit of my power to help them. Paul said, in effect: "I owe myself to humanity, to the men of all the other countries; I am debtor to humanity." Paul stated the correct life principle for everyone of us. The business of life is to translate our debtorship into the right kind of endeavor for the unlift of humanity. How shall we love God whom we have not seen, if we do not love men whom we have seen and about whose condition we are fully acquainted? Service to mankind is the test of the reality of our faith. "By their fruits ye shall know them." A tree is known by its fruit. The world cries out all along for the right kind of service. Wrongs cannot be righted by mere talk. Grievances cannot be corrected by mere talk. Service must enter into all of the domains of life, and our best must be expressed, not only in words, but in deeds for the betterment of our fellow humanity.

That is the sure way of happiness, as well as of usefulness. It is the way of gladness, of triumph, of conquering blessedness. It is the way of walking in the steps of Christ; going about ever to help our fellow humanity. But suppose these suggestions are disregarded? "Am I my brother's keeper?" Where is he? I do not know and if I did, is it anything to me? What have I to do with him? "Am I my brother's keeper?" Suppose I fail to regard my responsible relation to him, then what? The voice of thy brother's blood crieth against the unfaithful and the wrongly behaving man or woman everywhere. Oh, how solemn is that fact! That fact is inescapable. It is inexorably certain and sure.

Against whom does his blood cry? Well, it cries, I should say first of all, against unfaithful homes. Those of you who come to this church with anything like regularity, must be aware of my ever increasing concern for the home-life of the American people. "The voice of thy brother's blood crieth unto me," because of unfaithfulness in the home. Cain was unfaithful to his brother to the point that he murdered his brother. Parents can be unfaithful to their children to the point that they put cattle and land and business and society before the spiritual and eternal welfare of their children. Husbands can be unfaithful to their wives, and the wives sometimes can be unfaithful to their husbands. The sanctities of home and of marriage cannot be trifled with without a judgment day down the road. Oh, my soul, how I wish that men and women could realzie that down the road of life, there is a judgment day. I know about some of them who feel that their judgment day has already come because they have trifled with the sanctity of home and of marriage. "The voice of thy brother's blood crieth" against unfaithful homes.

God's first institution in the world is the home. Trifle not with the home, God's fountain head, the ultimate basis of a worthy society! It must not be mocked and scorned. The home is God's citadel of an enduring social order, above church or state; it may not be tampered with except with results, not far away, to the last degree appalling.

Oh, ye parents, what are all your physical achievements worth; if you get all your land, your cattle, your oil wells, your deposits in the bank, and your children go to spiritual doom? I had rather be a Lazarus in his rags with my children following in the wake of Christ, than to be in the king's palace with my children going pell mell into doom, without Christ! The unfaithful home! We must fight against it! Oh ye parents, what can I say to quicken your concern about your home? What are you doing about the boys and girls and the young men and maidens going forth to their homebuilding for themselves?

What are you doing about these great, deep-down, eternally momentous matters of the relations of human souls to the great God and Saviour? What are you doing about them? What is the wife, who is a believer in Christ, doing about that husband who is without Christ? You cannot win him by the wrong kind of life. You must be positioned; you must be definitely positioned, so that he will know that your highest loyalty of all is to Christ. Christ first! Christ before parents, or husband, or wife; Christ first!

The Christian woman sometimes has to pay a great price to win her husband, but she can afford to die any day if by death she might win him to Christ! And the father can afford to die for his boy and the mother for her girl and the brother for his brother. Oh, what about these families? They are beleaguered now; they are dreadfully beleaguered and assaulted now. Every kind of hostile invader enters within the circle of our loved ones. If we fail to watch the diversions, the education, the social activities, the spiritual life of our families, evil shall sweep them all from the right moorings down the stream. And the tragedy will be too deep for tears.

Some Vital Questions

"The voice of thy brother's blood crieth" against unfaithful citizens. I wish I might say the right word that would quicken the interests and consciences of citizens. Those who come here often, know that this pulpit never indulges in partisan, personal politics. Never! I am as concerned for the men and women of one political party and their spiritual welfare, as I am for another. I am concerned for universal humanity; for their salvation and their highest usefulness.

The Word of God does not allow the prophet of God to forget that the home is a divinely appointed institution, and that civil government is also divinely appointed. The Bible tells us, concerning the civil government, that the powers of civil government are ordained of God. Every man and woman possessed of the franchise is called upon to give the highest, worthiest, most patriotic, and most unselfish thought to citizenship.

I wonder if you have read that old and oft quoted statement from Ambassador Brice who came from the British Empire to be the Ambassador to our country in our National capital. He made it years and years ago and we may well remember it at this late date. He said: "The one conspicuous failure that I find in American life is the failure of your cities. They are not well governed." He apologized for criticizing our nation. If men and women have a modern city to grow up around them and they are indifferent to it, inattentive to it, unconcerned for it, drawing their cloaks a little closer about them, without regard to what is going on in the city, then all kinds of evils will spring up to decay and destroy the highest and best in the city.

Every man in his city should take the worthiest interest in the city's welfare. There should be no trifling, no compromising, no betrayal. Every citizen should be enlightened as to whom he is putting in office. The eye of God is upon everyone who casts a vote. What will this vote do for the city? Your vote may determine the issues of an election – your vote! You cannot play fast and loose with your vote.

AM I MY BROTHER'S KEEPER?

You must think of what is involved. You must think what standards should be exalted in a city and how they ought to be maintained and upheld. You are to pick out the men who will not fail, who will not yield to the seductive voice of the tempter. You must pick out the right kind of men to preside in the affairs of the city's life.

Do you remember the parable of the trees and the bramble told in the Book of Judges? Things were going from bad to worse in the city and the people called unto God's prophet and asked what was the meaning of the down-hill trend of their cities? What was the explanation? Do you remember what he answered them? He told them a parable and let them deduce from it what they would. He told of how all the trees of the forest got together and said to the olive tree, "Come thou and reign over us." And the olive tree said: "I cannot. I must bear olives." Then all the trees turned to the fig tree and said: "Come thou, and reign over us" and the fig tree said: "No, I must bear figs." Then all the trees turned to the vine, the simple delicate vine, and said: "Come thou, oh vine, and reign over us." But the vine said, "I must bear grapes; there must be wine for the people; I cannot rule over you." What next? Then all the trees of the field turned to the bramble. The bramble does not bear fruit nor give shade. It was of no use to the community. So, all the trees turned to the bramble and said, "Come thou, and reign over us." And the bramble said, "Very well, come and trust in my shadow. I will be your ruler."

Just as Ambassador Brice said, "The one conspicuous failure in America is that the people do not give worthy attention to their cities." We ought to have the best men in our cities to hold offices, the best men in state government, the best men anywhere and everywhere. This great matter cannot be cast smilingly aside. Let us guard against the "bramble rule."

Another great writer said: "America is afflicted with the bad citizenship of good men"; and he insisted that it is a sad incongruity for a vast citizenship of good men, high class in their home life, noble in their business relations, honored by their comrades and friends, to let the affairs of their city severely alone. "What is it to me? What is Dallas to me?" they say. It is a great deal to every citizen of this goodly city. Your relation to this city is a matter of colossal moment, and every man and woman ought to be wide awake and be highly resolved saying: "I am going to do my best this year to try to have the fairest and cleanest and worthiest city in the whole land, by the help of God." That ought to be the attitude of every one of us.

Now, I have another word. Our brother's blood crieth out, not only against unfaithfulness in the home and against unfaithful children, but it also crieth out against unfaithful Christians who say, "Am I my brother's keeper?" Yes, you are! You have denied knowing where he is, but you should know and by your own carelessness you have allowed him to stray away and his blood crieth from the ground unto the ears of God.

The voice without reserve crieth against the unfaithful preacher. The preacher who can be at ease, with the world in the plight it is in, with humanity in the plight that it is in, with his church members straying into paths of unrighteousness, let him go back to the shop or the plow or somewhere and leave this highest calling which God has for men. "I have made thee a watchman, O my prophet, and if thou art not faithful in thy word and testimony among the people, I will require their safety at thy hand." That is the teaching of God.

Think of a deacon imagining that a Sunday night's service is not for him at all! imagining that the prayer meeting is not for him; a deacon in the church of God, in the one institution fashioned by our Divine Lord! Think of him ignoring any public duty pertaining to the administration, the witness and the work of the church of God!

AM I MY BROTHER'S KEEPER?

And then the Sunday School teacher who fancies, "I have accomplished my whole mission when I get together a little group and have thirty minutes with them on Sunday morning, and let them go until next Sunday," without regard to the fact that example will do far more to stabilize the young people in ways of righteousness than all the teaching can do.

Oh, Christian! What did Jesus say? "Ye are the light of the world, but if the light in you be darkened how great is that darkness." "Ye are the salt of the earth, but if the salt have lost its savour, wherewith shall it be salted? It is thenceforth good for nothing but to be cast out and trodden under foot of men." "Ye are living epistles of Christ, known and read of all men." And you are seen of all men. Your example and the fidelity of it, the unselfishness of it, the high principle of it, count for far more than all the talk that could ever issue from your tongue.

"The voice of thy brother's blood," or thy sister's blood, crieth unto thee because of thy bad example. Oh, men and women, how serious it is that we are often careless concerning our testimony for Christ! Let us make the high resolve that, with God's help, we will live more consistent Christian lives, so that by word and deed we may glorify the matchless name of Christ.

Oh, this is a word for us all. There are fellow-Christians going down the toboggan slide because of inactivity. Inactive Christians lose followship with Christ. They lose contact with the church. They lose the joy of service. Do you know an inactive Christian? If so, that one is your responsibility. We are the keepers of our brothers and sisters. We must look about us and find the inactive, back-slidden Christians, and do all in our power to help restore them to the active life of the church. We can ask them: "How will you face your Lord? Is the careless course you are taking defensible? Is it helpful? Is it a course that will glorify God? Is it a course that will magnify the church? Is it a course that makes sinners say: 'That person has been with Jesus'? Is it a course that will help the lost to understand Christianity?"

This is also a time for the re-commitment, re-dedication, re-devotedness of active Christians; a time for the writing down in the secret depths of our hearts the highest resolves of our redeemed nature.

Is there somebody here who says, "I am the inactive one"? If you are here, come back into the line of duty and privilege. Come definitely, positively, obediently back to Christ's service. Come today. Is there someone who says, "I have never come out for Christ, but I know that this matter of being right with God ought to have my first, my supreme attention." Oh, how God invites TODAY while light is given. Today, definitely surrender to Christ, my friend! Will you say: "I yield, I choose, I vote, I decide, I surrender my needy life to Christ, who sayeth: 'Him that cometh unto me, I will in no wise cast out.'"

QUESTION IX

Despise Ye the Church of God?
A Stewardship Message

QUESTION IX

Despise Ye the Church of God?
A Stewardship Message

~~~~~~~~~~~~~~~~~~~~~~~~~~~

> *Despise ye the church of God?*
> I CORINTHIANS 11:22

THE attitude that one bears toward the church is a matter of very large moment in the earthly life. One of the most arresting questions asked in the Bible is asked by Paul concerning our attitude toward the church. This is his ringing, surprising question: "Despise ye the church of God?" Paul asked this question concerning the church, you will recall, in connection with the Lord's Supper.

It is a matter of vast importance that we have the right view concerning the two ordinances that we have in the church — baptism and the Lord's supper. We shall miss it most terribly if we take the wrong view concerning these two ordinances. They are not sacramental, but are symbolic. They do not have saving efficacy at all; they portray great facts of infinite moment to the life of mankind. It is a sad thing for these two ordinances to be misused, to be perverted, to be changed from their true meaning.

Baptism is a portrayal of great facts — historic facts — in the life, death, burial, and resurrection of our Lord, and is to be observed only once in the life of the individual. The Lord's Supper is to be observed again and again, in remembrance of Christ, and it reminds us of the spiritual help we get from our Lord. Under no circumstances should we ever misuse or pervert these two ordinances. They are not for the securement of the forgiveness of our sins. These ordinances

Some Vital Questions

are for those whose sins are already forgiven and who are saved already through Christ, the infinite Saviour. They are symbolic. They are not intended to save or be a part of salvation. They portray great truths touching salvation and our relation to Him who gives it — a matter of most vital moment. Certainly it goes without comment, as we interpret the Scriptures, that these ordinances are only for the true friends of Christ. How inconsistent to give a man the emblem of the Lord's death, burial and resurrection if such man is not the friend of Christ! What an incongruity!

These ordinances are for the true friends of Christ — for those who have repented of their sins, have personally accepted Christ as their Saviour and personally owe their lives to Him as their rightful Lord and Master — and they are administered by order of the church. These ordinances should have our worthiest attention. Always our habits and our attitudes concerning them should be well pleasing in the sight of God.

Paul saw those early Corinthian Christians perverting the ordinance of the Lord's Supper. They were making of it a feast. They were making themselves gluttons in connection with the observance of the Supper in the church of God, and his righteous soul rose in protest. He rang out this question: "Despise ye the church of God?" This Supper of the Lord is not for the satisfying of the appetite; it is not to be perverted, debauched, nor misused, and in that ringing question Paul sums up the real meaning of this Supper which is set in the church of God.

The question goes beyond the Supper; it can be applied to all our relations to the church, and I should like for us to think of it in this most comprehensive way today. That question, "Despise ye the church of God?" shocks us! Can it be possible that Christians would abuse this sacred institution? That word, "despise," has a far-reaching meaning which we discover when we turn to the dictionary. It means to contemn, to undervalue, to neglect. Now we *can* "despise the

Despise Ye The Church of God?

church," undervalue it, disparage it, pervert it, neglect it. Paul was telling about all that, and he used this forceful word — "despise." We *can* "despise the church of God."

What can be said of the church? It is the only institution fashioned and founded by our divine Saviour and Lord. He said, "The gates of hell shall not prevail against it," and they have not through the long centuries. Though sorely persecuted, the church has endured through fire and sword, and has risen up from the debris and has gone on conquering and to conquer.

> Oh where are those empires now,
> Of those that went and came?
> But Lord, Thy church is praying yet,
> A thousand years the same."

You ask, "How may the church be thus despised, neglected, disparaged, undervalued?" There are various ways that can be seen upon a moment's reflection. We can despise the church by non-attendance upon its services. Every one of us should have the most conscientious thought concerning the habit of church attendance. "Not forsaking the assembling of ourselves together, as the manner of some is," says the Word of God. People ought to go to church, and they ought to go with the habit marked by conscience and principle. A man misses the way of duty if he neglects the high privilege of habitual attendance upon the services of God's house.

It is a tragedy that many people never darken the doors of a church, save to attend some funeral or wedding held therein. The children of these people are being brought up without contact with the one institution which Christ deemed of such importance that He fashioned it and left it here for our edification when He went back to the eternal home. How distressing that people anywhere should neglect habitual attendance upon worship in God's house and how terrible that children — responsive, impressionable children — should be brought up without any attention being paid to the church and its teaching and preaching appointments, which con-

Some Vital Questions

tribute so vitally to the uplift and betterment of humanity! The matter of church attendance ought to be written deeply in the lives of men and women for their own sakes, for the sake of others, and for Christ's sake. Church attendance ought to be one of the great habits fixed resolutely, conscientiously and unwaveringly in men's lives.

We can "despise the church" by failing to make preparation for the worship services of the church. People say that a preacher ought to prepare for his message — and they are correct. He ought to think and pray and delve and study, ought to think of God and of the people as he broods over the Scriptures which he would seek to expound for the counsel and leading of the people. Even so, the congregation should prepare for public worship in God's house. There is all the difference in the world in congregations. It is like going into a very cold room or into a warm, comfortable room. People who are unsympathetic, prayerless, indifferent, cynical, critical, can create a frigid atmosphere. Jesus tells us we are not only to take heed to *what* we hear, but that we are to take heed to *how* we hear. You can hear with a sympathetic mind and heart; some listeners are indeed eloquent listeners. Sometimes the preacher is inspired to the depths of his soul by the serious attention even of a child whose eyes follow the preacher and glisten with interest, showing that the little fellow is getting what is said. Sometimes, it is an humble man, beaten and bludgeoned by the trials of life, who finds in God's house the hope and comfort that are needed for him. He feeds upon the preached Word of God, and upon the songs of praise, and the whole testimony coincident with public worship.

Eloquent listeners! There are some. Now, that means that we are to go to church with spirits attuned, prepared by prayer and meditation, hoping for a blessing for our own lives, and for the lives of others. Everybody ought to go to church with the prayer that the preacher be God-guided and that his subject be divinely appointed. That is godly prepa-

DESPISE YE THE CHURCH OF GOD?

ration for church worship. How immeasurably blessed it is! Time and again, when a preacher seems to flounder, a fervent prayer of a worshipper will restore the preacher. Sometime ago, I found myself in such a plight, but soon my thinking was cleared. I felt that God had given me light and leading. When I got home my telephone rang and one of the most timid, most modest little mothers of the church family said: "I saw that you were perplexed today and I bowed my whole being before God for you and in a minute or two you were recovered; and Pastor, I then said, 'Thank thee dear Lord, for thou has heard a poor old woman's prayer.'" And He had. "Keep thy foot, when thou goest to the house of God, and be more ready to hear," says the Bible.

We try to make much of reverence in this place. The glory and blessing of public worship are destroyed if reverence be absent. Everybody here is summoned, invited, entreated to put his or her best into the service always. The other day, when a child played with a paper noisily in the audience, the man sitting beside the child should have laid his hand quietly on the little fellow who made the noise. Everybody is a partner in a church service, and if all are wholeheartedly sympathetic, concordant, and prayerful, then, out of that kind of sevice, the very best will be had. We should prepare for the service. We can "despise the church" by the lack of worthy preparation.

We can "despise the church of God" in our lax religious beliefs and views and convictions. Men and women ought to know what they believe and why they believe. They ought to have a clear idea as to what is the significance of it all. Why do we stake our all on Christ, the Son of the living God? Why do we believe in His deity; in His lordship, and in His saviourhood? Why do we believe that salvation is had only through Christ? Men and women ought to be able always and everywhere to give a reason, to anybody who asks, concerning the hope that is in them. "As a man thinketh in his heart, so is he." Lax statements in the pulpit lead to lax views and behavior in the pew. The pulpit is no place for a religious stammerer, never! And the pew is no place for the religious stammerer. We are to know why we believe and what, and we are to give a reason to those who ask concerning such beliefs within us. The Apostle said, "We cannot but speak the things we have seen and heard," and the Psalmist of old said, "I believe, therefore have I spoken." Men are to know why they believe and what. They can "despise the church of God" by ignorance, by laxity, by incoherence, and by uncertainty, concerning the great truths of Christ and His church and His great salvation.

We can "despise the church of God" by wrong and inconsistent lives which do not tally with the professions we have made. The church is to hold up the standards and ideals and is always to summon people from the lower to the higher sphere of living. If a church makes the profession, "We are the friends of Christ," and lives below that profession, then the banners droop, for Christ has set proper standards for His people in His church. "Ye are the light of the world," but "if the light in you be darkness, how great is that darkness." "Ye are the salt of the earth, but if the salt have lost his savor, wherewith shall it be salted?" "Let your light so shine before men, that they may see your good works, and glorify your Father which is in heaven."

The best argument for Christianity is some Christian who lives it, foursquare and full length, because the world takes the measurement of everyone of us day by day and week by week. We can "despise the church of God" by ragged, wretched, irregular, inconsistent, unworthy behavior as professed friends and followers of the great Saviour and Lord.

Our lives should be lived for Christ. Our talents may be limited, perhaps just one; but we can live for Him. Some men came to Gladstone, that great British leader, who went to church every Sunday and said to him: "You know more in an hour than that rector in the pulpit can tell you in a year." Gladstone replied: "I would not agree to that. I would not agree to any of that, for I need the public service of God's house. I would like for all England to know, and for all the dominions of the British Empire to know, that I count the religion of Christ as the one important matter for man's attention and I want all men to take knowledge that I count the will of Christ and the work of His church supreme in men's lives."

That great Southerner, General Robert E. Lee, said: "I want my soldiers who were with me and my neighbors living around me and my students whom I am teaching, to know that the chief thing in my thought, in my adoration, and in the life I am living, is to know the will of Christ and to carry out His will." He was a great Christian. We can "despise the church of God" by living below the right standards.

Again, we can "despise the church of God" by unworthy giving to the church. If men think of giving as a kind of benevolence, or as a kind of philanthropy, they need to repent in sackcloth and ashes. Would you think it a philanthropy to pay your grocery bill, a philanthropy to pay your doctor, a philanthropy for you to pay the merchant for the suit of clothes that you bought for the coming Christmas — would you think that a philanthropy? A man's supreme business is his obligation toward God. God is the first Creditor to us all. If a man has irregular, desultory habits of giving, then all down through the years his giving will miss the high standards which Christ has set for His people. Men and women in the church "despise the church of God" by unworthy habits and standards of giving. Giving is a God-appointed duty, and to neglect it or to play fast and loose with it is to go directly against God's plan.

We heard last Sunday here, as we began our Stewardship Week, that the one high objective of life is stewardship. Everything about life is stewardship. God made it to be such. Our talents, many or one, our time, our influence — and we cannot trifle with our influence without great peril to others — and our very life, itself, constitute a stewardship, no less than do our material possessions. Our material possessions may be a large bank account, or just two mites, or a little alabaster-box hidden away for some great emergency; but our stewardship of property is fixed by our divine, atoning, buried, risen, reigning Saviour.

Every man and woman ought to come with noble thinking and highest behavior about the matter of giving to the church of God, and I will say that your gifts through the church will go further than through any other channel in the wide world. Jesus knew what He was about when He set in His church the right standards and methods for giving.

When a church puts her hands and hearts together in a great united effort for her own maintenance, and for missionary work, for educational work, for benevolent work, for sick and needy humanity, near and far, and brings her gifts unitedly, cooperatively, prayerfully to the altar in the church of God, these gifts will go further there than in any other possible place.

I have already said that a man ought to have a fixed principle in his giving. A man who says, "I will give as I feel," needs to be taught until his feeling will be right. His obligation to the Lord should be recognized. Christianity has accepted the Jewish standard of giving the tithe as a minimum. This is a working basis, because the tithe belongs to the Lord, anyway.

One of our young men here was wounded in World War I and, after a period of some two or three years, the government gave him in one lump sum his pension for all his service and suffering. The amount was $4,000.00. And he came to me and said: "Here is $400.00." I asked, "What for?" He replied, "My tithe." And I said, "You are married; you are young; you are wounded; you are crippled." I demurred. I hesitated to take it. "You are taking this $400.00 out of your $4,000.00, which is your tithe, you say; and you want this church here to have this?" For this was not his permanent home. And he said, "Doctor, what am I spared for? Why am

I alive? Why did not the gas kill me? Why did not the war put me into a grave? I am here to serve God. Certainly you will take this. I entered into a solemn pledge with God way back yonder, that I would give a tithe of my income as a minimum. Please take it." And he went on his way to a distant city to make his home, and every now and then I have a letter from the minister of his church saying, "We need more men like this man." He is a joy and a benediction to that downtown church in a far distant city.

A man ought to have a fixed percentage as a minimum, and over and above that, he should make thank offerings and love offerings, gratitude offerings. But he should have the tithe as a minimum. And then he ought to have that great habit of giving through the church as Paul urged First Century Christians to give: "Upon the first day of the week, let every one of you lay by him in store, as God hath prospered him." How glorious it is to give!

I wish to express my joy that our people are steadily improving in this God-appointed standard of stewardship. Heaven's blessings be on these hundreds of young people, who, out of their meager incomes, bring in their tithes. We have here a young girl who supports her helpless mother and father. I questioned as she brought her tithe here, but she said, "Why, this is the best way I can serve Christ." Sunday after Sunday she brings it. Oh, I fancy the cavalcade of angels hurried back to the heavenly heights to tell the redeemed of the Lord: "The kingdom is coming down yonder; a young girl supporting a helpless mother and father brings to the church of God a certain percentage of what she makes." With her it is a matter of principle.

Now, I have said enough. May I see the hands of those who have signed their budget-cards since last Sunday? Ah, yes, a great company! The officers will now come forward promptly to gather up these cards, while the congregation remains quietly seated for a few minutes. We are not overlooking the large company who have not yet signed their cards. You can

SOME VITAL QUESTIONS

sign them now, without hesitation; or if you need more time today, if you need counsel and prayer further, why of course take the time. We will pray for a moment.

We bless Thee, loving Saviour, for this appointment in human life, the privilege of bringing our gifts to the altar of our Lord. By giving our gifts unitedly, we can care for our local church work; we can help the orphan child, and the poor, afflicted, underprivileged mother, the overburdened and broken in health and mind. We can help the missionary in far-off, war-torn China, and in India, and in Japan, and in Europe, and in Africa. These people who go out to far-off lands and witness for Jesus, are thus our fellow-helpers.

Now as we plan for the new year to come, may our plans be worthy; may they be God-directed. May principle and conscience be put into the signing of every card, and, though there are just two mites that some may give, let them know, that if the two mites are honestly and sincerely the best they can give to Christ, that He will be as pleased with that gift, as with the largest offering.

Let us all measure our responsibility and appraise it as we ought, and all praise shall be given to Christ, now and forevermore. Amen.

After next Sunday, I hope to see your name on that voluntary roll, that honor roll, just your names, not the amount at all. The one who gives those two mites conscientiously will be just as precious in our appreciation and in the great Saviour's appreciation, as the one who gives his many dollars per week. The names only will be on that voluntary roll.

I would like to say another word. You can listen while these plates are being quietly passed. There are two other people who can "despise the church of God." Who are they? Two other people! One is the Christian who is detached from the church; the Christian who is not aligned with the church. Oh, it is a tragedy for a Christian to be on the outside, detached from the church, not aligned, non-cooperative! That hurts you and it hurts other people more than you

Despise Ye The Church of God?

know, and it grieves the heart of our Lord. Are you here? Come, link your life with Christ's church and people. Come, and thrice welcome!

The other one here who can "despise the church of God" is someone who is not a Christian at all! Oh, how you can despise and disparage the church, which our Saviour bought with His own precious blood! Do you, deep down in your heart, accept Jesus as your Saviour? Have you accepted Him but have not made it known? He wants you to confess Him before men and without hesitation or delay. Do you say, "I want to?" Well, Christ wants you to confess Him. Do yo say, "How shall I make the great surrender?" Give yourself wholly to Him, utterly to Christ! Do you say, "When shall I do it?" The answer is, "Today, if you will hear His voice: harden not your heart." Now is the accepted time! Now is the day of salvation!

Are there those here today who will say, "We will not despise the church of God; we will not undervalue it; we will not neglect it"? Come by letter, or come upon statement, having us get your letter. Or come upon open confession of Christ as your Saviour. Are you here? Are you here? Come on as we sing two stanzas:

> I gave my life for thee,
> My precious blood I shed —
> That thou mightest ransomed be,
> And quickened from the dead.
> I gave, I gave my life for thee,
> What hast thou given for me?
>
> And I have brought to thee,
> Down from my home above,
> Salvation full and free,
> My pardon and my love.
> I bring, I bring rich gifts to thee,
> What hast thou brought to me?

Who today says, "I come?" *Come* quietly, right now!

QUESTION X

Who Is My Neighbor?

QUESTION X

Who Is My Neighbor?

Who is my neighbor?
LUKE 10:29

I AM taking a moment to pass on to you expressions of gratitude from some of the soldier boys who have been in our services, from time to time, while they were students at the Aviation Center. They came to see me this past week and wanted to voice their deep gratitude to pastor and congregation for the consideration shown them in these weeks that they have been in Dallas. They were leaving for their homes in the East and North, and are to be transferred soon to other military camps. The words they said were as music to my heart, as they told of your beautiful consideration of them, your invitations to them to come here and your welcome when they came. Keep that up and make it deeper and sweeter all the time. Look about you constantly for the young men and women in uniform and, with all graciousness and cordiality, invite them to come with you to our church services. Do all you can to make them feel at home here in the house of the Lord. These are days of golden opportunity for our people to exhibit the most beautiful brand of Christian hospitality to multitudes of service men and women who spend a while in Dallas.

And now, turning away from these, we are to think together this morning on the one human example in the Bible which Jesus asks us to imitate, one of whom He says, "Go and do thou likewise." This sentence is found in the final statement of the parable of the Good Samaritan, from Luke's Gospel, the tenth chapter, which was read for you earlier in

Some Vital Questions

the service. Surely we shall do well to ponder often, and with all faithfulness, the parable of the Good Samaritan in which Jesus said to the lawyer, "Go and do thou likewise." He was referring to a man who gave his time, his money, his sympathy, his service, himself, to help his fellow-man. This parable will continue to challenge, and even startle, us by its lesson as to noble and unselfish behavior. Indeed, this story of the Good Samaritan is one of the most instructive and challenging to be found in the entire Bible. It is so simple that a child can readily understand it, and at the same time its message is so profound that the great ones of earth often stumble over it. This parable of the Good Samaritan is a pungent, profound, and powerful treatise on practical ethics. For it gives us in a few words the essential truth of man's proper relations to man.

Now the occasion of the parable is quite familiar to us all. A lawyer, listening to Jesus, said to Him, "Master, what shall I do to inherit eternal life?" Jesus replied, "What is written in the law, what readest thou?" And the lawyer said: "Thou shalt love the Lord thy God with all thy heart, with all thy soul, with all thy mind, and all thy strength; and thy neighbor as thyself." "Thou has answered right," said Jesus, "this do, and thou shalt live." But the lawyer, desiring to justify himself said, "And who is my neighbor?" And then it was that Jesus gave us this parable of the Good Samaritan, in which He evidently meant to teach us several things. He meant to teach all of us that our neighbors are all those who need us and the help we can give them, no matter who they are nor where they live. That teaching pushes back the horizons of our personal responsibility to the limits of humanity. If we are to obey the teachings of Jesus and follow His example, then there can be no room for those petty parochialisms and provincialisms, those racial prejudices and caste systems which erect barriers between us and those who need us and the services we can render them.

Who Is My Neighbor?

And then Jesus meant also to give that lawyer and to give all of us, for all time, an example of true benevolence, in this parable of the Good Samaritan. It is just as wonderful to me this Sunday morning as it was when first I heard it as a little child. Its truths stand out very vividly.

First of all, you have the picture of a man in suffering, a man afflicted, a very common thing. The world is filled with such. The world is filled with trouble, sufferings, and afflicted people. And ofttimes this trouble is through no fault at all of the one afflicted. For example, it is no fault of the little child if the parents are alienated and the little fellow is robbed of the blessings of a happy home. Such cases are brought again and again to the attention of the pastor of this church. It is no fault of the little child. I am thinking just now of four such little children. The father went in one direction and the mother in another. Heaven save the mark! It was through no fault of those four tiny tots that they were gathered into an orphans' home. There they will be mothered the best an orphans' home can mother them. But, even so, a dire tragedy befell them in their innocence. Alas, that so much trouble results from the wrong behavior of others! One thinks of the old saying: "Man's inhumanity to man makes countless thousands mourn."

Think of the trouble that the robber makes. Think of the trouble that the oppressor makes, the persecutor, the man using brutal strength against pitifully helpless people. Think of the awful tribulations that bedarken the world today because of the ruthlessness of evil men in high places — men led on by the lust of place and power, by greed for position and wealth. Think of the depths into which they plunge untold millions as they themselves seek to climb to power. Think of the tragedies inflicted upon helpless humanity right now, bombs falling on women and children, bombs falling on hospitals and church houses and orphanages. In London Spurgeon's great church house, where I have preached again and again, has been bombed and many another temple dedi-

Some Vital Questions

cated to the worship of Almighty God has been bombed and laid in ashes. If you can get man changed, you have changed the wildest beast of them all; wilder than any lion, wilder than any hyena is man, unrestrained, vicious, ambitious, sinful man. No beast of the jungle is more cruel than man. We have much evidence of this awful truth in this modern world.

We are told that the road from Jerusalem to Jericho, down which the unfortunate man of the parable traveled, has long been a perilous road. Jerome called it "the bloody way." Formerly, it was infested with robbers who came out from this side and the other — and woe betide the traveler who fell into their hands! That was what befell the poor fellow told of in the parable of the Good Samaritan. Certain ways may well be called the way of peril and danger. Think of the miner going down into the earth with all of the perils incident to that life. Think of the soldiers going to the battle front, and the sailors on the seas with the perils that face them. Think of our firemen and our policemen in our cities and the perils which they face.

Now two other men appear in the story. Down that road from Jerusalem to Jericho came a priest who saw the beaten, bruised, suffering and half-dead man, lying beside the road. But the priest passed by on the other side. There came down a little later a Levite who also saw the wounded man and also passed by on the other side. How wretched, how contemptible, how wicked the behavior of these two men! Their conduct was without excuse. Both of them came face to face with a case of desperate need. Both of them claimed to be religious men. They had an opportunity and a corresponding obligation to help a desperately needy human being. By their conduct they rejected the opportunity and denied the obligation. They were as guilty as the robbers who way-laid the traveler. Every rightful thinking person holds that ancient priest and Levite in utter contempt.

What of the motorists who step on the gas as they pass a wrecked car beside the road where there are bloody and injured people? We are to help bruised and mangled people, suffering people, distraught people. We are to help them without delay. The test of a man's character is his attitude toward suffering.

Now, there was another man of another spirit who came down this road and saw the victim of the robbers in his awful plight. He was moved with compassion, went to the victim, bound up his wounds, and poured in oil to heal and soothe. He lifted the man onto his beast and went along steadying him. He took him to an inn down the road and cared for him through the night. When the morning came he paid the innkeeper the bill and said, "Keep him here as long as he ought to be kept here, don't let him get out too soon. Look after him; I'll be back and pay the bill. Whatever it is, I will pay it." "Which now of these three thinkest thou," said Jesus, "was a neighbor to him that fell among thieves?" "Why, the man that helped him, of course." "Very well," said Jesus, "go and do thou likewise."

What was the difference in these men? It was a difference in spirit. A man is to build his life, not on petty rules, but on great principles. "As ye would that men should do to you, do ye also to them likewise." There is a great principle. How would you like for the other man to treat you if you were beaten and bruised and mangled on the roadside and he came along? How would you like for him to treat you? What would you like for him to do for you? That great principle will guide you in determining who is your neighbor and what your duties are in regard to him. This principle has been called the Golden Rule. Perhaps it were better to call it the Golden Principle. Jesus did not give us a set of rules or a code of statutes. Rather, He gave us great, universal principles which we are to apply to our individual problems. Take any of the great Christian principles. Take this one: "As we have therefore opportunity, let us do good unto all men." Or this: "Whether ye eat or drink, or whatsoever ye do, do all to the glory of God." Still another is:

Some Vital Questions

"Seek ye first the kingdom of God and his righteousness; and all these things shall be added unto you." The Christian life is based on great principles, constuctive, creative, cooperative principles.

The Samaritan who came down the road was not hindered by race. The man he helped was probably a Jew. The Jews and the Samaritans were not supposed to have dealings one with the other. But that long-standing, racial antagonism was no barrier to the Good Samaritan. He was a man of another spirit. That was why Jesus could say: "Go, and do thou likewise." All humanity, all races, all classes, constitute our opportunity, our obligation. We are not to be hindered by race, nor by creed. If anybody is in need you are not to stop and ask, "Do you belong to my church?" Instead, you are to say, "What can I do for you? I'm here to help you." We are not to stop and ask, "Do you go to my church?" Not at all; we are to help all in need. By his conduct the Levite said, "Why should I stop? I am in a hurry. Why should I carry him to an inn and pay the bill and look after him? I am a Levite." And to his eternal shame, the priest, in effect, said the same thing. Not so with the Samaritan. His reaction was: "Here is my fellow human being, half dead! He must have the best I can give him." The Samaritan was a true neighbor to the one who fell among the robbers. Thus we have the one human example which Jesus set as a pattern for all of us to follow. "Go, and do thou likewise!"

I trust each one of you has already been making personal application of this great parable of our Lord. Let each of you be thinking of someone whom you can and ought to help this very day. It may be that only a word of encouragement from you is needed. "A word fitly spoken," says the Bible, "is like apples of gold in pictures of silver." Full many a time the understanding word of sympathy is the vital thing. Or in the case of poverty, relief — fortifying and practical relief — is what is needed. Where there is affliction and discouragement and bereavement and aged loneliness, perhaps

Who Is My Neighbor?

you can bring a great blessing by a brief visit. There are numberless ways to help and many who need help.

I would like to direct your attention to a large group of children to whom you may play the part of good neighbor. I refer to the more than six hundred children in the Buckner Orphans' Home. In several respects they are our neighbors. For one thing, as you know, that blessed institution is on a great and fertile farm just east of our city. In that respect, those children are our neighbors. And the fact that their very livelihood is dependent upon the good and generous people of Texas makes them our neighbors. Their need is a recurrent and challenging appeal to every generous impulse of our hearts.

Should you visit this Home, you would be amazed at how little of crying there is, even by the tiny tots who have not long been orphaned. Of course their little hearts are sometimes very heavy. One day some friends were visiting at the Home and they noticed a little six-year-old girl off by herself on the playground, looking very sad and lonely. One of the friends went to her and began to pet her and said: "Dear, do you sometimes cry about all this?" And the little tot said: "I've nobody to cry to. Mama's gone and Papa's gone. I used to cry to them. But now I've nobody to cry to. I'm in the Orphans' Home." Bless her little lonely heart! There were many at Buckner Orphans' Home to whom she could cry. But, even so, they could not be quite like Mama and Papa, no matter how hard they tried.

Oh, men and women, privileged as we are, here, right at our door, is an institution which calls for this congregation and its friends to bring a gift, to the last degree worthy of such a cause. Let our gifts be worthy of Christ who said: "Inasmuch as ye did it unto one of these least, ye did it unto me." At this glad season let every one of us have a part in adding to the gladness, the comfort and the care of all at Buckner Orphans' Home. Your generous and loving gifts will bring gladness out there, they will bring gladness to you, and they will gladden the heart of Him who delighted to take little children into His arms and bless them.

My neighbor is anyone in all the world who needs the help that I can give. From our own community and the wants of so many of its citizenry we could go to far-away China, with her teeming millions in dire distress, caused by war or famine or both. How the heart of our Saviour must bleed as He looks upon babes and mothers — innocent victims of this world holocaust — going to bed hungry, many of them to die before another sun shall rise! How inexpressibly great must be His sorrow as He sees young men, with all their possibilities and expectancy for great usefulness in the world, mowed down in the prime of life! And what is true of China is true of nations around the globe. Scarcely a home in this land of ours has not felt the poignant sorrow of separation or the hush of death during these troublous days through which we are passing. We are neighbors to the world and we must share its physical burdens.

But most important of all are the spiritual burdens with which we can help our neighbors, near and far, in this sorely bludgeoned world of ours. We have Christ to give them — our matchless, loving Redeemer and Saviour of men. In Him is Life; in Him is Hope; in Him is Power. From Him come words that could issue from no other lips without rankest blasphemy: "Come unto me all ye that labor and are heavy laden and I will give you rest." "For God so loved the world that he gave his only begotten son that whosoever believeth on him should not perish, but have everlasting life." "Him that cometh unto me I will in no wise cast out."

God help us, that we be not negligent in our divinely appointed mission of giving to our neighbors — near and far — the great Glad Tidings of Him who loved us and died on Calvary's tree that we might have everlasting life.

QUESTION XI

How May We Know Christ Better?
A Message to College Students

QUESTION XI

How May We Know Christ Better?
A Message to College Students

> *"That I may know him . . ."*
> PHILIPPIANS 3:10

FOR A moment, you will let me speak personally and say that the privilege of coming again to this college campus and chapel is a privilege that warms my heart very deeply. Years ago it was my privilege to speak twice to the assembled students in this same chapel, and the memories of those brief visits have lingered with me for years to gladden and bless me. These fellow students will allow me in one brief moment to offer them my most cordial congratulations upon their rare privileges here as students. It is a glorious privilege to be linked with a worthy college family, and the far-reaching influence of this college family I have felt from one end of this country to the other. You will allow me to adjure you to turn to the highest and best account all these rare privileges. Education, once considered a luxury for the few, is now known to be a stern necessity for all.

That great leader, Foch, of France, once said laconically, "Battles are won the day before." Wellington said of Waterloo, "That battle was not won on the battlefield but back in Cambridge, Oxford and Eton." One of the old Troy generals, when asked by a group of young men how they might succeed, made this simple reply: "The secret, young men, of every victory is in getting a good ready." Get ready, my fellow-students, for the great times ahead. The world is now one big neighborhood, with all its trained men and women increasingly needed for the duties and battles of life.

Some Vital Questions

In recent months it has been my privilege to speak to thousands of college students, both in North and South America. My heart has been warmed more than I can say by the eager quest of these students for the chief knowledge of all, which is spiritual knowledge. That is your quest today, I trust.

The Apostle Paul has stated it for us in one of his great epistles. Let me quote it: "But what things were gain to me, these have I counted loss for Christ. Yea verily, and I count all things to be loss for the excellency of the knowledge of Christ Jesus my Lord: for whom I suffered the loss of all things, and do count them but refuse, that I may gain Christ, and be found in him, not having a righteousness of mine own, even that which is of the law, but that which is through faith in Christ, the righteousness which is from God by faith: that I may know him, and the power of his resurrection . . ." [American Standard Version]. That I may know and may have the knowledge most desirable and necessary, the knowledge of Christ. Our constant peril in these stressful times is that we will allow the things about us to crowd out our *consciousness of Christ*. The question emerges for our brief meditation this morning, "How may we know Christ better?" Let me give you several familiar, but I think vital, answers.

We must know the Bible better if we are to know Christ better. There can be only *one* best. The gift of His only begotten Son is God's best gift to mankind and the Bible comes next among His precious gifts to humanity. The great, sane, conserving book of civilization is the Bible. All rational people should read the Bible every day, whether they read the daily papers or not. The supreme book for human society is this Book from God and every rational person should read it every day.

One of the greatest problems that confronts us is that many clever people are neglecting and ignoring the Holy Word of God. That is true among groups of college students. I have been surprised in the various colleges throughout

How May We Know Christ Better?

America to find how well-informed the student body was with Shakespeare, Tennyson, and with the more modern writers, but how little they knew about the Bible. The Bible tells us that people are destroyed by their lack of knowledge of this great Book.

Chinese Gordon, that great English soldier, took with him his library when he went down into the Sudan. Later, he wrote that he had need down there for only two books, first, the Bible, and next the concordance that enabled him quickly to find any passage in the Bible.

If we are to know Christ better, we must find time for meditation. One wonders if the art of meditation is not nearly lost in these times of hurry and rush and superficiality and extravagance. The habit of meditation is one to be magnified continually by us all. They told me at Wellesley that the most important time, of all the hours of the day, is that little quiet half-hour when every girl in the college goes to herself and is alone with her own thoughts . They got more from that half-hour of meditation than from any other period that came to them through their entire college life. The Bible enjoins us to magnify this habit of meditation continually. "Wait on the Lord and he shall strengthen thine heart. Wait, I say, on the Lord."

The prophet Ezekiel gives us a picture of certain living creatures which, when they stood, let down their wings. There are times when we should "let down our wings" and let our thoughts dwell truly for a while upon Him who is the Light of the World.

If we are to know Christ better, we are to magnify daily the habit of secret prayer. I wonder if we do not fail at this point more than at any other. Arnold of Rugby was, in my judgment, the greatest teacher of boys the world has ever seen, and he used to say to his boys, "Whatever your troubles, your difficulties, your doubts, your temptations, your sins, if you will give yourself faithfully for a few minutes every day to secret prayer for divine direction, you will be victorious." I think he was undoubtedly right. Jesus calls us to prayer in these words: "But thou, when thou prayest, enter into thy closet, and when thou hast shut thy door, pray to thy Father which is in *secret;* and thy Father which seeth in secret shall reward thee *openly.*"

It was when Moses was thus alone that God gave him the sight of the burning bush, which was not consumed. It was when Isaiah was alone that he received the vision that transformed his whole life. Paul was alone with God when given power to bear the rigid thorn in the flesh. All down the years men and women have sought to be alone with God and bare their secret souls before Him for His guidance and mercy. Madame Guyon speaks of the great creative hours of life, and tells us that, when we try to abandon ourselves in the secret places to the knowledge and leadership of God, *these are the supremely creative hours of life.*

If we are to know Christ better, then we are to magnify our associations in life. Life is largely made or lost by our associations with our fellow-men. The Bible tells us that "he that walketh with wise men shall be wise; but a companion of fools shall be destroyed." The Bible tells us that "evil communications corrupt good manners." Life is largely set in right ways or wrong ways by our associations. Stanley, who went down into Africa to find Livingstone, tells us that his associations with Livingstone truly transformed his whole life. I adjure you to make much of the right kind of friends and of the reflex influence of such friends.

If we are to know Christ better, then we are to watch with uncompromising warfare against the commission of sin. The Bible tells us, "Blessed are the pure in heart: for they shall see God." It also asks: "Who shall ascend into the hill of the Lord? or who shall stand in his holy place?" And it answers: "He that hath clean hands and a pure heart, who hath not lifted up his soul unto vanity nor sworn deceitfully. He shall receive the blessing from the Lord." If we

How May We Know Christ Better?

are to know Christ better we are to watch with rigid, uncommising diligence against every wrong thing.

If we are to know Christ better, then we are to be busy. One of our chief faults is that of idleness. "An idle mind is the devil's workshop." Satan still finds mischief for idle hands to do. We are to watch with uncompromising opposition against idleness in the wrong times and ways and places.

I heard that great leader, John R. Mott, perhaps known to more college students in this country than any other man, I heard him tell the students again and again how his own spiritual life was once cut to shreds by a period of idleness, and how his usefulness was restored. This was his advice: "In all your doubts about Christ and the Bible, if you will go out and do your task of helping the needy world, your doubts will disappear as do the clouds with the rising of the morning sun." He told of going to a penitentiary one morning, where were incarcerated all types and ages of men, guilty of various crimes, and as he stood on the platform and began to speak to them, hoping to help them, he was flung back upon the necessity for divine power. As he talked to those men, there came pulsing through his own being again the conscious sense of Christ, and again was he strengthened in his faith and fellowship with Christ.

We are to make much of activity in the service of Christ. "If any man will do his will, he shall know of the doctrine whether it be of God."

If we are to know Christ better, we must have the necessary *desire and purpose* to know Him better. Christ has a plan for your life as real as He had for Paul, or Peter, or Wesley, or Livingstone, and the great quest is for you to find that plan and the great business of life is for you to complete that plan. Do not be afraid to venture your all upon Christ.

George McDonald, a famous Scotchman, has emphasized this truth in these lines:

I said, "Let me walk in the fields."
  He said, "Nay, walk in the town."
I said, "There are no flowers there."
  He said, "No flowers, but a crown."

I said, "But the sky is black,
  There is nothing but noise and din":
But He wept as He sent me back —
  "There is more," He said. "There is sin."

I said, "But the air is thick
  And fogs are veiling the sun."
He answered, "Yet hearts are sick,
  And souls in the dark undone."

I said, "I shall miss the light,
  And friends will miss me, they say";
He answered me, "Choose tonight
  If I am to miss you or they."

I pleaded for time to be given.
  He said, "Is it hard to decide?
It will not seem hard in Heaven
  To have followed the steps of your guide."

I cast one look at the fields,
  Then set my face to the town;
He said, "My child, do you yield?
  Do you leave the flowers for the crown?"

Then into His hand went mine,
  And into my heart came He,
And I walk in a light divine
  The path I had feared to see.

Oh, my fellow-students, be not afraid to follow Christ without stint or reserve, with all love and loyalty. Give to God your best to the end of the way!

QUESTION XII

Who Knoweth What Is Good for Man in this Life?

QUESTION XII

Who Knoweth What Is Good for Man in this Life?

> *Who knoweth what is good for man in this life?* ECCLESIASTES 6:12

THE question for our meditation today is a question which suggests to us how little we know of the earthly life and how little we can know while we are in the flesh. "Who knoweth what is good for man in this life, all the days of his vain life which he spendeth as a shadow?"

The thought that we do really know so little in the earthly life and, so long as we are in the flesh, we shall be able to barely skirt the realm of what is to be known, is a thought that is ofttimes doubly serious for earnest men and women. Paul put it truly when he said, "Now we see through a glass darkly," or through a blurred glass! Mysteries confront us on every side. We cannot sound their depths nor scale their heights. Our ignorance abashes us whichever way we turn. Since that is true, we should not give range to foolish talk or speech. In these recent years, when conditions everywhere have been abnormal, there has been a flood of foolish writing and talking on all subjects, including religion, the highest and most vital subject of all. Since we know so little and while in the flesh shall ever know so little, let us not quarrel with God — let us not complain and rebel and talk foolishly.

Job teaches us wisely at this point. When every earthly prop seemed taken from the grand old Patriarch of Uz, he turned to God and would not be deflected from God. When his children, not simply one but all, were taken from Job, the

Some Vital Questions

grand old man of faith said, "The Lord gave and the Lord hath taken away; blessed be the name of the Lord." Later, when not only the children were taken and every piece of his property was taken and his erstwhile friends forsook him, and his own wife said to him, "Curse God and die," Job simply said, "Let come on me what will; though he slay me, yet will I trust him." Job teaches us gloriously the proper way for us to behave in the mightiest of the perplexities and problems that come to vex us in the earthly life.

President Theodore D. Woolsey of Yale exhibited wonderful and Job-like behavior when all five of his children died of a dread disease within a few hours. The great educator followed them out to the last resting place and was overheard to quote from Psalm 38 the words which later were carved on the gravestone marking the resting place of those five children: "I was dumb; I opened not my mouth; because Thou Lord didst it."

That was a wonderful word flashed out in 1865 when Lincoln was assassinated — the great, patient, mighty Lincoln. An excited throng of thousands and thousands had gathered in the streets. They were utterly bewildered, going to and fro as sheep without any shepherd. They were overcome by questions and emotions incident to that tragic hour. You perhaps recall that one man gave out the statement: "God reigns and the government at Washington still lives." The crowds dispersed quietly. The right word had been said: "God reigns." God loves and He pities and He cares. We are not to indulge in querulousness and contention with God and foolish talk, but we are to draw nearer and still nearer to Him today and forever.

Now, the text from the Book of Ecclesiastes asks: "Who knoweth what is good for a man in this life, all the days of his vain life which he spendeth as a shadow?" There are two great, central truths suggested by this question and one is that we do not know much about the earthly life — not much but something — and that little something that we know is

Who Knoweth What Is Good For Man in This Life?

enough greatly to humble us. What is it that we do know about the earthly life? We know for one thing that it is very brief. Its brevity is brought to our attention whichever way we look. Very, very brief! If one should live to be as old as Methuselah — nine hundred and sixty-nine years — yet, would that last year come quickly. I was talking the other day to an old man, now past ninty-four, and his comments were to the effect that the earthly life was so brief. Now past ninety-four, he said, "The earthly life is so brief. I was a child the other day, sitting on mother's lap — now my great-great-grandchildren are here — it seems as rapid as the fight of an arrow — the earthly life is so brief!" We know the earthly life is painfully brief! How quickly come and go the Christmas seasons, the Thanksgiving seasons, birthdays and anniversaries! Solomon in our text likens the earthly life to a shadow. "Who knoweth what is good for a man in this life, all the days of his vain life which he spendeth as a shadow?" What is so fleeting and uncertain as a shadow? While you look at the cloud it dissolves and is gone. James asks, "What is your life — the earthly life?" and answers, "It is even a vapour, that appeareth for a little time, and then vanisheth away." The Bible teems with figures and similes suggesting the brevity and frailty and uncertainty of the earthly life. The great Psalmist speaks of it as "grass growing up in the morning but in the evening of that same day is cut down and withereth." So is the earthly life. In another place he compares it to the swift ships at sea. In one place you see the ship as it plows through the great waters and, lo, while you look, it passes beyond your vision and is gone. The earthly life is compared to the breath of one's mouth. It is also compared to the flight of the eagle. While you look, the proud bird lifts himself higher and higher until in a moment more he is lost in his upward flight. Death is the one certain thing; oh, the uncertainty of life. More uncertain is life than the spider's web woven across our window while we sleep! Yet it is hard for us to lay this truth to heart. Charles Dickens in his own inimitable way tells us of a lawyer who was constantly declaring that every man should make his will. The lawyer was correct; every man should make his will. But Dickens said this same lawyer died without making his own will. Most men think of life only in terms of today. If we will only pause to think, surely the frailty and brevity and the utter uncertainty of the earthly life, will be borne in upon us all.

We also know that this earthly life does not satisfy. We rise early and toil late and gain things at great pains, patience and cost; and when we have gained them they do not suffice. Take wealth, for example. When men have gained it, it does not give peace to their restless spirits. It does not satisfy. One of the richest men in the world was quoted the other day, when the interviewer asked him about his state of mind, as saying, "I would give all my fortune for the stomach of my chauffeur, as nothing I eat, morning, noon or night, gives me any pleasure but rather causes me pain."

One of the leading college men of America tells us about his boyhood friend, his chum of the early years. He tells us that this boyhood friend, who is now a multi-millionaire, said to him recently: "My friend, the only thing in print in all the world that interests me at all is the column that has the stock market reports." How pitifully poor is that man!

And then the quest for fame is equally unsatisfactory. Men rise early and toil late to win for themselves chaplets of glory. How sad the spectacle! How unsatisfactory to win crowns that fade! Fame is both fleeting and futile.

Men also toil for earthly pleasure and it palls on them. They become jaded and their spirits are tossed, troubled and disquieted. The sense of loss and weariness, of defeat and reverses, comes down upon them like some menacing cloud.

Not even knowledge — that great power for which we strive — not even knowledge can suffice. "Much study," this Book truly tells us, "is a weariness of the flesh." One of the world's great authors, Rudyard Kipling, when in this country

Who Knoweth What Is Good For Man in This Life?

the last time, became desperately ill. He was far from home and the great sea was between him and his loved ones. They carried him to one of the Eastern hospitals and one of the nurses heard him pitifully sobbing in the night and saying over and over again: "I want — I want." She bent over him and said, "What is it you want, Mr. Kipling?" And he said, "I want Christ — I want Christ. Nothing can suffice me now but Christ." A prominent sick man said the same thing last Sunday as he was hard by the gates of death. To the doctors and nurses he said: "I am at the place now where only Christ can suffice men. I want Christ. Nothing on earth can satisfy."

Since that is so, what are we to do? Just what the Lord tells us to do. We are to come with unfaltering submission of life, soul and will and all to Him who offers to be Saviour, Master, Pilot, Guide and Helper today, tomorrow and forever, for those who trust Him.

This question of the wise man suggests still another thought and that is that there is much about life that we cannot know. "Who knoweth what is good for a man in this life?" That is what Solomon asked.

Who knoweth which is better for a man, wealth or poverty? Do you know? Both have their perils. Who knoweth which is better for a man? Wealth is noisy, often arrogant. Wealth is often proud and self-sufficient. It often hardens the heart, dries up and shrivels and withers the finest things in the lives of its possessors. No wonder this Book says that the love of money is the root of every kind of evil. No wonder Jesus says, "How hard it is for them that have riches to enter into the kingdom of heaven!" And He explains in the next sentence that their peril lies in the fact that they are prone to put their trust in their riches. That is why it is so hard for them to enter the kingdom of God.

Poverty likewise has its perils. One can call to mind easily and visualize the most painful pictures concerning poverty. Especially pitiful it is to see a gentle woman undergoing the burdens of poverty! It stabs the heart to see a frail woman without enough to eat or wear. Poverty has its pains and its perils. Perhaps that prayer of Agur's, given in Proverbs 30:8, 9, is the best prayer for us all to pray: "Give me neither poverty nor riches; feed me with food sufficient for me: lest I be full, and deny thee and say, 'Who is the Lord?' or lest I be poor, and steal, and take the name of my God in vain." Who knoweth which is better for us, poverty or wealth?

Who knows which is better for us — health or sickness? Each has its compensations. Who knows which is better? Do you have health? Go your way and take care of your health. How rich a boon in the earthly life is health! Then we can work early and late for humanity. Then we can put hands and feet, heart and brain and life on the altar in a gracious way for human service! How great a blessing is health!

But I remind you that likewise sickness has its remarkable compensations. The Psalmist said: "It was good for me that I was afflicted." He learned about God as never before. One of the finest men in this country said: "I had to go blind in order to see Christ. I was foolish, selfish, self-sufficient, until my sight was taken and in the darkness I looked for Christ and I saw Him and found Him. My heart rests on Him without a shadow of fear." Sickness has in it often the enrichment, enlargement and quickening of our sympathies. Who knows which is better for us — health or sickness?

Who knows which is the better for one, prominence or obscurity? Oh, the perils of prominence! A man is a very foolish man who struggles to be prominent. If it ever comes, dear friend, let it come naturally. If it comes, let it come in response to the method of Jesus: "He that would be greatest among you, let him be the servant of all." That one will rise early and toil late and help humanity without any regard to prominence or reward or fame or notoriety. He will serve at his maximum and leave the result with God. "Uneasy lies the head that wears the crown."

Who Knoweth What Is Good For Man in This Life?

Prominence! What is there in that? Obscurity! Some of the greatest heroes and heroines the earth has known are men and women not recognized beyond their own neighborhoods. They are patient, truthful, honest, noble, good, loyal and they give their lives for home, neighborhood and Christ. The world does not know how worthy they are. Great shall be their reward.

The most prominent Negro in the world some years ago was Bishop Scott of Algeria. I saw an old Negro porter on a pullman in the East. The conductor said, "Take a good look at that Negro porter as he comes back down the aisle. I will tell you a story about him." Presently when the white-haired porter, over eighty years of age, passed by I searched his remarkably fine face. Then the conductor said, "His brother is a wonderful man, the great Bishop Scott of Algeria. Our porter was the oldest child in the family. When he came to young manhood, he had a notion he wanted to preach Christ's gospel to the world. But his father died and left him and his mother with a houseful of young children and he had to give his life to the support of the family. He educated all the younger children. One of his brothers whom he educated is the great Bishop of Algeria." Continuing, the conductor said: "This old Negro said to me the other day: 'Maybe when I come to the gates above the Master will say: "There is a place here for you." Then he said, quite wistfully, "How little I have done for God in the world."'" He was mistaken — he was a full-fledged partner with his famous brother, the distinguished Bishop of Algeria.

Who knows whether it is better to sail on the quiet seas through the world or to meet violent storms? The Apostle Paul said he was given a thorn in the flesh and that thrice he besought the Lord to take it away. But the Lord did not remove the thorn. Instead, He said: "Paul, I will give you more grace than ever, since you have the thorn." No more account have we of Paul asking for his thorn to be taken away. But we find him saying, "Most gladly therefore will I rather glory in mine infirmity, that the power of Christ may rest upon me." "It is better," thought Paul, "to have that thorn with the added grace from God than to be without that thorn and without that added grace."

Since we know so little and must ever know so little in the flesh, there is one infinitely wise thing we can all do. We can commit ourselves trustfully to Him who is the Light of the World, who is our Saviour, our Master, our Guide, our Almighty Brother, our adequate and infinite Redeemer. We can put our trust in Him and follow Him gladly to the end of the day.

Have you done that? If so, then rejoice forevermore! Have you not done that? Have you held back from reliance on Him who made you, who died for you, who upholds you, who blesses you with every blessing, from the largest to the least? Have you held yourself back from submission to that great Saviour and Lord? Give Him that submission before it is too late! Surrender to Him now!

The best possible thing any human being can do in this life is to make complete surrender unto Christ, the all-sufficient Saviour. I beseech you to make that surrender to Him now.

QUESTION XIII

What Is Your Attitude Toward Life?

QUESTION XIII

What Is Your Attitude Toward Life?

"Then I looked on all the works that my hands had wrought, and on the labor that I had labored to do: and, behold, all was vanity and vexation of spirit, and there was no profit under the sun."
ECCLESIASTES 2:11

". . . The time of my departure is at hand. I have fought a good fight, I have finished my course, I have kept the faith: henceforth there is laid up for me a crown of righteousness, which the Lord, the righteous judge, shall give me at that day: and not unto me only, but unto all them also that love his appearing."
II TIMOTHY 4:6 8

LET ME begin my message by asking every one of my auditors, "What is your attitude toward life, your dominant attitude?" One's attitude toward life is a matter of eternal moment. What do you conceive to be the answer to the fact that you are here in the earthly sphere for a little while and that you are to pass from this stage to another land? What do you think it is all about? What is your attitude toward life?

Jesus reminds us that He has a plan for every life, large or small, brave or humble. "To every man *his* work" says He — not to every man *a* work, not to every man *some* work, but to every man *his* work, to every woman *her* work. Have you found the plan God has for you? God has a plan for every life. It is not a matter of caprice, or chance, or accident, that you are here. God made you and put you here. "For what purpose?" is the eternally important question. Have you found out what that is? Have you found out what niche God would have you fill? He has one for you. Have you found out the work that God would have you do? He has a definite work for you to do. The great, important matter is your attitude toward life.

Many authors have their writings marked by cynicism and pessimism when they talk about life. Again and again we hear the cynical question, "Is life worth the battle?" or "Is the game worth the candle?" Wretched questions! It is the echo of Hamlet's soliloquy, "To be or not to be — that is the question." You are here now, and you are going to be somewhere, conscious and personal, forever. What is your attitude toward life?

Your attitude toward life, as I have said again and again, is a matter charged with eternal moment, even more important than all other things in the world. "What shall it profit a man if he gain the whole world, and lose his own soul?" Your soul is worth more than all the money in all the banks, and all the jewels on the whole globe. What are you thinking about life? What is your attitude toward life?

Today I should like for us to think together about the attitude toward life of two outstanding men told of fully in the Bible: Solomon in the Old Testament and Paul in the New.

Through the years Solomon made disastrous abuse of life and became one of the most cynical pessimists the world has known, although finally he was recovered out of it before his day was done. But for many years his plight was wretched beyond words. "Then I looked on all the works that my hands had wrought, and on the labor that I had labored to do; and, behold, all was vanity and vexation of spirit, and there was no profit under the sun." He was right in the hey-day of his worldly surroundings, when these words were written. They reveal his spirit and his attitude toward life during those years.

How different was the attitude of Paul! As he looked out upon the vast beyond toward which we are all traveling, Paul said with triumph which we can feel in his words this hour, "The time of my departure is at hand. I have fought a good fight, I have finished my course, I have kept the faith:

What Is Your Attitude Toward Life?

henceforth, there is laid up for me a crown of righteousness, which the Lord, the righteous judge, shall give me at that day: and not to me only, but to all them also that love his appearing." What a contrast between the life of Solomon and the life of Paul! It is poignantly impressive.

We would like to compare these men for a little while today. For a season, quite a long season, Solomon was in the grip of cynicism and pessimism and dark despair, in his outlook on life, toward that great chapter of immortality, the life that shall never end. I am a citizen of this world for sixty or seventy or eighty years, more or less, and then I shall go to be a citizen of that other world forever and ever. The doctrine of immortality is not a dead doctrine. It is not simply some vague philosophy, some abstract proposition, some misty dream. The doctrine of immortality is a great, moral dynamic which lifts life to a high level and drives it to great ends.

What is our attitude toward life today? We may step from the stage of action before next Sunday and be somewhere else, or before tomorrow's sun shall rise, we may be in the great beyond. What is your attitude toward life? We are here for a few, fast-fleeting years and then we step from the stage here to be somewhere else forevermore. What is our attitude toward life?

For years and years Solomon was utterly self-centered in his life. It would seem, as we read his story — his unfolding and remarkable story — that he was probably the most self-centered man in all the world of his day, and probably there was never a more self-centered man in the world from that day to this. He began, he built, he carried forward, he planned, he acted with an eye to his own pleasure, his own honor and his own ease. Go read his book, *Ecclesiastes*. It is the most pessimistic book in the Bible. Turn to it and read of Solomon's awful plight, and then his final recovery, his wise conclusion. At the last he said: "Let us hear the conclusion of the whole matter: Fear God and keep his commandments; for this is the whole duty of man." This *is* the whole of man, this is what man lives for. Fear God reverently and keep His commandments, promptly and faithfully.

Look at Solomon's personal life for awhile. He trod the whole gamut of life and its paces here. He said, "I have tried all of it." He was a learned man; he was called the wisest man of his day. He was an author; he searched near and far and delved into all sources to get information; he ransacked all avenues of learning; but he came back and said it was all weariness of the flesh: "All is vanity and vexation of spirit."

Then he devoted himself to pleasure. Read his story and see how he spent his life — how he went all the gaits. He gave full reign to his eye and looked on all the evils and pleasures that man can concoct in the world. He gave full rein to his five physical senses, full rein!

He turned to dissipation of the body — sensualities, gross and life-destroying. He turned to drink. Look at his writing and you will see where he says: "Wine is a mocker, strong drink is raging, and whosoever is deceived thereby is not wise." In so saying, he uttered a great truth. What folly there is in drink! What madness! What enervating, accursed, down-dragging weight is drink! America needs to wake up on that matter before the currents of evil carry us much farther down the stream than we are now; and Heaven knows we are far enough down now.

He followed all the pleasures he could think of. He had his house full of wives of all kinds, from all lands and of all faiths, and he came back and said: "All is vanity and vexation of spirit."

Then he tried power of all kinds. He gathered wealth from all the ends of his great kingdom. He built up the outstanding kingdom of his day, a powerful army, a vast retinue of servants. A mighty company thronged about him and gave him applause and praise and bowed before him. He tried

What Is Your Attitude Toward Life?

power in all of its forms — wealth and rulership and kingcraft; and yet he came back from it all and said: "All is vanity and vexation of spirit." His reaction to it all was: "I hated life. It were better never to have been born." He was in an awful plight. He was horribly enmeshed and overborne. He loathed himself and he loathed life and he loathed all the things to which he had clung; he loathed all the power with which he had surrounded himself and he looked back on his life and said, "I hate life." Oh how this man of ability, of tremendous power and of wisdom, in a worldly sense, had missed the whole conception of the meaning and mission of life!

After he had run the whole gamut of sin and recklessness, he knew that his life had been all "vanity and vexation of spirit." He realized that God had set eternity in the human heart, and that nothing but the eternal could survive and satisfy the human heart.

> This world can never give,
> The bliss for which we sigh,
> 'Tis not the whole of life to live,
> Nor all of death to die.
> Beyond this veil of tears,
> There is a life above —
> Unmeasured by the flight of years,

In his old age, Solomon became conscious of the fact that he was a citizen of two worlds and it was then that he said: "Let us hear the conclusion of the whole matter: Fear God and keep his commandments; for this is the whole duty of man." He was recovered by the might of God, ere his day was done, and he gave that great counsel before his sun was set.

Now, set over against him, Paul. Paul was the mightiest man of the New Testament, the greatest single credential that Christianity has had from the first Christian up until now; the mightiest apologetic of the Christian faith in the two thousand years of Christian history. His attitude toward life was as far different from that of Solomon as the east is from

SOME VITAL QUESTIONS

the west. Just as different. Just as far removed the one from the other. Paul started out as a noted unbeliever in Christ and Christianity. He was guilty of the sins of self-righteousness, of pharisaism, of bigotry, of fierce hatred, of bloody persecution. He went to and fro seeking to exterminate all the Christians of his time who dared to utter the name of Christ. The Scripture says he journeyed along the Damascus road and Christ met him and spoke to him these words: "Saul, Saul, why persecutest thou me?" Saul, all trembling and astonished said: "Who art thou, Lord? Is it possible that I am persecuting the promised Messiah? Is it possible that He has come? Who art thou?" And Jesus answered: "I am Jesus whom thou persecutest." And Saul, trembling and astonished, had only one question to ask: "Lord, what wilt thou have me to do?" And from that very hour Paul obeyed Christ, trustfully and joyfully, until death.

I doubt not that the most joyful man who ever lived was this man Paul. The most joyful. His tribulations were overwhelming. Turn to his second letter to the Corinthians and there in the eleventh chapter he tells of his tribulations. He had been beaten five times, with forty stripes save one, each time; he had been shipwrecked again and again; he had been imprisoned again and again; he had been scorned and despised times without number; he had been hungry; he had often been in fastings; he had been betrayed; but he had come through it all victoriously. "I am more than conqueror," he said.

Again and again Paul was able to write down the words: "Rejoice, rejoice, and again I say rejoice, evermore." He was irrepressible; he was unconquerable; he was the most joyful man that ever lived.

Solomon said, "I hate life." Paul said, "I rejoice in Christ." Solomon had for a long season the conception of life that: "It is all for me, and I am going to get out of it all that I can for myself." Paul's thought was: "All that I am and have and can be, is for the making of humanity wiser, safer,

WHAT IS YOUR ATTITUDE TOWARD LIFE?

surer, happier." The two men were poles apart in their conceptions of life.

How vastly important your attitude toward life, you eternity-bound men and women! What are you living for, Paul? "I am living to pay a debt." And what is your debt? "Why, I owe every kind of service that I can give to everybody. I owe everybody. I am a Jew, but I owe a debt to the Gentiles. If I am a wise man, I owe a debt to the ignorant masses. I am a poor man, but I owe a debt not only to the poor, but to the wealthy, the ease-loving, the God-forgetting. I owe myself to humanity and while I am here I must live to pay this debt. I must do all the good I can to all the people I can, just as long as ever I can." What a conception of life!

That is the attitude toward life which makes heroes and heroines. That is the conception that made Livingstone and Matthew T. Yates and General Booth and D. L. Moody! That is the conception of life that made Robert E. Lee the mighty personality who grew more vibrant and strong with every rising sun. Do you say, "I will live for humanity. All that I have and am is not for myself, it is for humanity, for its uplift, its salvation and conservation, for the highest today and for the unending tomorrow"? Is that your attitude? If you have not that feeling, you have missed it from beginning to end. That is the meaning of life.

Attitudes toward life and toward religion and toward all the important things of life, have their beginning in the home. Often the very humblest home is a great blessing to the world. I was reading recently the story of Pasteur, the world famed scientist yonder in France. When I was in France, I saw his tiny home. If you are ever in Paris you should go and see that little, poverty-marked house in which Pasteur was born and lived; he, the world-famed scientist. His discoveries in science have alleviated suffering and marvelously aided a needy world. He went back to that little home, after he was a world figure, and put a tablet on the little house where he was reared. Here it is:

Some Vital Questions

> "Oh my father and mother, who lived so simply in this tiny house, it is to you that I owe everything. Your eager enthusiasm, my mother, you passed into my life; and you, my father, whose life was so toilsome, you taught me what patience can accomplish with prolonged effort. To you, my father, I owe my tenacity and daily labor."

There was a mother and father who put their best into their son. They tried to shape, to mold, to direct, and to inspire that boy. His success and his attitude toward life go back to that father and mother. You are building for the world in that home of yours. The influence that goes out from your home will help shape the world. Will it help lift the world upward, or will it pull it downward?

Then, there is the man with money, with property. Oh, what an incongruity in the world is the man who has property, who imagines he can feed his soul, which is to live forever, on corn and meat. We are stewards of everything that we have. That is the conception of life at its best.

I was in Atlanta, Georgia, not long ago to preach the opening sermon for the First Baptist Church there, a beautiful building. Some time later the pastor told me of a modest old lady who had died. She had said before she went away, "I am a steward for my Lord. I am a steward of all this property that my husband left me." She gave one round million dollars to that church, saying, "I will ask that the officers of this church invest this million dollars as wisely as they can and make the interest on it go on and on in every wise way." Then she gave the other million, left her, to the hospital center there, and said: "I will ask the trustees to take the interest of it and make it last until time shall be no more." How great! "Go thou, and do likewise," living on and on when this earthly life is over. You can live on by the right kind of example, the right kind of influence. You can live on in the lives of people even though you have no money to leave.

There came to me once a godly man and his wife saying: "We want to talk to you about our property. We do not

What Is Your Attitude Toward Life?

have a great deal, but we want to talk to you about it. We want to live on after we are gone. We are looking toward the sunset hour and we want to live on. How shall we bequeath our modest estate so that Christ may be glorified and His cause be advanced?"

Give to the fullest right now, today. When we live with an eye for the unseen we are laying up treasure for ourselves, "where neither moth nor rust doth corrupt, and where thieves do not break through nor steal." When you invest in the Lord's work, often you may not see immediate results, but you may be greeted by someone in the hereafter, whom you never saw, who will tell you: "It was because of you that I was healed or helped, because of what you did, said, or planned, that I am here."

What is your attitude toward life? Oh, man and woman, there is only one attitude to have toward life. How ghastly, how down-dragging for a life to be a selfish life! We are in the world to do all the good we can, in all the ways we can, to all the people we can and just as long as ever we can.

Selfishness is not of God. Selfishness is the suicide of all lasting greatness. The unselfish man or woman shall go on and on, making the world a better place in which to live. They have the right attitude toward life. Oh, men and women, get this right attitude, trust obediently this divine Saviour and Lord. Turn from the things that enslave and debauch and drag you down. Turn from the sin that poisons and enervates. Turn to the great and gracious Saviour who died for us all, and say to Him: "Be my Saviour. I choose; I yield; I decide; I surrender to thee. What wilt thou have me to do? Here I am awaiting thine order. Point the path in which I should go and my feet shall tread it without delay." And you who are Christ's declared friends hearken to the lines which say:

> Rise up, Oh men of God —
> Give heart and strength and mind and soul —
> To Christ the blessed King.

Some Vital Questions

> Rise up, Oh men of God,
> Christ's church for you doth wait --
> Have strength well equal to the task;
> Rise up, and make her great.

Who wants to follow this glorious Saviour and Lord and toward life. I am Christ's friend now, and I want to link myself with His church and His people just as He commands me to do"? Or, "I am His friend deep down in my heart, but have never stepped out, but now, I step out before all these people just as He commands me to do"? Or, "I want to be His friend and I want to make unconditional surrender of my life to Him and I make it today." Who comes today into the church, making open confession of Christ as your Saviour?

> Would you live for Jesus
> And be always pure and good?
> Would you walk with Him,
> Within the narrow road?
> Would you have Him bear your burden,
> Carry all your load?
> Let Him have His way with thee.

Who wants to follow this glorious Saviour and Lord and say, "His attitude is mine. His way is mine. His will is my will and I make my surrender to Him"? Who wants to follow Him today into the church, coming by letter or coming upon statement or upon your confession of faith in Him as your personal Saviour? Will you yield to Him, confess Him, own Him, register your surrender to Him?

QUESTION XIV

What If Christ Had Not Come?
A Christmas Message

QUESTION XIV

What If Christ Had Not Come?
A Christmas Message

~~~~~~

> *If I had not come . . .*
> JOHN 15:'22

BEFORE coming to our message of the morning, I would like to voice for you, all and each, a wish for a joyful Christmas season, not only for this company within these walls, but also for all who may be listening in throughout radio-land. As we come again to this happy season, may all our hearts be deeply grateful and humble, and may we all join fervently in the prayer of Tiny Tim when he prayed, "God bless us, everyone."

At this happy season it behooves us very wisely to remember that the true Christmas spirit is the spirit of unselfishness. All about us there are those whose condition challenges our wisest and worthiest attention. There are the needy, whichever way you turn your eyes. Who can think of a little child being hungry and cold, undernourished, under-privileged — or a mother in the same plight, or any human being anywhere in like condition — except with emotion of deepest sympathy? Then there are the aged and the infirm, the bereaved and the lonely. How easily can they be neglected, overlooked, passed by! At this season there should be a summoning of all our best thoughts to the end that all these groups mentioned, and our fellow humanity on every side, of all classes and conditions, may have from us the right message in word and deed.

Some Vital Questions

The apostles, when they were asked for alms, answered by the mouth of Simon Peter: "Silver and gold have I none; but such as I have give I thee: In the name of Jesus of Nazareth rise up and walk." And the man rose up and leaped for joy and went his way. That was better than to have given him a sack filled with gold. The old proverb from the Book of Proverbs comes to mind, namely: "A word fitly spoken is like apples of gold in pictures of silver." A beautiful expression, isn't it? Words are real things. They can cut like a knife or they can soothe like the sweetest music. Let us through all this joyful Christmas speak the word, with our lips and with our pen, as wisely and faithfully as possible.

And now turning away from these personal expressions, let us remember that the Christmas season chronicles the chiefest event that earth has ever known, or shall ever know — the coming of the only begotten Son of God in human flesh, the God-man, to be the Saviour of a sinful world.

History discloses numbers of great instances where mighty personalities came back who were supposed to have been sunk in oblivion. For example, one recalls the coming back of Napoleon. You will remember that he was banished in 1814 to Elba, and it looked like that amazingly brilliant soldier was finished. But in March 1815, barely a year later, he went back to France. He had kept close watch on events transpiring in Europe while he was away at Elba, and he knew of the unpopularity and the weakness of Louis XVIII. He was aware also of his own personal power and influence over his fellow-countrymen, so he went back to France.

The Emperor sent an army out to capture Napoleon, who alighted from his carriage and advanced toward the army without any army of his own, without even an attendant — one lone man against whom an army was sent. He went toward the army quietly, confidently; and when he was near enough, he opened his coat that the bullets of the enemy might reach his heart if they chose to fire. Napoleon quietly

What If Christ Had Not Come?

said, "Frenchmen, it is your emperor." And they went wild. They kissed his hand, they fell at his feet, they picked him up and carried him on their shoulders, and they shouted until the heavens were filled with their shouts: "Vive l' empereur!" "Long live the emperor!" It was the most thrilling scene that history ever recorded of the return of one whose day-star seemed to have set.

Some years ago there was a remarkable book written by that eminent writer, William P. Stead — who later went down, you will recall, with many others, on the ill-fated Titanic. The book he wrote bore the title, "If Christ Should Come to Chicago." It is a thrilling book. Imagination is set free as you read and one's deepest soul is thrilled and challenged. If Christ came to Chicago, what would He see and what would He hear and where would He go and what would He say and what would He do?

We can bring it closer and say, "If Christ came to Dallas" — today or tomorrow morning, Christmas morning — where would He go, at whose house would He stop, at whose door would He knock ? Oh my soul, would He knock at my door? Would He knock at your door? Where would He go if He came to Dallas tomorrow — where would Christ go and with whom would He talk and what would He say, if He came and talked to the individual or group? If Christ came to Dallas — what a startling thought!

A more startling thought would be if Christ did not come to Dallas or to Chicago or to New York or to London, or to the Americas, or to Europe, or Asia, or Africa, or the islands of the sea — what if Christ did not come? That would be a far more startling thought! He Himself raised that question, the night before He was crucified. "If I had not come" — He used those very words. Now, let the imagination go on the wings of fancy and thought: "If Christ had not come!"

Nearly two thousand years ago He came to this world, and His spirit has made an impact deeper than that of any other personality that has ever touched this world. His spirit pervades all the realms of life. His spirit pervades literature and government and law and religion and art and music. All the spheres and realms of life have been influenced by Christ and Christianity. What if He had not come? Where would the world be, at this moment, if Christ had not come?

Fancy the actual conditions if you will, when He came. The conditions were appalling throughout the world, nearly two thousand years ago when He came in the flesh. Three-fifths of the world was in slavery. The clanking of chains could be heard and slaves — human beings — were bought and sold as oxen, and they were beaten and bludgeoned and killed without any hesitation or compunction. There was a law among the Imperial Romans, that if a man killed an ox — just an animal — the death penalty followed for such an awful thing; but if he killed a slave, his fellow-man, it was passed by and nothing thought about it.

In ancient Greece and in Imperial Rome, slavery to an awful degree held high carnival. Masters, numbers of them, had from ten to twenty thousand human beings as their slaves. The coming of Christ sounded the death-knell of slavery, and as He and His principles are held aloft in the world, the clanking chains of slavery will sound less and less until their echoes finally will be heard no more.

Call to mind the condition of childhood when Christ came. Often children were not welcome in the day when Jesus came. They were regarded as a burden, they were in the way in many cases. They were troublesome, they were vexing, they were unwelcome. Oh, how that is all changed! The most interesting object in the whole world is a little child. The sweetest music heard is the laughter of a little child. The most beautiful vision is the joy in the eye and on the face of a little child. Christ changed our conception of childhood when He came. He glorified the latent, measureless possibilities in a little child. Therefore, we are caring for children

What If Christ Had Not Come?

better all the time, with orphanages, with hospitals, with all kinds of conveniences and arrangements and improvements for their betterment.

Think of the condition of woman when Jesus came! She was a slave, she was a burden-bearer. One man would have a houseful of wives, so called, and they were burden-bearers; he drove them to and fro as men drive their beasts of burden, their oxen that pulled their plows or their wagons. Christ changed all that!

I have said it again and again, and I say it again today: how any woman can keep from loving Christ, can keep from bowing before Him, from accepting Him as her Saviour and serving Him as Lord and Master, is a mystery deeper than I can understand. The supreme champion of womanhood is Christ! There is not in the New Testament the account of one harsh word that He ever spoke to a woman. When there was dragged into His presence the poor woman who had sinned, defiled in life by her own ill-behavior, and when self-righteous men cried their bitter speech against her, Jesus wrote on the ground and then He said: "Let him that is without sin, cast the first stone." And He wrote on the ground again, and looked up and they had all gone. "Let him that is without sin, cast the first stone," but none were there to cast the stone, and gently he said to the poor woman, trembling in His presence, "Where are thine accusers? Hath no man condemned thee?" And she answered: "No man, Lord." Oh, the wonderful words of Jesus to her! "Go and sin no more." Is not that just like a divine Saviour, an all-gloriously divine Saviour? He has glorified womanhood, and when womanhood is lifted up, all civilization is lifted up. Marvelous transformation came to womanhood by the coming of Christ into the world.

But most of all, the coming of Christ Himself, this personal Christ, changed and is changing all history, even as His purposes are ripening with the rising and setting of every

Some Vital Questions

sun as the days come and go. Socrates, the wise man of his day, cried out in his darkness: "We look for a god, or a god-inspired man, who will teach us our duty and help us to live as we ought." The cry of men through the generations is the cry for somebody higher, better, abler than themselves.

They said to Jesus, when He came and before they understood Him, "Show us the Father and it sufficeth us." His answer was, "Have I been so long time with you, and yet hast thou not known Me, Philip? He that hath seen Me hath seen the Father." Jesus came to reveal God. "God was in Christ reconciling the world unto himself." Jesus came that men might understand God, not as a God of cruelty, not as a God of ill, but as a God of love, of grace, of compassion, of sympathy, of ever abounding interest in humanity, in all humanity. Jesus came to reveal God! "Behold, I bring you good tidings of great joy, which shall be to all people" — white and black, rich and poor, high and low, noble and ignoble, lovely and despicable, "I bring you glad tidings of great joy which shall be to all people, for unto you is born this day in the city of David, a Saviour, which is Christ the Lord," said the angel. The birthday of Christ! This is the supreme event to entrance and enthrall and challenge the world forever and ever.

But look a little further. What if He had not come? If Christ had not come, where would the world be now? We would be in paganism, deep, dark, desperate paganism! The world, through all its wisdom, did not know God. Even Socrates, the wisest man of his time cried out: "We look for a god, or a god-inspired man, who will teach us our duty and help us to live like we ought to live."

If Christ had not come, we would not have the stories recorded here in this Book of His sympathy for the distressed and the distraught, and the suffering of all ages and classes and conditions of humanity. We would have no story of His pity and compassion for the leper, for the blind, for the igno-

What If Christ Had Not Come?

rant, for the bereaved, for the broken-hearted, for the poor. God sent Christ to preach good tidings to the poor, counting that as the supreme thing. The blind receive their sight, the lepers are cleansed, the dead are raised up, and the poor have the gospel preached to them. Here is one champion for every poor man and woman in the world. He is unforgetting, unfailing, all-sufficient, and He is Christ. We would know nothing about God's care for the poor, if He had not come. We would never have heard of the story of His grace and delivering mercy in behalf of these distressed and unfortunate groups about us, if He had not come.

If Christ had not come, we would not have the parables in the New Testament which so enrich and enlarge our lives. How much poorer the world would be, if we did not have the Parable of the Prodigal Son! Whose heart does not start afresh, with a sense of humility and feeling out after God, when he goes over that Parable of the Prodigal Son?

And how much poorer the world would be if we did not have the Parable of the Good Samaritan! Oh, the enlightening, the illuminating, the enlargening power of that parable! From it the question emerges, "Who is my neighbor?" Your neighbor and mine is anybody in the world who needs us. Maybe he lives close to us, maybe he lives far away, maybe he is a black man or a red man or a yellow man or a white man, of your race or another race, in sympathy with your creed, or not in sympathy with it at all. Your neighbor is anybody in the world who needs you. He may be in darkest Africa, he may be in age-old China, or in Japan, or in beaten, blungeoned India, or in America, North or South — anybody in the world who needs you is your neighbor. You cannot draw your robe around you and say, "It is nothing to me." It is something to you, and you will find it out at the judgment bar of God if not before. We are in the world, bound together in the bundle of humanity and we may not, dare not, must not, ignore the welfare of any human being in all the wide world.

Some Vital Questions

We would not have all this teaching if Christ had not come. And we would not have the right estimates and appraisals of humanity if He had not come. It is easy to evaluate things as more important than human beings. It is easy to imagine that gold, stocks and bonds, houses and lands, well-filled granaries, and all such things constitute the chief values in life. Christ does not so teach. More important than all the grain that fills the granaries, and all the gold that fills the banks, more important than all this, is a human life—humble, ignorant, undeveloped though it may be, just a human life. "What shall it profit a man, if he shall gain the whole world, and lose his own soul? Or what shall a man give in exchange for his soul?" Christ, and He alone, gives us the right appraisal of humanity.

The correct test of a civilization is the kind of people that the civilization produces. What will it profit a civilization if it build towering skyscrapers and crowd its granaries with grain, and fill its banks with gold, if such civilization loses sight of the truth that yonder little child, under the wagon or shivering this morning in a cold tent, is worth more than all these material possessions that civilization can bring together? Christ gives us the right appraisal, the right estimate, the right measure of a human being. Somewhere such human being is to go on, consciously and personally, forever. Wheat will not last, money will not last, houses and lands will not last. Here is a human being that is to exist forever. Christ gives us the right appraisal of humanity.

If Christ had not come, we would have no adequate atonement for sin. Men were trying to fix up their own atonement, they were beating themselves, they were torturing themselves, they were offering all kinds of crude and terrible sacrifices, if haply they might ease the ache at their hearts which tormented them when there was an accusing conscience. If Christ had not come, there would have been no adequate atonement for sin.

What If Christ Had Not Come?

The day that changed the world was the day of the Cross. "God forbid that I should glory, save in the cross of our Lord Jesus Christ." Jesus alone has made adequate atonement for sin; and now the person with the vilest, the lowest, the most wretched, the most terrible life in the world, can be pointed to the Cross and can be assured — if he will turn penitently to Christ who made atonement for all men, and accept Him — that person will be forgiven and will be saved. Oh, the great message in the Cross of Christ!

> In the cross of Christ I glory,
>   Towering o'er the wrecks of time.
> All the light of sacred story,
>   Gathers 'round his head, sublime.

The Cross is our hope.

If Christ had not come, we would have no door of hope beyond the grave. Men had wondered about it, speculated about it, and guessed and sighed and sobbed and gone on wondering: "Whether there be anything more, we cannot say." They said, "Whether the grave is the final chapter, we do not know." But Jesus came and comforted the brokenhearted. "Your brother shall rise again," He said to Mary and Martha. His own tears were shed with theirs out of the compassion and sympathy of His loving heart. "Thy brother shall rise again. I am the resurrection, and the life: he that believeth in me, though he were dead, yet shall he live: and whosoever liveth and believeth in me shall never die." Who can weigh the worth of these precious words from those lips divine?

The three great matters that concern mankind are life, death, eternity — and Christ alone has the only definite, clarifying, authoritative, satisfying word concerning all three. You need not be afraid of life. Trials may be in it daily for you. Do not be afraid. For He said, "I am he that liveth and was dead: and, behold, I am alive forevermore." Be not afraid of life's checkered experiences. It is given unto you, not only to believe on Christ but also to suffer for His sake. And do not be afraid of death; do not be startled nor overborne at the thought of death. The "black camel" will kneel at your gate someday and bear you away. "It is appointed unto men once to die"; do not be afraid. Only see to it that your trust is in the Christ, "who hath abolished death and brought life and immortality to light through the gospel." Cling to Him and do not be afraid of how or where you shall die; leave all that to Him, who will turn your death into a triumphant march. And do not be afraid of eternity. Christ is out there! We are going where He is. "I go to prepare a place for you. And if I go and prepare a place for you, I will come again, and receive you unto myself; that where I am, there ye may be also."

Oh, dear men and women, are you not glad that Christ came? gladder than word of man or angel could ever tell, that Christ came? Where would we be? In a pagan land. Where would you be, if Christ had not come? He is the one who gives us the right estimate of humanity, the right appraisal.

One of those poor Russian soldiers driven into battle, or a Finnish soldier fighting for his independence, or a German or an Englishman, or a Frenchman — anyone of these brave men, helpless, driven by the powers superior over them, anyone is worth more than all the countries about which these men are fighting and all the assets and materials these men are grasping for. Old Dr. Knox sang the right song:

> When wilt thou save the people?
>   Oh God of mercy, when?
> Not thrones and crowns, but nations,
>   Not kings and czars but men!
> Flowers of Thy heart, Oh Lord, are they,
>   Let them not pass like weeds away;
> Their heritage is a sunless day —
>   God save the people.

What If Christ Had Not Come?

And Edward Markham sang also:

> Then clear the way there, clear the way,
>   Blind kings and creeds have had their day.
> Break the dead branches from their path,
>   Our hope is in the aftermath.
> Our hope is in heroic men,
>   Christ led to build this world again —
> To this event the ages ran,
>   Make way for brotherhood, make way for man.

What is your attitude toward Christ? Oh woman, young woman, or older woman, young man or older man, happy girl or boy, how can you keep from giving your all, trustfully to Him, who alone can save? Have you done it? Will you do it now? And today, does not your heart stir with gratitude that things are as well with us as they are? That we are the recipients of such goodness and mercy? And does not every man, and woman and child in this place want to open his purse and bring a worthy offering to Christ? If He should come upon this platform now, our divine Saviour, the Son of God and say: "I would be pleased if you would make a Christmas gift to me," you would open up your purse and pour out your gifts as the Magi did of old, a gift worthy of Christ. Very well: "Inasmuch as you would do it unto Me, do it unto these!" These orphan children out at Buckner Orphans' Home, whose parents have gone on. Surely you want to make a gift to them this Christmas time. Surely everyone would like to. Maybe you had rather write on a slip of paper that you will come in later during the week and make your gift. Let us start now, before Christmas is here and make our gift to the Buckner Orphans' Home. Let the officers come forward promptly, and take their places while the organist plays that grand old song:

> I gave my life for thee.
>   My precious blood I shed:
> That thou mightest ransomed be,
>   And quickened from the dead.
> I gave, I gave my life for Thee,
>   What has thou given for me?

Some Vital Questions

As the officers pass among you, are there those here today who say, "I want to follow Christ at this Christmas time"? or "I have already accepted Him as my Saviour, and am a member of the church and have recently moved to Dallas and want to join this church"? Today as these men move among the audience, gathering up these gifts, come and thrice welcome as you come!

Christ came in the long-ago as Saviour. Christ is here now in power to save and bless and empower all who will trust Him and surrender unto Him. Christ will come again some day in person to judge the world in truth and righteousness. In this present day and hour of golden opportunity will you not take your stand with Him and for Him, whole-heartedly and without reserve? Come humbly, penitently, trustfully and He will receive you and bless you for time and eternity. Surrender to Him yourself, your heart, your all! Come now!

The Inspiration of Ideals

THE INSPIRATION OF IDEALS

GEORGE W. TRUETT, D.D., L.L.D.

Compiled and Edited by
Powhatan W. James, Th.D., D.D.

Copyright 1950
by the William B. Eerdmans Publishing House

Reprinted 1980 by Baker Book House
with the permission of the copyright holder

FOUR-VOLUME SET
ISBN: 0-8010-8854-2

PHOTOLITHOPRINTED BY CUSHING - MALLOY, INC.
ANN ARBOR, MICHIGAN, UNITED STATES OF AMERICA

DEDICATION

This and other volumes
of sermons and addresses
in this series by Dr. George W. Truett
are dedicated to
his beloved
First Baptist Church, Dallas, Texas
where most of them
were delivered

FOREWORD

The first four volumes of the *Truett Memorial Series* were composed of fourteen sermons each. There has been a widespread request that at least one volume of the series contain some of Dr. Truett's addresses delivered on special occasions during his eventful life. Accordingly, ten addresses which are more or less typical of his whole ministry have been selected for Volume V. They range over forty-four years of his ministry, beginning with his graduating address at Baylor University in June, 1897, and concluding with an address he delivered in February, 1941, at the dedication of a church building in South Carolina.

The footnotes found on the first page of each address will quickly disclose the fact that the compiler and editor sought to select addresses which would cover a wide range of subjects and occasions, such as many ministers are called upon to face frequently. To them and other readers it will be of interest to observe how Dr. Truett dealt with these varied subjects and audiences across the years.

Several of these addresses are reprints. The one on the Lord's Supper was printed in tract by the Baptist Sunday School Board and had an extensive circulation in the Seventy-five Million Campaign of Southern Baptists during the years 1920-25. *Baptists and Religious Liberty, The Leaf and The Life* and the address at the funeral of Dr. J. B. Gambrell were printed in the volume entitled *God's Call To America,* compiled and edited by Dr. J. B. Cranfill and copyrighted by the Sunday School Board of the Southern Baptist Convention. Dr. T. L. Holcomb, Executive Secretary of that board graciously granted permission to reprint and expressed the judgment that these several addresses were altogether worthy of reprinting at this time.

It is hoped that The Truett Memorial Series may ultimately contain ten volumes.

PRESIDENT'S OFFICE
BETHEL WOMAN'S COLLEGE
HOPKINSVILLE, KENTUCKY
OCT. 1, 1950

POWHATAN W. JAMES

TABLE OF CONTENTS

Chapter	Page
I. The Inspiration of Ideals	11
II. The Leaf and the Life	23
III. The Power of Convictions	47
IV. The Supper of Our Lord	63
V. Baptists and Religious Liberty	83
VI. The Greatness of Service	113
VII. Dr. J. B. Gambrell: The Great Southern Baptist Commoner	131
VIII. C. H. Spurgeon Centenary	147
IX. The Dedication of a Church	167
X. Civic Righteousness	185

CHAPTER I

The Inspiration of Ideals

CHAPTER I

The Inspiration of Ideals*

EVERY intelligent life must be a journey toward an ideal. This ideal is a pattern in the mind, held up before its eye, for imitation, realization and guidance. Aspiration is life's universal law. What we call progress is but society following after and translating into life the visions of the mind. As a definite plan is essentially needful to the workman in the erection of his building, so are ideals in the fashioning of anything worthy in all the realms of human achievement.

It is language divine which says: "Where there is no vision, the people perish." As the star guided the wise men of the East to the place where the Christ-child lay, so God has hung starry ideals — visions of the ever unattained — before men and nations, by which He ever beckons them on, in the working out of their destiny. The hope of this world has always been fashioned into some vision of what ought to be and may be; and the individual or nation, unstimulated by such vision, is speedily hastening into decline and the grave.

This practical age sneers at "visions." It asks for something practical; for houses and horses — for rail-roads and factories — for lands and gold. We forget that visions are the materials out of which all progress is fashioned. The builder of states is the one who sees visions and dreams dreams.

---

* The graduating address of George W. Truett delivered at Baylor University, Waco, Texas, June, 1897. Its subject and contents constitute a clear prophecy of this graduate's future.

The Inspiration of Ideals

Every human invention was first a thought in some mind. For years, there was working in the mind of James Watt a vision which in time became a steam engine. So with the telegraph in the mind of Morse, the telephone in the mind of Bell, and the countless other inventions of men. For years, in the mind of Michael Angelo, there worked a vision of earth's mightiest tragedy and at last an admiring world gazed enraptured on his matchless painting of the Crucifixion. The great artist, Millet, gazed for twenty long years upon the flying clouds. The people pushed him aside as a "dreamer"; but by and by he made an investment of 60 cents for canvas, brush and colors; and upon that canvas, he spread the glories he had seen in the heavens, and that vision gave him a painting worth $105,000.00.

What are the vast volumes of literature, but the fastening upon the printed page. the visions of some thinker's mind? What are inventions and factories and institutions but the incarnation of ideals?

Yea, more, what is this wondrous, whirling planet, adorned with flowers and harvests and mountains, but the material embodiment of the thoughts of God?

These visions of the mind hold the secret of all progress whether of individuals or nations. Napoleon believed that every battle must first be fought in the mind; and so, while his soldiers slept, he marshalled his armies, and led them against his foes, and triumphantly saw the victory hours before the battle began.

When only a dozen years of age, waking one midnight hour, John Milton beheld the vision of a poem which he fain would write and which the world would never allow to die. From that hour he ever followed the gleam of that midnight vision. He toiled seven long years in Cambridge, never closing a book before midnight. He made a tour of Italy, the better to study that land of story and song. He hastened back

The Inspiration of Ideals

to England to join his country-men in the conflict for liberty. The years hurried on, bringing slander and old age and blindness; but the midnight vision persisted and finally became the immortal poem — *Paradise Lost*.

While Henry Clay's youthful hands hoed corn on the old farm, he had visions of standing in the halls of Congress. With every weed that fell before his stroke, his mind cut down an opponent with an argument. Ah, what battles in every age the plow-boys have fought in dreams! These plow-boys are the hope of the world!

It has often been said that the history of civilization is the history of great men. It is largely true. What would Israel have been without Moses? Athens without Socrates? Carthage without Hannibal? Rome without Cicero and Caesar? Paris without Victor Hugo and Napoleon? England of the past without Milton and Shakespeare? England of the present without Spurgeon and Gladstone? America without Washington and Lincoln and Lee? Texas without Sam Houston? The characters of a few men leaven the life and mold the destiny of every nation. Their lives are as universities to the multitudes. They become beckoning beacons, pillars of cloud by day and fire by night to guide the peoples in their wilderness wanderings. The primary fountain of every country's greatness is not in the extent of her territory, not in her imperial enterprises, not in her vast populations; all these a country may have, and her seeming prosperity be but as a feast of Belshazzar, flaming with wine and crowned with flowers, while speeding on to irretrievable doom. After all, Emerson's test of civilization is the only true one: "The kind of men the country turns out."

And the history of great men is only the history of their ideals. The history of every epoch of the past is but the history of some great ideal, embodied in a leader.

The ideal of individual responsibility and consequent freedom of action in religion, dropped into the life of

The Inspiration of Ideals

Martin Luther, set tyrants to trembling and thrones to tottering, and led to the banishment of the dark night of the Middle Ages, and the advent of a mighty mental and moral reformation.

It was the ideal of personal rights in church and state, which in the hands of Cromwell, became a weapon powerful enough utterly to destroy that citadel of iniquity: "The divine right of kings."

It was his ideal of the structure of the globe that shaped the career of Columbus and determined the destiny of millions.

It was the ideal of the possibilities of free institutions and self-government, first dropped into the minds of the Founding Fathers that in its working has changed the course of all history and turned hopefully to our nation the eyes of the oppressed of every land.

During our American Revolution, when the English Secretary of War urged such an increase of English troops in Boston as would make England's guns outnumber the guns of the Americans, the farseeing Pitt replied: "We must reckon not so much with their guns as with their sentiments of liberty." Not rifle balls but sentiments win battles.

Nations as well as individuals are fashioned by their ideals. When the ideal of Sparta was grace and symmetry of body, then she produced the most splendid physique that has ever graced the earth. When her ideal fell to that of mere brute force, then her civilization was "red with the fierce fires of animal passion." When the ideal of Athens was philosophy, there was produced her Socrates, Plato and Aristotle.

When the ideal of France was glory, then "glory sat with the eagles on her victorious banners." But when her ideal was agnosticism, then anarchy took the place of government; patriots were exiled and murdered; scholars were proscribed and banished; licentiousness held high carnival in her first homes, and lovely womanhood was degraded and despised.

The Inspiration of Ideals

The ideal of empire and commerce made little England, "the mistress of the seas; the ruler of vast and varied populations; the banking-house and workshop of the world."

The great ideal of the worth and freedom of the individual has made the United States an asylum for the earth, and put her flag foremost among all that float in the galaxy of nations.

But I pause to say that there are ignoble ideals in our incomparable country, which forebode evil and threaten the well-being and the permanency of our beloved nation. Is it not time for patriots to inquire anxiously about our future when the press and the public give greater prominence to the pugilist than to the poet, to murder trials than to meetings of great religious bodies? The race horse is often glorified more than the gospel preacher and the unprincipled politician too frequently displaces the unselfish statesman. These things occur when low ideals are in the ascendancy.

A still more dangerous enemy to great and noble ideals lurks in the well-nigh universal passion for money. Unquestionably, this passion is today the Black Plague of America's individual, social and national life. Stealthily but surely it is corrupting our highest ideals of education, literature, statesmanship, and religion. No tongue among us is able to describe the direful effects of this gloomy trend of American life. The transcript of it may be seen in the glory and fall of ancient Rome. When the pagan Emperor of China was petitioned to license the opium traffic, he at once replied: "Nothing could induce me to desire a revenue from the vice and misery of my people." And yet Christian England gladly derived an immense income from this very traffic; and Christian America "jumps at the chance" of obtaining revenues from business still more infamous and destructive. We talk much of heathen idolatry, but there was never a heathen temple crowded with more eager devotees, than is the temple of mammon in this land of alleged civilization and Christianity.

The Inspiration of Ideals

This passion for money is even now dictating terms to society; it is freezing patriotism to death; it is absorbing life's higher aims; it is stifling intellectuality; it is consuming the vitality of our manhood and lowering the standards of our morality. For money men claw each other like vicious beasts. For it, they stand on yawning precipices that overhang the bottomless abyss! For it, they trifle with the judgments of God and lend their souls to deeds of infamy.

No greater service could I offer today to my class and comrades, than to hold up before them life's noblest ideals, to urge obedience to them as the steady motives of their lives. They are the visions that lift life above its toils and seeming defeats, into the peace and hope of the unseen. History would be robbed of its glory if from it were stripped the story of the mighty men who have endured, through seeing afar off the realization of their visions. Moses long endured the hardships of the desert and wilderness because he foresaw the time when his people would be clothed with the qualities of patriots. It was this that sustained Paul chained in a dungeon, while bloody Nero lived in a palace of marble and gold. It was this that enabled John Huss to look out from behind prison bars, upon a massed mob of men, and calmly endure his trials, by the foresight of that day when the arms then wielded for repression of liberty should flash for its emancipation. It was this that sustained Savonarola, living in his garret and eating crusts, while Lorenzo was robed in purple and lived in a palace. It was this that enabled Dante to live exiled from his own vine and fig tree and at last to endure the scaffold while licentious kings drove in chariots and revelled in palaces. It is this that sustains the heroes of liberty and religion in every age, hunted as they often are as partridges upon the mountains — their lives one unceasing struggle against tyranny and sin. Through these noble ideals the whole manhood is vitalized, the mind is stirred to sublimest aspiration, the heart is nerved to all-conquering courage and endurance.

The real worth of noble ideals is that by mere reflex influence they tend to mold men into their likeness. In the market-place of an Italian city, there once stood a beautiful statue of a Greek slave girl. It represented her as graceful, well-dressed and beautiful. Wandering through the streets was a homeless child, forlorn and ragged, who one day came before this statue, and for hours gazed upon it. On other days she came to admire it and drink in its inspiration. By and by the little street girl is herself a transformed child. Her face is now clean, her hair well combed, her tattered clothes washed and mended. That statue was an ideal to that wandering child, which acted as ideals always act; it revealed possibilities, it awakened new longings, it transformed her entire life.

It was found out thousands of years ago, that what men long gaze upon admiringly, transforms the heart and life. Moses went upon the mountain summit and for days was in fellowship with the God of light. When he came down again to the people, though Moses knew it not, the people saw in his face the reflected life of God. It was said of England's great poet, John Keats, that his face was the face of one who had seen a vision. So long had there been before his mind some glorious ideal, that not only did his inner soul receive its loveliness but its awe-inspiring beauty was chiselled into every lineament of his face. Swiftly does man become like the thoughts he loves. He whose habit it is to think on things ugly and base will by and by expose the foulness of his character in every glance of his eye, and in every expression of his face. Faithfully does Dickens depict this power of thought. One of his characters, Monks, begins his life a guileless, beautiful child, but ends it with a face as eloquent of bestiality and sin, as hunger was ever written upon the countenance of

THE INSPIRATION OF IDEALS

of a wolf. Constant thinking upon vulgarity and iniquity has transformed the sweet face of the guileless child into the countenance of a demon. It matters much upon what you think — "As a man thinketh in his heart, so is he."

An artist cannot avoid putting himself and his own character into his work. A vulgar artist cannot paint a virtuous picture. It is said of one of our greatest artists that he would instantly turn away from a bad picture for fear the defect might impart itself to his brush. A low, aimless ideal leaves its mark upon the character as truly as God put upon Cain the brand of guilt. This is the reason why God forbids the worship of idols — man becomes like the things he admires and worships. Cruel idols have in every age made cruel men; effeminate idols have made effeminate men. There necessarily comes a paralysis of power to every one whose life is wedded to some narrow-minded, little hearted, superficial ideal. And as the rose becomes red by exposing its bosom to the sun and soaking each tiny petal in its rays of light, so constant thinking on noble things comes at last to transform the character into the image of the ideal comtemplated.

Hawthorne illustrates this profound truth in his allegory of "The Great Stone Face." On the side of a mountain overhanging a village where a young man lived, there was a great stone face. The people of the village oft talked of the prophecy respecting this face, that by and by, a great and noble man, having an exact resemblance to that face, was coming to the village, bringing blessings to all her people. While this prophecy touched only the surface of other's thoughts, it sank to the depths of this young man's soul. Day after day he would go out and for hours gaze upon the face in the mountain, thinking long and faithfully of what it stood for and of the coming of the great and good man who was to bless all the people. As he thought, he began to long to prepare the way for his coming. He strove to be himself what that great stone face would wish him to be, and here and there he went, scattering kindly looks and hopeful words. And lo, as the young man grew old, the gray about his face was like the mists about the stone face on the mountain and at last the shout went up from the people: "The prophecy is fulfilled — the man resembling the great stone face is even now with us."

Comrades of the Class of '97,

passing by all the ideals of men, many and mighty as they are, — I hold up before you the one ideal and inspiration for every day and duty of life. "He is no empty abstraction nor bloodless theory," but He is Jesus of Nazareth, "in whom dwelleth all the fulness of the God-head bodily." In Him alone is fulfilled those needs of highest manhood and noblest character, that forever enthrone Him the one Master and Model of the world. As you see His faithful portrait drawn in the simple words: "He went about doing good" — know that all education that aims only at self-improvement, stamps its possessor as a twin brother to the miser who gloats over his gathered gold. Study Him, and know that there can be no heroism save in self-sacrificing interest for others. From Him learn the strength of patience, the glory of self-control, the nobility of self-denial. Study him as against mighty odds, he resists temptations and holds up the great truth that bread and power and fame are not so vital as fidelity to principle. Plant your feet where His have walked, and let His great, unselfish, magnanimous life flash out its rebuke to every lull of conscience and every sordid vision that may assail you. And when your panting lives shall pass through that valley whose waters moan with the soul's last struggle, may His glory rest upon your face and may His welcome make you happy forever!

CHAPTER II

The Leaf and the Life

CHAPTER II

The Leaf and the Life*

THE topic upon which I am to speak is, "The Leaf and the Life." It at once suggests the wide influence of the printed page upon all human life, whether upon the individual, the home, the State, or the Church.

In thinking upon this subject, a scene of the olden days passes before me. An old man is confined in the dark, cold, noisome Mamertine prison. Upon him are marks of feebleness by reason of advancing age and also the scars of many a hard-fought battle. The time of his departure is almost at hand. He has fought a good fight, and is now complacently awaiting the summons to go hence. But, before he goes he must write to his son in the ministry, Timothy, the gifted young pastor of the church at Ephesus. It is all a very realistic picture. See the old man as he slowly writes: "Do thy diligence to come shortly unto me." Poor, old lonely soldier, while the shadows are so heavily gathering about him it is no wonder that he yearns for the companionship of his dear young friend. He goes on to write: "The cloak that I left at Troas, with Carpus, when thou comest, bring with thee." You see, Paul was no Christian Scientist. He was just a plain, sensible man, recognizing that he had a physical body, and that he needed his cloak in order that he might be somewhat protected against the cold. Then he added these significant

---

* An address delivered at the annual meeting of the American Baptist Publication Society, St. Paul, Minnesota, May 23, 1902 and reprinted by permission.

words: "Bring with thee the books, but especially the parchments." Just what these books and parchments were, of course, we may not positively say, but it is probable that they were the Holy Scriptures, together with other noble books that had wrought mightily in their influence over Paul, and were unspeakably precious to his great heart.

Though he was first and foremost in all the works and triumphs of Christianity, though he was marvelously endowed by nature and by grace for his incomparable work as an apostle, yet Paul prized beyond all human computation his books. They were his constant companions and fellow-helpers through all the eventful years of his matchless ministry. Paul was not only a flaming evangelist, he was a glorious teacher of doctrine as well. The two should always go together. In his far-reaching outlook for the work of the kingdom, Paul employed the leaf as well as the voice. Indeed the crowning work of his life was the writing of his Epistles.

This scene of the olden days suggests some lessons of measureless moment to the people of God. Prominent among these lessons is that of the possibility of preserving and disseminating truth by means of the printed page. The printing press is man's greatest mechanical triumph. By this means we not only become the heirs of the thoughts of the wisest and best men of all the ages, but we have also the transcription of the very thoughts of God. This is a triumph beside which none other of man can begin to compare. Though one may be poor, seeing never the wise and great of the earth, yet by means of the printed page they enter his humble home and become his personal companions and friends. Thus Franklin enriches him with his practical wisdom. Shakespeare reveals to him the worlds of imagination, and Milton sings to him of Paradise. Nobly has Milton said of a good book that, "It is the precious life-blood of a master-spirit treasured up unto a life beyond." And strongly does Emerson say, in his great "Essay on Books," that "there are books which take rank in

THE LEAF AND THE LIFE

our life with parents and lovers and passionate experiences, so medicinal, so stringent, so revolutionary, so authoritative."

We are never to lose sight of the truth that it is utterly impossible for the printed pages to take the place of the preacher. The progress of civilization, the vast increase of schools and learning, the amazing triumphs of the press, mighty as are all these agencies, they can never supersede the divinely sent preacher. "It pleased God by the foolishness of preaching to save them that believe." Let not Christ's minister for one moment lose sight of the divineness of his mission. Of him it has been truly said: "He holds a divine commission, he proclaims a divine revelation, he is animated by a divine purpose, he accomplishes a divine result, he is dependent upon a divine Spirit." As in the past, so shall it ever be in the future, that God's foremost instrument in both the evangelization and civilization of the world is his preacher.

But it is just as true that the preacher can never take the place of the printed page. The preacher and the printed page are correlatives. Hand in hand they always need go, and their union should be as vital and as indissoluble as was that of the Siamese twins. Their conjoined influence finds striking illustration in the rise of Protestantism. The preacher alone did not bring about the great Reformation, and could not have brought it about. The printer had to come in. Luther was the preacher, Erasmus was the writer.

This truth is still more strikingly illustrated in the union of Christ the Incarnate Word and Christ the written word. The Incarnate Word was not enough, neither was the written word enough. Therefore, the Word Incarnate and the word written stand or fall together. The two storm centers of all religious history and controversy have been Christ and the Bible. The Bible is the complement and counterpart of Christ. They are one and inseparable — the binomial word of God. The porch of Solomon's Temple was upheld by two mighty pillars of brass, the names of which were Jachin, meaning strength, and Boaz, meaning continuance. When the ancient Jew went to the Temple, though faint and weary from his journey, the sight of those two pillars always brought confidence to his heart and strength to his arm. The leaf and the life, the word written and the Word Incarnate, are the Jachin and Boaz in the whole scheme of the Christian religion. They must stand or fall together, for the veracity of the one stands pledged for the perpetuity of the other. We do not have one iota of fear as to the destiny of either, but our deepest conviction is that if Jesus Christ is to reign throughout all the world, — an ultimate triumph of which we have not a doubt, — to a marvellous degree the propaganda must be carried on by the dissemination of the written Word of God. Its leaves, like the leaves of the tree of life, are for the healing of the nations. Those leaves are to be sent upon the four winds of heaven, bearing the tidings of salvation to those who sit in darkness and in the shadow of death.

Would you see the influence of the leaf upon national life? Then you have only to open your eyes to behold illustrations without number. The circulation of the Bible in France, Switzerland, Germany, Holland, and England, in the several stages of Protestant development, exercised an immeasurable influence. The iron preacher, the press, could go where the flesh-and-blood preacher could not go. And when assemblies were unlawful and speakers would be arrested and imprisoned, the leaves from the press were being silently carried from country to country, from city to city, and from house to house.

Take the nations of the earth, and the dividing line between barbarism and civilization, between slavery and liberty, between the shadow of death and the light of life, is the open Bible. In the coronation exercises of Edward VI, three swords were brought to him, the signs of the three kingdoms under his rule. The young ruler demanded that they bring him still another sword, and, when his nobles asked him what it was, he answered that it was the Bible, the Sword of the Spirit, which he preferred to all other swords.

That demand of Edward VI was the precursor and prophecy of the coming Reformation. Of this Reformation Carlyle has truly said: "The period of the Reformation was a judgment day for Europe, when all the nations were presented with an open Bible, and all the emancipation of heart and intellect which an open Bible involves. England, North Germany, and other powers, accepted the boon, and they have been steadily growing in national greatness and moral influence ever since. France rejected it, and in its place had the gospel of Voltaire, with all the anarchy, misery, and bloodshed of the revolutions of which that gospel is the harvest." France would not recognize the indisputable fact that the Bible is the franchise of all civil and religious liberty, and by the same token the security of all national perpetuity. In her *Corps Legislatif* she condemned the divine book, and by resolution said that God should no more have any recognition at the nation's hands. Instead of the Bible, "Chambers' Encyclopedia," with infidel interpretations by Diderot and others of similar views, was scattered all over the land. A tidal wave was thus and then set in motion that has left its disastrous blight upon France, even to this hour. The Reign of Terror was an inevitable consequence, when mobs marched through the streets of Paris, and the heads of the bravest and the best fell under the guillotine, and the people were plunged into unutterable woe, and their ill-founded temple of freedom went down in fire and blood. All that the leaf can do for a nation's life or a nation's death.

The Reformation began when Luther, rummaging through the library at Erfurt, came upon a dusty copy of the Scriptures and opened it. There he read, "The just shall live by faith," and again he read, "Search the Scriptures, for in them

The Inspiration of Ideals

ye think ye have eternal life, and they are they which testify of me." He had read enough to change the whole of his life. Here was the search warrant which God himself had put into his hands, entitling him to read for himself, and, without the intervention of priest, pope, or church, to interpret for himself God's revealed word. From that came the Reformation. Hitherto the Scriptures had long been hidden away in monasteries, while monks swung their censers and chanted their prayers. But Luther unchained the book, and lo, the truth flew abroad like Milton's angel with the flaming torch. The flying abroad of that truth set tyrants trembling, and thrones tottering, and led to the banishment of the dark night of the Middle Ages, and the mental and moral reformation of Christendom.

England's noble queen, when she was asked the secret of her country's greatness, explicitly and instantly avowed that it was the Bible. The preamble of our own Declaration of Independence was unquestionably borrowed from Paul's sermon on Areopagus, and our whole political fabric is permeated with the teachings of the Bible. Put it down as an inevitable and unalterable truth that wherever God's Book has been honored, there national life has been glorious. Wherever it has been dishonored, upon such people have fallen blight and shame and death.

Not only is it true that national life is very largely directed and moulded by the printed page, but it is equally true of social life. Do you not recall the influence that was wrought upon London by Thomas Hood, as he wrote in simple verse of the wrongs inflicted upon the seamstresses of that great city:

> *With fingers weary and worn,*
> *With eyelids heavy and red,*
> *A woman sat in unwomanly rags,*
>   *Plying her needle and thread —*
> *Stitch! stitch! stitch!*

The Leaf and the Life

Oh, men, with sisters dear!
Oh, men, with mothers and wives!
It is not linen you're wearing out
But human creatures' lives!
Stitch — stitch — stitch.

Those simple words fastened upon the printed page, stirred the world's greatest city to its deepest depths. And the leaf has wrought this same result, in greater or lesser degree, in the social life of every community.

None the less true is it in individual life. The world is filled with illustrations of the truth that individual life is often shaped and its destiny determined by the reading of just one book, or even a tract. Let us dwell for a moment upon some well-known instances. Take this oft-mentioned one: An old Puritan doctor wrote a book on the *Bruised Reed*, which fell into the hands of Richard Baxter, and led him to the saving knowledge of eternal life, and thus was begun a ministry of world-wide power. Then Baxter wrote a book, *The Call to the Unconverted,* which speaks on and on to uncounted millions, though the author's lips have long been silent in the dust. Baxter's book got into the hands of Philip Doddridge, and was the means of leading him to a broader knowledge and a richer faith and a deeper experience of the things of God. Then Doddridge wrote a book called *The Rise and Progress of Religion in the Soul,* which book fell into the hands of William Wilberforce, and so impressed him that he wrote a book called *Practical Christianity*. And this book in turn made its way into the sunny Isle of Wight, and there thrilled the heart of Leigh Richmond. Then Richmond wrote the *Dairyman's Daughter,* which book has been translated into more than fifty languages of the earth, working, wherever it goes, an immeasurable influence for the extension of the gospel. Still again this book of Wilberforce made its way into a secluded parish in Scotland, and its reading worked an epoch in the life of a young man, who was afterward to thrill the world with his glorious ministry — the eloquent Thomas Chalmers. There it is, not a break in the chain — Baxter, Doddridge, Wilberforce, Richmond, Chalmers, and after these names another word needs to be added — eternity.

Note again the example of Peter Waldo with his great cargo of tracts which he scattered in the Piedmontese valleys, the outcome of which was the Waldensian churches, which through thirty-five persecutions, held fast to the truth of the Bible, although "Gashed by the spear of Savoy, and scorched by the fagot of Rome."

Look again at John Wycliffe, the great tract writer and distributor, one of whose tracts was carried by a Bohemian nobleman into Bohemia, and loaned by him to a man who read it and was converted to God and gave to the world his glorious testimony and service, the immortal John Huss.

Notice that it was a little leaf written by Luther that reached the heart of the Bedfordshire tinker, John Bunyan, who was later to write an allegory unmatched and forever matchless.

Then, again some of these tracts made their way into a convent where the lady abbess, Charlotte de Bourbon, was converted to God by reading just one of them, and so thoroughly converted was she, that she fled from France and took refuge at Heidelberg, in the court of Frederick III, of the Palatinate. By and by this good woman did the sensible thing and was married, and her husband was the famous Prince William of Orange. Who knows but that a vast deal of the positive, glorious stubborness of William of Orange of the Revolution, was inherited from the blood of his ancestress, who was led to God by the reading of this one little tract?

Take a nearer illustration: Yonder upon the upper banks of the Delaware, more than a hundred years ago, a lonely missionary to the Indians, David Brainerd, daily jotted down

The Leaf and the Life

in his diary the struggles and hopes and triumphs of his checkered experiences. This was probably not written for any other eyes than his own; but after the body of that heroic missionary had been laid away in the grave, that simple diary crossed the ocean, reached England's great university at Cambridge, and was there read by a most gifted student. The student was Henry Martyn, who, through the reading of that little diary, was led to the winning of a wide immortality as a foreign missionary.

You do not have to go beyond your own experiences to observe the measureless influences of the printed page. A tract, dropped into a man's hands between scenes at a theater, led to his salvation. A tract put into the hands of a humble ploughboy, shaped the destiny of the great preacher and editor, Jeremiah Bell Jeter, of Virginia. A tract on "Stewardship and the Foreign Missions," enclosed in a letter to a plain business man in my own State, led him to realize for the first time his duty as God's steward, and, at once, out of only a modest income, he gave five thousand dollars to foreign missions.

A tract led to the founding of the great Bible Society in England. If I mistake not, the founding of our own great American Baptist Publication Society was suggested by so little a thing as the dropping of a tract from the hat of Samuel Cornelius, which event suggested to Noah Davis the need and power of a great tract society which should send throughout the land a wholesome, God-honouring literature. Ah, it is true that

> *Many a shaft at random sent,*
> *Finds marks the archer never meant.*

Mr. Spurgeon tells the incident that one day a cabman drove him home, and when the great preacher paid his fare, the cabman said, "A long time since I drove you home, Sir." "But," said Mr. Spurgeon, "I do not recollect you." "Well," said the cabman, "I think it was about fourteen years ago," and then he pulled from his pocket a worn and faded copy of the New Testament, and holding it up to the preacher he said, "Perhaps you will remember this. You gave it to me and asked me to read it, and I read it and it led me to the Saviour, and I have been trying to serve Him through all these years." Ah, a simple deed was that; who could not do it? And yet, by service as easy and simple, we may daily batter down the strongholds of sin and Satan, and enthrone righteousness and the Lord of life.

These simple illustrations reveal to us the amazing expansion of thought by means of the printed page. The reproductiveness of truth, by means of the press, may never, even approximately, be measured. Truth may thus be looked upon as a seed, with limitless powers of self-propagation. The author of a good book may die, but his thoughts, being fastened on the printed page, live on to cheer and inspire the reader to noblest endeavour. Milton was therefore right when he said: "For books are not absolutely dead things, but do contain a progeny of life in them, as active as that soul whose progeny they are; nay, they do preserve as in a vial the purest efficacy and extraction of that living intellect that held them."

The printed page preserves thought. Homer, though dead these hundreds of years, lives far more widely today than when first he wrote his poems. Milton and Dante still sing on to the succeeding generations through the *Paradise Lost* and the *Inferno*, though their bodies have long since been returned to the dust whence they came. Shakespeare passed away nearly three hundred years ago, but his thoughts breathe on and influence today with an incomparably greater power than they did in the days of the Tudors. Longfellow sleeps yonder beneath the blooming flowers, but his beautiful songs of Indian life and Puritan history live on with undiminished power.

The Leaf and the Life

Tersely has Dr. Strong declared: "A book is the greatest leveller. It is utterly democratic. As Shakespeare makes Buckingham say in scorn of Wolsey, 'A beggar's book outweighs a noble's blood.' The bookcover is a door without bolt or bar, which swings open to all alike, admitting the ploughboy and the shopgirl to intimacy with the world's four-hundred."

Dr. Pierson has nobly said of the power of the printed page, that, "It unlocks the doors to the treasure houses of the race. It introduces all readers, without invidious distinctions, into the inner circle of authors, admitting all alike to the privilege of communing with them. In other ways we may seek in vain their acquaintance and audience, hindered by the forms of polite society, or their own seclusive and exclusive habits. Many authors are dead and therefore are out of reach; others, yet living, are too remote to be accessible. But the intelligent reader finds himself shut out by no wall of exclusion. He has the right of entrance and of converse, and none can forbid him. The palaces of the kings of letters stand with open gates, and there are no sentries or guards. The beggar's attire, the slave's bonds, or even the taint of crime prevents no seeker after knowledge from this instructive and elevating communion with the good and the great." He goes on to say that: "Books are the undying bodies in which authors continue to live and breathe, speak and act, and so find a sort of perpetual and potential incarnation, moving among men with immortal life."

The destiny-shaping power of the printed page is almost miraculous. The temporal and eternal destiny of many a boy has been determined by one hour's reading. A book fell into his hands, the reading of which charmed his mind and gave him a distinct and sublime purpose for all his after life. He rose up from the reading of its pages, to follow after his ideal as a lawyer, or statesman, or teacher, or preacher. No influence will ever undo the work of those few pages.

The Inspiration of Ideals

They gave the boy his bow of hope and nothing will ever turn him away from their enchanting influences. It was this that led Henry Drummond to say:

> To fall in love with a good book is one of the greatest events that can befall us. It is to have a new influence pouring itself into our life, a new teacher to inspire and refine us, a new friend to be by our side always, who, when life grows narrow and weary, will take us into his wider and calmer and higher world. Whether it be biography, introducing us to some humble life made great by duty done; or history, opening vistas into movements and destinies of nations that have passed away; or poetry, making music of all the common things around us, and filling the fields and skies and the works of the city and the cottage with eternal meanings; whether it be these, or story-books, or science, no one can become the friend of even one good book without being made wiser and better.'

No tongue is among us that is able adequately to describe the epoch-making influence of the leaf upon the life. Let it be repeated, a good book put into a boy's hands at a certain hour, saves him for time and eternity. Another book of opposite character leaves the boy a skeptic, and sends him through life a foe to men and a hater of God, and into eternity with soul unclothed and doomed. Franklin traced his entire career to the reading of Cotton Mather's "Essays to Do Good," which fell into his hands while he was yet a boy. Faraday attributed the arousing of his genius to the reading of a few books when he was an apprentice to a bookbinder. Carey's great decision to be a missionary was made as he read *The Voyages of Captain Cook*. Emerson's book on Nature made Tyndall a naturalist. Samuel Drew tells us that Locke's *Essay on the Human Understanding* transformed him from low and grovelling views of life to just the opposite. An English tanner of great excellence ascribed the pre-eminent value of his leather to the reading of Carlyle. The book of Proverbs, used as a first reader in the schools of Scotland, has largely made that people the practical, virile, stalwart people that they are.

THE LEAF AND THE LIFE

Who can ever measure the influence of one little American leaf, the Declaration of Independence? It is a model unapproachable in its simplicity, its fearless arraignment of tyranny, and its bold assertion and wise limitation of the rights of men. The echoes of that paper, that all men are created free and equal, with certain inalienable rights, have reverberated throughout all the earth and will yet, please God, find an acceptance by every government in the world.

Just in proportion as good literature has the power to uplift and ennoble and transform, does bad literature have the power to corrupt and drag down and destroy. The assassin of Lord Russell said that the reading of one bad book had made him a criminal and a murderer. John Angell James, one of England's greatest and noblest Christians, said, when an old man, that he had never fully recovered from the ill effects of fifteen minutes' reading of a bad pamphlet when he was a boy.

The great thing about the leaf is not so much the information it gives, as the effect it leaves upon the character. Every stream has what is called its residuum. For instance, where iron is in solution, it is seen in the reddish hue of the stones in the bed of the stream. Or, where sulphur is deposited, there the green tints may be seen. So it is with the leaf — it leaves its residuum on the life. A strong, stalwart body cannot remain so, if it be fed on dainty viands, with here and there a bit of poison impregnated in them. Neither can the mental and moral nature flourish when it is fed on corrupt food, however attractive and sugar-coated it may be. "Let it be observed and remembered," says Noah Porter, "that a book is always written by a man, and that it is never by any magic or mystery, any better than its author makes it to be."

Holy Writ has told us that, "Evil communications corrupt good manners." And, again, "He that walketh with wise men shall be wise, but the companion of fools shall be destroyed." There is a companionship of books as real as is the compan-

The Inspiration of Ideals

ionship of men. And a man's character may be judged as much, if not more, by the books he reads, as by the men with whom he associates. If it be deleterious in the formation and training of noble character to keep company with people who are vicious and bad, equally if not more deleterious is it to read bad books.

There is a psychological reason for this, since impressions made upon the eye are much more lasting than those made upon the ear. Sight appeals strongly to the imagination, while sound does not. The written word abides because it is seen, while the spoken word soon passes because it is only heard. H. Clay Robinson tells us in his diary that when he was a boy he was corrected for misspelling a word. He consulted his spelling book and proved that he had spelled the word according to the book. When told that it had been printed incorrectly, he said, "I was quite confounded. I believed as firmly in the infallibility of print as any good Catholic can in the infallibility of his church. I knew that naughty boys would tell stories, but how a book could contain a falsehood was quite incomprehensible."

What a revelation and testimony this is to the power of the printed page! O you editors of papers and you authors of books, with what scrupulous care should you seek ever to write the truth, the whole truth, and nothing but the truth, since the printed falsehood, whether subtle or glaring, never fails to get in its diabolical impression. It is well-nigh impossible for the young not to be impressed by what they see in print, however ridiculous or wicked the printed statement may be. There is a kind of sacredness about the printed page that is the foster-child of faith. Who does not know that the most glaring immoralities have been clothed in poems of enchanting beauty, and that the most deadly infidelity has been so deftly presented as to corrupt the morals of a whole generation? There is not the shadow of a doubt that bad reading furnishes the leading instruction in the school of plunder, licentiousness, and all manner of lawlessness.

My heart is heavy here. Oh, if parents and teachers and preachers would but realize as they ought what the young people of our land are reading. A very flood of false and foul literature is being pressed upon the people. There are popular books abroad today, that are pestiferous in their influences, damaging in their tendencies, and harmful in their results. They ought never to be seen on a lady's table or tolerated in a decent home. I am ready to affirm that women had far better spend their time fondling poodles and playing with kittens, than to give it to the reading of such soul-stupefying, mind-enervating, jaundice-hued, false-coloured, sin-besmirched literature. As one cannot touch pitch without being defiled, or take fire into his bosom without being burned, so neither can he read foul literature with impunity.

No other question is fraught with the possibilities, both for good and for evil, as is the question of the literature of the people. And the devil knows this and takes every possible advantage of it. Somehow he always finds plenty of money with which to print every species of false and corrupting literature, and plenty of agents to see that it is widely circulated. In this way, more than in any other, he poisons the minds and hearts of all classes against the highest and noblest and best.

It was the marvellous possibilities of the press that led Cowper to write his ode to it:

> *How shall I speak thee, or thy power address,*
> *Thou god of our idolatry, the press?*
> *By thee religion, liberty, and laws*
> *Exert their influence and advance their cause.*
> *By thee, worse plagues than Pharaoh's land befell,*
> *Diffused, make earth the vestibule of hell,*
> *Thou fountain, at which drink the good and wise,*
> *Thou ever-bubbling spring of endless lies.*
> *Like Eden's dread probationary tree,*
> *Knowledge of good and evil is from thee.*

THE INSPIRATION OF IDEALS

The only antidote for a bad press is a good one. The only cure for bad and cheap literature is to make good literature and much of it and give it to the people as cheaply as possible. This is the only way that a scavenger press can be suppressed and overcome. It is God's way, for his word to us is, "Be not overcome of evil, but overcome evil with good." You have read the dream that Gutenberg had of the power of the press. He once dreamed that as he wrought in his cell in the St. Aborsgot Monastery, he heard a voice warning him that the power of his invention would enable bad men to propogate their wickedness and sow dragons' teeth. The voice further told him that the time would come when men would profane the art of printing and posterity would curse the inventor. And then Gutenberg hurriedly took a hammer and broke the type into pieces. But then another voice was heard, and this voice bade him desist from the work of destruction, and to persist in perfecting his invention. The voice went on to tell him that though his invention should be the occasion of much evil, God would make it the fountain of infinite good, and finally give to the right the ultimate triumph in all the earth.

A passing word needs to be said about our religious and denominational papers. Who can estimate their meaning to the home? The home may be ever so humble and far removed from the maddening crowd's ignoble strife, but the weekly visit of a noble religious paper, supplemented by the occasional visit of a good book, shapes the life and determines the destiny of that home. The picture of such a home passes before me now. Its inmates were poor and lived in a section where they must toil through all the seasons in order to provide a livelihood. But, though all had to toil, from the oldest to the youngest, and though the home in which they lived was exceedingly humble, yet they held converse with the men and movements of the great, wide world. The parents turned every extra dollar into good literature for their children. They believed with Erasmus when he said, "I buy books first; after that, if I have any money, I buy clothes." They believed with a great theological teacher, who said to his class, "Young gentlemen, shirts are important, but books are indispensable."

And so into that home a choice book came as often as it could be afforded, and several of the great religious papers came every week. Those papers and books silently wrought their destiny-shaping power upon all that large family of children, and though far removed from the scenes of the world's great movements, yet they thus became vitally real to all those children and entered into their lives. And when they went forth to the work and warfare of the world all of them had been won to Christ and do joyfully walk in his blessed service to this day. Is this a mean or ordinary result? No, it is the sublimest result possible in the history of an earthly home. And more than all things else, the literature provided out of a scant purse for those children, during the plastic years of their childhood and youth, shaped their characters and determined their destiny. Oh, how can parents and teachers and preachers be oblivious to this transcendently important matter of right literature? Carelessness here is worse than foolish, it is wicked.

A further word needs to be said about the denominational paper, and a plain word it needs to be. It is the bane of some so-called religious and denominational papers that they have lost their great religious purpose and have gone off after matters sociological and semi-political. I could name such papers that were once as Samson for religious strength, but now are like him when his locks were shorn. Once they wrought mightily for the distinctly religious welfare of the churches, but now they are religiously nerveless and palsied and their power is gone. You ask the reason why. There is but one answer — they have lost their distinctively religious passion and purpose.

The Inspiration of Ideals

A denominational paper ought to be the counterpart in spirit and purpose of the Acts of the Apostles. Instead of a little "missionary corner" in the paper there ought to be a pulse-beat in every line for missions. The supreme trouble with the missionary work now is that it is crowded off into a little corner. We want a missionary literature that will enthrone the one great passion and purpose of Jesus Christ, and do this in every issue of the paper and in every column of every issue. Until that is done by our papers, our preachers, and our churches, the continuing black plague upon all our religious efforts will be the anti-missionary spirit. We are not here primarily to cultivate sociology or to build up civilization. Our primary business is to give the gospel to the whole world. On no other basis has a church the moral right to the plot of ground on which her building stands. What was our Lord's conception of his church? For what did he build it? His church, he tells us, was to be his body, the instrument of his will, the medium through which he would manifest himself to the world. It is the business of the body to execute the purpose of the head. Christ's church is his body, and it is his purpose that the body shall carry forward the work that brought him from heaven to earth. For what did he come? "It is a faithful saying and worthy of all acceptation that Christ Jesus came into the world to save sinners." This was his supreme mission, and that of his churches is identical with that of their divine founder and king. For this cause he brought them into the world, and for this cause he keeps them here.

Our supreme danger is that we shall perish, not so much from our wickedness as from the littleness of our conceptions and efforts for God's kingdom in the earth. It was Archimedes who said, "Give me a lever sufficiently long, and a fulcrum upon which to rest it, and I'll turn the world over." Yes, and let the hosts of our Baptist people enthrone as their dominant purpose and passion the salvation of this whole world for Christ, and sound this forth, in every possible way, by leaf and by voice, and ere long the banner of Emmanuel will wave over the whole earth.

May I refer for a moment to colportage work? It suggests a prospect that is thrillingly glorious. It is getting back to first principles. It is the gospel way of going into the highways and hedges to reach the people. Brethren, the wheels of the chariot will drag on, oh, so slowly, and the coming of the kingdom will be so long delayed, unless we go back to the Christ-appointed way of reaching the people. The colporter has this opportunity as has no other man. Therefore every Christian ought to be a self-appointed colporter. Every church ought to be a lighthouse for the constant distribution of life-giving literature. It is indeed a sad day for Christianity when churches or individuals become too dignified to do this work.

All hail to the colporters! They are doing for God and for men a work, the greatness and glory of which may only be read in the golden glory of the land and life eternal. If the vendors of foul literature can find money to print it, and agents to scatter it, will not Christ's blood-bought people see to it, by the grace of God, that all needed moneys are provided for the printing of life-giving, God-honouring literature, and that every man of us shall be an unceasing colporter in its widest distribution?

Some earnest words need also to be said about the circulation of the Word of God. The fields of such opportunity today are surely white unto the harvest. We marvel at the progress of Christianity in the early days, when few individuals owned a copy of the Holy Scriptures. The multitudes could not own it since it took years to write one complete copy. Even one hundred years ago the printing of the Bible was amazingly expensive, and its circulation was therefore correspondingly limited. A copy of Carey's Bengali Bible

The Inspiration of Ideals

cost about twenty dollars. Now it may be had for only a few cents.

What is to be our reply to all the attacks made upon the Bible? It is to print and scatter it all the more. When men tell us that it is not inspired, or if inspired it is only in spots, and nobody knows where the spots are, we are not to waste our lives in cavilling with them. We are to go on printing and scattering it all the more, and God will see to it that it will survive every conflict.

Voltaire said that he would pass through the forest of Scriptures and girdle all the trees, so that in one hundred years Christianity would be only a vanishing memory. The hundred years are gone, poor Voltaire also is gone, with none to do him reverence, while Christianity is still here, and the leaves of the forest of Scriptures are filling all the earth. The very press upon which Voltaire printed that direful prophecy is now used for the printing of Bibles, and the very house in which he lived has become a great depository from which is scattered the Word of God. On the very spot in London where the council condemned the bones of Wycliffe to be dug up and burned, there the great British and Foreign Bible Society has its central offices.

Gloriously does Cumming speak of the Triumph of God's Word: "The empire of Caesar is gone; the legions of Rome are mouldering in the dust; the avalanches that Napoleon hurled upon Europe have passed away; the pride of the Pharaohs is fallen; the pyramids they raised to be their tombs are sinking every day in their desert sands; Tyre is a rock for bleaching fishermen's nets; Sidon has scarcely left a wrack behind; but the word of God still survives. All things that threatened to extinguish it have only aided it; and it proves every day how transient is the noble monument that man can build, how enduring is the least word that God has spoken. Tradition has dug for it many a grave, intolerance has lighted for it many a fagot, many a Judas has betrayed it with a kiss, many a Peter has denied it with an oath, many a Demas has forsaken it, but the Word of God still survives."

> *A glory gilds the sacred page,*
> *Majestic as the sun.*
> *It gives a light to every age,*
> *It gives and borrows none.*
>
> *The hand that gave it still supplies*
> *The gracious light and heat.*
> *Its truths upon the nations rise;*
> *They rise, but never set.*

O brothers, I pray Almighty God that we may give and pray and toil and lay our every power under tribute to magnify and glorify and make known the written Word of God to all the peoples of every tongue and every clime even as we seek to exalt the Incarnate Word, Jesus Christ our Lord.

CHAPTER III

The Power of Convictions

CHAPTER III

The Power of Convictions*

IT IS the lesson of all history that the successes of men and women in all the walks of life have been according to the character and the degree of their convictions. What you are to be and accomplish in this life will be determined largely by your conviction with respect to life's character and conduct.

You will readily recognize that whatever of conviction you may have must of necessity be personal. No man can have your conviction for you any more than he can have your mind or heart. Your conviction is yours. Into every warp and woof of your life this great dominating element must needs be woven until it is a part of your very being.

This conviction, you will also understand, is always the result of investigation and hence the deep meaning and responsibility of all education. Beasts act from instinct, men act from reason. Conviction is not instinct but is always the product of earnest, individual investigation. As well might you expect to see the rich, ripe harvest without any sunshine or rain as to see men and women of noble convictions without the precedence of earnest, individual investigation. Faithful, persistent toil must be the price paid by everyone who aspires to the possession of intelligent, strengthful convictions.

Mental laziness is the cause of the nerveless, strengthless indecision and fickleness of these modern days. In church

---
* The Commencement Address delivered at the University of Texas, Austin, June 5, 1904.

and in state, in the gravest questions that touch men's temporal and eternal welfare, overwhelming multitudes of men and women pin their faith to the apron strings of the few and trust their destinies largely to the behests of others rather than pay the price for intelligent and strong convictions.

This conviction of character takes hold of the very heart of one's life. It spans the entire manhood or womanhood. It is the backbone of your every hope and aim and prospect and purpose. Over everything that you will ever think or say or do it is to sway the scepter.

I. *Convictions Determine Individuality*

Show me a man who has no convictions and I will point you back to the same man as one who lacks individuality. Did you ever stop to note the reason why a great many people go in gangs like so many dumb driven cattle? Why some are the slaves of every passing fancy? Why they change with every new moon and even oftener than that? Why they are attracted by every passing lightning-bug and obey the behest of every new-fangled notion? Why they one day shout: "Hosannah to the Lord of Hosts," and the next day shout: "Away with him, crucify him!" It is because they have no real convictions and hence have no individuality of character. They are not decided about anything. They do not believe anything. And like so many birds they sit with wide-open mouths waiting for them to be filled with anything that may be dropped into them.

Henry Ward Beecher fitly described them when in effect he said: "They drift through life performing no higher function than the swine at the trough or the beasts of the jungle. The faculty that God gave them to will, to restrain, to choose, to decide, they never exercise and hence they have no conviction or strength of character. Round and fat they are, sleek and comely they are, good eaters they are, good sleepers

THE POWER OF CONVICTIONS

they are, and good diers they are, for when they are dead they are out of the way."

Can you conceive of any value attaching to such a life? How much does it honor God? Of what profit is it to men? And yet this great throbbing, suffering world is crowded with lives that seem almost as aimless and useless as the one just described. Hear me this hour, young men and women, as with comradely sympathy I plead for the development of individuality in every one of you. Face personally the momentous questions that are all about you. Study them for yourselves. Do your own thinking. Have your own convictions. Believe them so strongly that they will become as real a part of your being as is your hand or your heart. That should be the import of all your education from whatever source it comes. The sublime meaning of all true education is the development of individuality — the leading out of your own inherent powers.

No man is truly educated, even though he may have been graduated from every university in the land, if his training has not resulted in the development of his own individuality. Any attempt to be educated otherwise thwarts the very aim of education and makes impossible the attainment of any large success in life. Any attempt to put all men in the same mould or grind them all out through the same machine can never result in the making of men. Such a method only makes "things."

Visitors at the seaside may often see a strange substance floating near the surface looking like a vegetable but moving like an animal, a flabby mould of jelly without bony structure, consisting of a mouth and a stomach, apparently without a heart. This substance is commonly known as jelly-fish. These float in and out with the flow and ebb of the tide, betraying no sign of life until they are taken up in the hand when the numerous tentacles close about the palm and leave a sting. And so it is that there are human jelly-fish who live without either a life choice or a life work. They float along with the popular current, living to eat and to drink, apparently of no use, simply existing, knowing nothing of life's dignity and power.

No, men are not mere machines to be run by the will of superiors. God's plan is the opposite. "Work out your own salvation with fear and trembling." "Every man must give account of himself to God." God calls for the highest possible development of the individual. We are hearing a great deal of talk these days about evolution. They are telling us in the clever books and magazines about a man's being descended from a monkey. Why, they have it all backwards! The tendency is far greater in men to become monkeys than in monkeys to become men!

The call of suffering, dying humanity which is but the higher call of God, pleads for men and women, real men and women of individuality. To be sure the development of individuality may sometimes make "cranks," but let them be made. Cranks move things. The commerce of the world would be palsied in a day but for cranks. Every liberator on earth has been branded as a "crank." The leader of every reform has at some time been branded as a "crank." The matchless Man of Galilee, the only Redeemer of a sorrowing, sinning, suffering world, was deemed to be "beside himself" by some of his contemporaries and has been branded by some people through the succeeding generations as a "crank."

Young men and women of the University, whatever you may or may not be, do be yourselves! Have your own convictions, intelligent and worthy, then live up to them, and you will be the men and women this suffering world so desperately needs.

II. *Right Convictions Should Be Avowed*

There are those people in the world, who, if they have convictions, never avow them. However much they may be-

THE POWER OF CONVICTIONS

lieve or know, they do not avow anything. They are always "on the fence." They are, as they call themselves, "conservatives," or "non-partisans" — smooth, high-sounding names, aren't they? And that is about all the world ever knows about them. Nobody feels the force of their convictions for they are never made known. There they sit on the fence, inert and self-satisfied. Battles may come and go, but they prefer not to fight. Great crises must be met — crises in which men, women, and children are mightily stirred, crises in which both heaven and hell are interested, but they prefer to be neutral.

These gentlemen believe in moderation. They would have us remember that there are two sides to every question and that one side is just about as good as another. They caution everyone to be careful while they sit on the fence and do nothing but look wise. The powers of falsehood and darkness are all afield and thoroughly arrayed against the powers of truth and righteousness but the men on the fence quietly look on and mildly criticise both sides, one about as much as the other. They wish it distinctly understood that they are broadminded. These fence-riders are a burlesque on manhood!

What are the causes that keep men from the avowal of their convictions? Among the many only a few may be mentioned:

1. First of all I would name *fear*. Holy Writ expressed it with faithful candor when concerning the conduct of certain people it declared: "They denied the truth for fear of the Jews." I do not hesitate to say that there are men all about us who are consciously belying their own heart convictions of truth and right and marching under the black banner of falsehood because they are afraid of the people. President Theodore Roosevelt uttered a suggestive sentence when he said: "One individual who is not entitled to exist in a community like ours is the timid, good man."

THE INSPIRATION OF IDEALS

2. Another reason for the non-avowal of convictions is the inordinate and wide-spread greed for money. That story of Jesus and the rich young ruler finds repetition on every hand today. You recall that the young man came with the most momentous question ever asked by a human soul: "What shall I do to inherit eternal life?" And when Christ's answer was given him, "Consecrate thy money to human betterment," he turned sorrowfully away. Dearer to him than his obligations to his fellow man, dearer to him than heaven itself, was his love for money.

3. Perhaps one of the most potent causes of the stifling of right convictions is the ambitious desire of many for promotion to office. Questions that go to the very foundation of our civil and religious life are being too lightly regarded by many of the office-seekers and office holders. A new note of worthy patriotism and citizenship needs to be sounded.

If good men sit at home complaining that affairs of state do not go as they ought, they need to be reminded of the words of George William Curtis: "Ours is not a government mastered by ignorance; it is not the victory of the slums; it is not the surrender of the schools. It is not that bad men are politically shrewd; it is that good men are political cowards."

4. But a still greater reason for the non-avowal of convictions is the thought that one's conduct may be ridiculed. There are those whose physical courage would remain undaunted before the open mouth of the cannon but whose moral courage fails completely at the first sign of ridicule.

There was conviction in the character of Martin Luther. Nobody doubted that he believed what he said, for he spoke with the voice of thunder and there was lightning in his faith. Reared as he was, it was very difficult for him to accept the scriptural doctrine that "the just shall live by faith." But when he did accept it, in the face of tremendous odds, he thundered his convictions throughout Europe. He believed something and he faced not only ridicule but death to make it known. When he went to the Diet of Worms his friends sought to dissuade him from the journey. They warned him of the danger of such a course, but he replied: "I would go to the Diet of Worms and there tell out the convictions of my soul if every tile on every roof in Wurtemburg were a devil."

John Wesley had convictions. Over and above the dead forms and lifeless ceremonies that had fastened themselves upon the religious services of England and America his clarion voice rang out the deep convictions of his great heart for holiness of character and conduct instead of dead forms and lifeless ceremonies. By the sheer strength of those convictions he brought about a revolution in the religious life of two continents.

John Knox had convictions. And so strong were they that he agonizingly prayed: "Oh, God, give me Scotland for Christ, or I die!" And back from the dead formalities of her religion and the deadlier shadows of her infidelity, God gave him Scotland in answer to that prayer. Go read again his life and you will understand the glory of the epitaph which marks his tomb: "Here sleeps a man who never feared the face of mortal."

The call to us to be bold and decided is as imperative today as it was when it came to the souls of the men before us. I am not a pessimist. I do believe with all my heart that the reign of righteousness is waxing stronger and that its ultimate triumph will be complete. And yet I confess to a deep trembling of heart for the future when I behold some elements that beset our country's life. This is a time of feverish energy and fierce competition. Speculation about everything is in every passing breeze. Doubters swarm through the land as ancient Egypt swarmed with frogs. On every side men are halting, vacillating, doubting.

The Inspiration of Ideals

The pulse of the world beats with a feverish restlessness. All is stir and change. Great potentialities throb in the air and undreamed of shapes peer out of every cloud. Never before was there greater need for strong convictions. Amid the tempest that sweeps about us it is of eternal moment that our faith be stayed on Christ, the solid Rock, for all other ground is sinking sand.

The gospel of Jesus has been criticised as an impossibility. The cross on which he died, making expiatory atonement for human sin, has been caricatured as nothing more than a bloody farce. We need not talk about the bold and blatant infidelity of the days of Tom Paine and Voltaire and Rousseau. We are confronted by an infidelity today that is as subtle and as damning as ever cursed the souls of men. But it wears a different dress from that of the skepticism of former days. It comes under the garb of great "liberality." It softly tells us that the Bible is the most remarkable book of the ages, but that it could not be divinely inspired, or, if inspired by God at all, it is inspired only in spots and no one knows what the spots are! It softly whispers again that Jesus of Nazareth was the world's most splendid man but that he could not be the divine Son of God dwelling in human flesh. That would be an inexplicable mystery and therefore the claim must be dicarded. This liberality laughs at the antiquated and vulgar idea of a hell; or, if there be such a place, it is proposed that it be recognized as a way station where all the sinning sons of men shall pause for a brief time and get real inspiration and preparation for the eternal enjoyment of heaven! If there be such a vulgar place as hell, it is proposed that there shall be a grand alliance between it and heaven, an amalgamation of the two establishments upon terms of mutual compromise, allowing truth and falsehood to lie down side by side like the lion and the lamb!

Infidelity, atheism, materialism, agnosticism, Christian Science, theosophy, spiritualism, and a thousand other "isms" stalk through the land every day and everywhere. The Bible whose principles and teachings come from God is being taken like a lump of wax and shaped by men according to their selfish wills; or, like a roll of cloth cut according to prevailing fashion.

In this trying hour it is of eternal import that our hearts be surcharged with the convictions of right and truth and that we avow such convictions with all the strength of our lives. In these convictions we should live and with them we should walk and by them we must stand. Let them be embodied in every action of our lives. Let our words speak them, let our faces reflect them, let our actions proclaim them, let our hands be true to them, let our feet tread their path!

This age is impressible. It will be moulded by something, anything which is advocated by aggressive lives. Falsehood will mould this age unless it be routed by truth incarnated in men and women of tremendous energy and living convictions, who refuse to compromise with error. Truth abhors compromise as light abhors darkness. Compromise is always wrong when it requires a violation of principle or duty or truth. Those possessed of truth have a sacred right, responsibility, and obligation to declare and exemplify that truth cost what it may. The uttering of one's convictions concerning eternal principles and truths may lead to a dungeon, a cross, or death. The cross was no surprise to Jesus. He knew that there was no other way whereby a lost world could be redeemed and moulded according to the mind and purpose of God. Therefore He refused to compromise and did not hesitate to declare the whole counsel of God. And His friends must follow His example if they want to have a worthy human part in the redemption of sinning, suffering, confused, lost humanity.

THE INSPIRATION OF IDEALS

III. *Fidelity to Right Convictions Brings Ultimate Victory*

During the Revolutionary War a British officer dined with General Marion. The meal consisted simply of roasted sweet potatoes. The British officer frankly asked General Marion if he and his forces did not generally have better food than that. "No," said Marion, "not better, but rather worse, for we do not get even enough of this." "Then," said the officer, "you surely draw large pay." "Not a cent," said Marion. "Then how on earth can you stand the life you are leading?" the officer asked.

Hear General Marion's reply: "When the heart is deeply stirred a man can do anything. Many a youth would think it hard to make himself a slave for fourteen years. But let him love deeply such a woman as Rachel and he will think no more of fourteen years' servitude than young Jacob did. That is exactly my case. I am in love and my sweetheart is liberty. I would rather fight for my country and feed on roots than keep aloof and enjoy all the luxuries of Solomon. For now, Sir, I work the soil that gave me birth and exult in the thought that I am not unworthy of it. The children of future generations may never hear my name but it gladdens my heart to think that I am now contending for their freedom and all its countless blessings." Ah, that is fidelity to conviction undaunted by difficulties, invincible in its triumphs.

When the British officer returned to headquarters that day his superior officer asked him why he looked so serious. "I have cause, Sir," he said. "Has Washington defeated Sir Henry Clinton?" "No, Sir, not that, but worse." "What could be worse?" demanded the officer. And this was the significant reply: "I have seen today an American general and his men without pay and almost without clothes, living on roots and drinking water and all for liberty. I do now

THE POWER OF CONVICTIONS

resign my position in the army for we have no chance against such men."

John Bunyan would never have written *Pilgrim's Progress;* Columbus would never have discovered America; Sam Houston would never have successfully met the overwhelming hosts of Mexico; Henry Grady would never have brought men from each section of the divided nation to stand side by side with uncovered heads at his grave, had not he and they all been men who were utterly loyal to their convictions. Right convictions lie back of the faith that overcomes the world.

But I would hasten to remind you that there are battles to be fought in your own heart which will mean more to your life than every other battle of earth. The most responsible battle you will ever fight will be fought in the secrecy of your own soul, single-handed and alone when you meet the tempter of life. Then you will be grappling hand to hand with the hardest foe you will ever meet. That is the hour when you will reveal your real manhood or womanhood. The real battle of life is the battle within your own heart.

Read the life of William Lloyd Garrison and from him learn afresh the power of persistent fidelity to conviction. When he began his crusade in Boston against slavery they hooted at his presence in every street in that city. They boycotted his business. They burned him in effigy. They threatened his life. But over and above the waves of excitement he sounded out these words: "I am in earnest. I will not equivocate. I will not retreat; and I will be heard." Ah me! he was heard! Through a long war the roar of whose artillery shook the world he was heard. Through four long, weary years from the bloody grounds of Bull Run to the smouldering embers of Atlanta, he was heard. In the shouts of four million human beings freed from slavery he was heard — and all because of the dauntless persistence of the man's convictions.

The Inspiration of Ideals

Let not men talk of poverty, of their disadvantages, of their lack of talents. Rather let men steadily and courageously follow right convictions and their pathway to success is as certainly marked as is the pathway of the planets about the sun. What are life's difficulties but the challenge to become their master? When a man chooses to wipe out "I can't" from his vocabulary and in its place put, "God helping me, I will," then it is that mountains are reduced to mole hills right before his eyes.

Few men in American statesmanship have wrought so valiantly as Alexander H. Stephens of Georgia. His body pinched and dwarfed, a life-long sufferer, he had to remain seated when he made his speeches before state and national senates. Yet to the day of his death men knew that underneath that shrivelled, dwarfed body there was housed a man whose firm convictions had mastered every circumstance and obstacle.

> *If thou canst plan a noble deed,*
> *And never flag till it succeed,*
> *Though in the strife thy heart must bleed,*
> *Whatever obstacles control,*
> *Thine hour will come — go on, true soul,*
> *Thou'lt win the price, thou'lt reach the goal.*

Guided by right convictions the young people of today stand in the opening gateway to the noblest possibilities ever offered to the children of men.

Benjamin Franklin expressed the wish in one of his charming essays that he might awake at the end of one hundred years to see the marvelous changes a century would produce. But far-seeing as was that great man's mind, his prophetic dream fell far short of the realities you and I behold today. Emerson was right when he said: "We live in a new and exceptional age. America is another name for opportunity.

THE POWER OF CONVICTIONS

Our whole history appears like a last effort of the divine Providence in behalf of the human race."

This great West, especially, is still largely virgin soil. The sons and daughters who now enter her fields find infinite possibilities. I sincerely believe that there is no such arena elsewhere offered in all the world, as is today offered in our matchless West. Under the inspiration of a thousand thrilling memories and incentives you, my young friends, are summoned to your life battles. To the world of letters, to the domain of science, to the busy marts of trade, to the forum, to the teacher's altar, to the sacred desk — earth and heaven together call you to go forth with right convictions to meet life's solemn and tremendous trusts. What will be the answer of your lives to this mighty call?

> *God give us men! A time like this demands*
> *Strong minds, great hearts, true faith and hands —*
> *Men whom the lust of money does not kill,*
> *Men whom the spoils of office cannot buy,*
> *Men who have convictions and a will,*
> *Men who have honor, men who will not lie.*
> *Men who can stand before a demagogue*
> *And down his treacherous flatteries without winking,*
> *Tall men, suncrowned, who live above the fog*
> *In public duty and in private thinking.*

The supreme questions for every human soul are these: "What do I think of Jesus Christ?" and "What shall I do with Him?" The noblest possible choice for a human being is the right answer to these two questions. It was the right answer to these questions that made Gladstone one of the foremost men of the last century. It was the right answer to these questions that made Robert E. Lee forever the peerless man of the South. It was the right answer to these questions that enabled Queen Victoria to give to the British Isles such a glorious reign.

Many beautiful stories are told of the world-famed Victoria. But there is one incident which more than any other thrills

The Inspiration of Ideals

my heart. It was arranged that Handel's *Messiah* should be sung as a climax to the coronation exercises. Though it was customary for everyone to rise during the singing of that great oratoria the Queen was instructed that she must not rise as that was not the proper procedure for royalty. The music began and the sublime strains swept on, thrilling every heart.

> *He shall reign forever and ever,*
> *Hallelujah, Hallelujah!*

At those words the young queen was seen to tremble with deep emotion, but according to instructions she did not rise. Finally when the great chorus reached those all glorious words: "King of kings and Lord of lords," the young queen could no longer remain seated. She rose, lifted her eyes heavenward, then bowed her head and wept. How appropriate and beautiful and glorious!

> *Bring forth the royal diadem*
> *And crown him Lord of all.*

O my young friends, fix your heart on Him as your soul's sufficient hope and as the only true inspiration for rightly meeting the intricate questions and momentous duties of human life. And thus trusting in him and striving to do his will while you tarry here, may you at the close of your earthly pilgrimage have his glory rest upon your face and may your welcome by him be such as to make you glad forever!

CHAPTER IV

The Supper of Our Lord

CHAPTER IV

The Supper of Our Lord*

THERE are two ordinances in the church of our Lord, and only two — Baptism and the Lord's Supper. They do not come from men — they are of divine appointment. Since they are teaching ordinances, through which the deep, gracious meanings of Christianity are symbolized, their observance cannot but be fraught with far-reaching moment to both the church and the world. Unceasing controversies have gathered about them for hundreds of years, with results often sadly misleading and hostile to the truth. They have often been wrested from their true position, and their solemn and far-reaching meanings have been disregarded and perverted.

The plea is here made for an earnest restudy of these two ordinances, by all Christ's friends, not in any controversial or prejudicial spirit, but with the deeply sincere and prayerful desire to find and to follow Christ's will respecting these ordinances.

In such frank and prayerful spirit let us give ourselves to a restudy of the Supper of our Lord. May the Holy Spirit himself teach us and guide us into the truth, for Jesus' sake.

There are three vital questions concerning this ordinance that we need to consider: Whose is this Supper? To whom was it given? What is its meaning?

---
* This address was first delivered as a sermon in the First Baptist Church of Dallas. Some years later it was printed as a tract and received wide circulation.

The Inspiration of Ideals

Whose Is This Supper?

What is your answer to this question: Whose is this Supper? There can be but one mind concerning it, if we allow God's Word to answer it. Matthew, Mark, and Luke all speak of it, and this is their unvarying testimony: "And Jesus took bread and blessed it, and brake it, and gave it to the disciples and said, Take, eat: this is my body. And likewise He took the cup, and when He had given thanks, He gave it to them saying, This is my blood of the New Testament, which is shed for many." The question, then, is settled as to whose is the Supper. It does not belong to Moses, or to the prophets, or to the apostles. This is the Lord's Supper. Then since Jesus instituted it and for the specific purpose just named, isn't it beyond every question His table? He so designates it in every reference made in His Word.

When our Lord instituted it and gave it to the eleven, His language leaves no doubt that this Supper in every sense is His: "I appoint unto you a kingdom, as my Father hath appointed unto me; that ye may eat and drink at my table in my kingdom." (Luke 22:29-30.) Plainly it is here stated by Him that this table is His. If, then, this Supper is the Lord's, He alone must prescribe the rules regulating and governing it.

Your neighbor proposes to give a dining. It is for him to make every regulation, specification and limitation concerning it. These regulations he carefully makes and commits to his servants. What are these servants to do? There is nothing else for them to do except follow literally the instructions of their master. They cannot legitimately say: "Now, this is not our table — it is our master's — it is not for us therefore to say who shall or shall not come to this table — every man in the community must pass on this matter for himself."

To suppose this case is at the same time to suggest its absurdity. Those servants are literally and fully to follow instructions, just as the trust was committed to them by their master.

So it is with Christ's people concerning His Supper. They have no authority or option in this matter. This is not man's table. This is the Lord's table. Human sentiment, long established customs, prejudices, tastes, or feeling are not to govern it. Will you say that a command or an appointment of God may be governed and decided by the people as they would regulate some public enterprise? Then you forget that this Book is as unchanging and unchangeable as God. You may as consistently talk about your right to change the doctrine of regeneration as to talk about your right to change the place and purpose of this Supper. He who placed it in His church has alone the indefeasible right to prescribe every regulation for its government. He either has or has not done this.

If He has, then any talk about "courtesy" and "liberality" concerning it surely cannot be in place. Shall we talk of "liberality" concerning things that are not ours? That neighbor cannot wisely talk of "liberality" concerning his neighbor's dining. So this table is our Lord's, and if he has put regulations and limitations upon it — and that this He has done cannot be denied — then His regulations are not only wise, but their strict observance is vitally necessary to His own honor and the well-being of His churches. For God's people to do otherwise is to be unfaithful to Him and to be treasonable with the trust that He committed unto them.

To Whom Was It Given?

Our second question is, To whom did our Lord give the Supper? For whom did He intend it? He certainly gave it to somebody. To whom? Did he give it to his enemies? To those who would sneer at it and pervert it? To men yet blind and lost in sin? To ask these questions is at the same time to answer them. Our Lord gave this Supper to His disciples, and not to the world. There is no disagreement among Christian people here. We are all agreed that the Lord gave this ordinance to His own people and not to the world.

Then the first prerequisite in coming to this table is that one must have been regenerated by the Holy Spirit. No other one can in spirit either partake of this Supper or be really baptized. These two ordinances symbolize spiritual things, and spiritual things must be spiritually discerned. Regeneration is the first and an inexorable prerequisite to this table. Let God's Word here speak on this matter. Matthew, Mark, and Luke all unite in saying that "Jesus gave the Supper to the disciples" — to the disciples and not to the world. He gave it to the eleven men who were with Him on that sad, lone night. To these apostles, the nucleus of His church, the Supper was committed. That it was committed to His disciples and not to the world is seen from this record in Acts 20:7: "And upon the first day of the week, when the disciples came together to break bread" — that is, to observe the Supper. Then, clearly it was committed to Christ's people and intended only for them.

The two ordinances, baptism and the Supper, symbolize the entire gospel of the Son of God. The Supper symbolizes the constant feeding of the soul that has been begotten unto a spiritual life by the power of God. Bread and wine indicate nourishment. This new life must have nourishment. That is the reason why we often observe this Supper. Baptism symbolizes another thing. It symbolizes our death and burial to the old life, and our resurrection to walk in the new life. This death, burial and resurrection take place but once. Hence, we are baptized but once. But the new life just begun has to be sustained and nourished. Therefore, often do God's people come to this table, and only His redeemed people may come. A lost man is a dead man. The dead cannot eat. You feed only the living. So this Supper, by its very consti-

THE SUPPER OF OUR LORD

tution and character, is intended only for those washed in Christ's precious blood.

But again, not only was it restricted to Christ's disciples, but these same disciples must previously have been baptized. I beg you to pause and think on this a moment. Do the Scriptures teach that baptism is prerequisite to this Supper? Plainly and fully they do so teach. In this Word, baptism always goes before the Supper. There is practically no disagreement among Christian people on this point. All the great bodies of Christian people are agreed that this Supper is to be observed only by the baptized, and that no one has the scriptural right to observe it who has not been baptized. A few small bodies dissent from this view, but there is but one mind about it among the many large bodies of Christians throughout the world. They are thoroughly and earnestly agreed that only baptized people ought to come to the Lord's table. This proposition is true historically, denominationally, and scripturally.

What, then, is the issue between our Baptist people and others concerning this ordinance? The answer may be stated in one brief sentence. The issue mainly gathers about the ordinance of baptism. We believe that only baptized people — and but one thing to us means scriptural baptism — may scripturally come to this table. Here, then, is the chief issue between us and other people. I have said that baptism always comes before the Supper. This is historically true. The great historians who have written about it confirm it. Let me quote three or four brief sentences from them. Mosheim, speaking of Christians in the first century, says: "They were such as had been solemnly admitted into the church by baptism." Justin Martyn wrote, 150 A. D.: "It is not lawful for any to partake of the Lord's Supper, but such as believe the things that are taught by us to be true, and have been baptized." Gibbon, in his "Decline and Fall of the Roman Empire," says: "With the early Christians the

THE INSPIRATION OF IDEALS

Lord's Supper followed baptism." Neander, a leading church historian, says: "No man could be present at the communion who was not a member of the church and incorporated into it by baptism."

Not only is it true historically that baptism goes before the Supper, but it is true denominationally. Baptists, then, are not alone who propose "close" or "restricted communion," as it is commonly called. Every great denomination of Christians throughout the world does identically the same thing. There is not a scintilla of difference between Baptists and others on this point. They, with us, demand that before one comes to the table, he must have previously been baptized. The issue then is not about "close communion" — it is "close baptism." With Baptists, immersion alone is baptism, and the immersion of one who has already been saved. With them, nothing else can be scriptural baptism.

Our people are unyielding and immovable in their contention that a person to be scripturally baptized must have first believed on Christ and been saved by Him, and then immersed. They believe that nobody can be scripturally baptized, even though he be immersed, if he has not already been saved by Christ. Therefore they are compelled to deny the scripturalness of sprinkling or pouring for baptism. To them neither has even the semblance of scriptural baptism. And furthermore, they would also reject as fundamentally unscriptural the immersion of infants, if that were even proposed in the place of sprinkling or pouring, because the Scriptures demand personality, voluntariness, and spirituality in all the duties of Christianity. Baptism and the Supper are for the saved alone, and only the saved can scripturally observe either ordinance.

But some good man who thinks differently from what I have said, says: "My baptism is not immersion, but I am sincere in believing that it is scriptural baptism." I will not question his sincerity, but I do not believe that he has been scripturally baptized. I must be governed, therefore, by my own convictions of the teachings of God's Word, and not by his. It is not enough to say because one is sincere that therefore he is right. If that were true, then Paul was as right before his conversion as afterwards, because he was sincere in his conviction that, in his bitter persecution of the church, he was serving God. If that were true, the heathen in his idolatry is safe because he is sincere. Do you not see that this standard alone might pervert all truth? No, this whole matter with us is a question of the interpretation of the Word of God. Frankly, candidly and lovingly we differ from our brethren as to "what saith the Scriptures" concerning these two ordinances.

Though we are compelled thus to differ from them in our interpretation of God's Word, yet we differ in tenderest Christian love. God pity Christian men who otherwise differ and who magnify their differences by unchristian wrangling and spirit! Differing, as we thus do fundamentally, we would not only be inconsistent, but we would also be dishonorable in the sight of God and men to ask those to come to this table whom we solemnly believe have never been baptized.

Let me read some brief quotations from other denominations that you may see how they are coming to appreciate the position of our Baptist people. I quote these words from the *American Presbyterian*, as printed some years ago:

> Open communion is an absurdity, when it means communion with the unbaptized. I would not for a moment consider a proposal to admit an unbaptized person to the communion, and can I ask a Baptist so to stultify himself and ignore his own doctrine as to wish to commune with him while he believes I am unbaptized? I want no sham union and no sham unity, and if I held the Baptist notion about immersion, I would no more receive a Presbyterian to the communion than I would receive a Quaker. Let us have unity, indeed, but not at the expense of principle; and let us not ask the Baptist to ignore or be inconsistent with his own doctrine. Let us not either make an outcry at his 'close communion,' which is but faithfulness, until we are prepared to be open communionists ourselves, from which stupidity may we be forever preserved.

The Inspiration of Ideals

Henry Ward Beecher used these words in the *Christian Union* some years ago:

> A Pedo-Baptist who believes that baptism is a prerequisite to communion has no right to censure the Baptist churches for close communion. On this question there is a great deal of pulling out of motes by people whose own vision is not clear.

The late Dr. John Hall, of New York, one of the leading Presbyterians of the world, said:

> If I believe with the Baptists, that none are baptized but those who are immersed on profession of faith, then I should, with them, refuse to commune with any others.

Dr. Hibbard, the great Methodist leader, thus speaks:

> It is but just to remark that, in one principle, the Baptist and Pedo-Baptist churches agree. They both agree in rejecting from communion at the table of the Lord and in denying the rights of church fellowship to all who have not been baptized. Valid baptism they consider as essential to constitute visible church membership. This also we (the Methodists) hold. The only question then, that here divides us is, What is essential to valid baptism?

The distinguished Episcopalian, Dr. Wall, says:

> No church ever gave the communion to persons before they were baptized. Among all the absurdities that were ever held, none ever maintained that any person should partake of the communion before he was baptized.

These expressions are truthful and noble and Christian, and they state the case just as it is.

But, waiving all the historical and denominational testimony to the proposition that baptism is a prerequisite to the Supper, let us ask: "What saith the Scriptures?" Does this Word teach that men ought to be baptized before they come to the table? Here are its answers:

"When therefore the Lord knew how the Pharisees had heard that Jesus made and baptized more disciples than John (though Jesus himself baptized not, but his disciples),"

John 4:1-2. There is Christ's law: (1) Making disciples; (2) baptizing them.

When Jesus gave the Great Commission (Matt. 28:19-20), this was the order of its development: (1) Make disciples; (2) baptize these disciples; and (3) properly teach them. Is it thinkable to you that Jesus would have these apostles and early Christians demand of others what He did not demand of them? And we find the early church at Jerusalem literally carrying out this commission. Here is the record: "Then they that gladly received His word were baptized; and the same day were added unto them about three thousand souls. And they continued steadfastly in the apostles' doctrine and fellowship, and in breaking of bread (i.e., the Supper), and in prayers." (Acts 2:41-42). How clear this record: Men are convicted of sin under Peter's preaching. He points them to Jesus, who saves them. They are then baptized. Next, they are steadfast in the apostles' doctrine and in fellowship. All these things occur before the Supper. Perfectly clear, then, is God's Word, that the first duty of the believer is baptism and that baptism comes before the Supper.

Not only did Jesus give this Supper to His disciples, who had been previously baptized, but He gave it to the baptized disciples in their organized capacity; that is to say, He gave this Supper to His church. Then, a third prerequisite to this table is orderly church membership.

Note the order: Regeneration, baptism, church membership. To His curches, then, Jesus committed this ordinance. He did not commit it to preachers, as such, nor to individuals, as such, but to His churches, in their church capacity. I put this question: Who is to judge of the qualifications of people who come to this table? There can be but two answers. One is that it is an individual matter, and that the individual must wholly pass upon it. The other view is that this ordinance was committed to the churches, to be preserved by them in all its pristine purity and meaning. Shall the individual desiring to come to this table be the sole judge of his qualifications, or shall the church be the judge? If you say the individual shall be the sole judge, then you cannot keep any man away from the Lord's table. Let me show you the utter inconsistency of it. In your church is a man guilty of insubordination to church authority, or some gross immorality, or some serious heresy. Fidelity to God's Word compels you to withdraw from him, and you obey that Word. The solemn act of withdrawal is taken by the church, in obedience to God's command, and for the preservation of the church. Next Sunday the excluded man comes again into the worship of God's people. And now they come to observe the Lord's Supper. Every man present is told to be his own judge, and come to the table if he chooses. There sits the excluded man, whose immorality is odious to the community, and whose heresy seeks to subvert the very fundamentals of the gospel, and yet he is included in the invitation to the Lord's table. Is it consistent? Is it righteous? Can it be honoring to God? How dare His people do it?

Just here is answered another question: Why do not Baptists invite the immersed of other denominations to the Lord's table? The answer is at hand: Immersion only, as before said, does not constitute scriptural baptism. One must be immersed because he is already saved, and not in any sense to secure salvation. Just here we are compelled to differ, fundamentally, from some who agree with us as to the proper act of baptism. One of the fundamental designs of baptism is to symbolize the great fact of the believer's death to sin and his resurrection to a spiritual life that has already taken place. And still again, baptism must be administered by a proper administrator. This ordinance, as well as the Supper, has been committed to the church. Then the church alone can administer it. But suppose a body of Christian people inveigh against immersion as the scriptural act of baptism, and give their influence in writing against it, speaking against it, and teaching against it; and if, to secure a member, or for any other cause, immersion is administered by them, against their consciences and against what they conceive to be the teaching of God's Word; and if, as is unwaveringly held by Baptsts immersion alone is the proper act of baptism; then can such baptism be orderly, consistent and scriptural? Our convictions of God's Word compel us to answer in the negative.

The Bible not only plainly specifies certain prerequisites to the Supper, but it also just as plainly specifies certain disqualifications. Now, since the Supper is an ordinance of the church, it must inevitably follow that whatever would debar a man from the church must also debar him from the Lord's table in the church. It is logically inconceivable that one should be deprived of membership in the church and yet not also be deprived of coming to the Lord's table in that church, since the first privilege is the source and foundation for the second.

Among the causes mentioned in the Scriptures, for which a church should withdraw from members are these: Insubordination to church authority, immoral conduct, a schismatical spirit, heresy, and disobedience to the commands of Christ. Do we see schism, heresy and disobedience to the commands of Christ in the teachings of other Christian people who believe and teach so differently from us? Our separate existence is a sufficient answer. Then the question is answered by the two points of valid baptism and scriptural doctrine, as to why Baptists do not invite the immersed of other denominations to the Lord's table.

That the local church is the custodian of this ordinance, and must judge of the qualifications of those desiring to partake of it, is shown by the fact that the command to observe it was given, not to individuals, but to a company. On the night of its institution, Jesus said to the eleven, themselves His incipient church: "I appoint unto you a kingdom, as my

THE INSPIRATION OF IDEALS

Father has appointed unto me; that ye may eat and drink at my table, in my kingdom." (Luke 22: 29-30). Manifestly, this table is inside and not outside the church. The church alone can, therefore, be charged with the responsibility for its government.

Writing to the church at Corinth, Paul uses this language: "But I say, that the things which the Gentiles sacrifice, they do sacrifice to devils, and not to God; and I would not that ye should have fellowship with devils. Ye cannot drink the cup of the Lord, and the cup of the devils; ye cannot be partakers of the Lord's table and of the table of the devils." (1 Cor. 10:21-22). What was Paul talking about? He was talking about the influence that idolatry was insidiously wielding upon the church at Corinth. He found there, for example, this condition, a husband and a wife — the one an idolater, the other a Christian. The idolater proposed to the Christian: "Come with me to my table, then I will go with you to yours." This, Paul declared to be fundamentally wrong. Not for the sake of husband or wife, or mother or child, could the Christian sit, now at one table and then at another. The place and purpose of the two tables imperatively forbade such inconsistency and compromise.

Writing further to the same church, earnestly does Paul bring out the thought that the observance of this ordinance is not an individual act, but the joint act of the church. "When ye come together in the church . . . when ye come together therefore into one place . . . when ye come together to eat [i. e., to observe the Supper], tarry one for another." (1 Cor. 11:18-20-33.) Not individually, therefore, but in her collective capacity, may the church observe this Supper. Therefore I always instantly decline to carry these emblems out to the sick and the dying.

Writing elsewhere to the same church, Paul says: "For we, being many, are one bread and one body." (1 Cor. 10:17.) As it takes the separate states of the Union to make the

United States, so the members of a church, not individually, but "being many are one bread, and one body," must act collectively in order scripturally to observe this ordinance. We have seen at length that the answer to our second question is, that a local church is the only body known to the Scriptures which has any competency or jurisdiction in the government of her two ordinances.

The Meaning of the Supper

Our third question is, what is the meaning of this Supper? What is our design in our observance of it? That is a question of great moment. Some of the most grievous evils that have ever afflicted the world have grown out of the perversion of the design of this Supper. Three distinct views are held with regard to its nature. There is the view of the Romanist, called transubstantiation, which view is that this bread and wine are literally changed, by the consecration of the priest, into the very body and blood of Christ; and that, by thus eating Christ's body and drinking His blood, God's saving grace is received by the communicant. The view of the Lutheran, and, perhaps some others, called consubstantiation, is that though the bread and wine are not changed, yet along with them is present the real body and blood of Christ, so that both are eaten at the same time by the communicant. So palpably do these two theories contradict the plain nature and purpose of this ordinance, and the whole gospel, that I do not need to stop to refute them.

Let this simple statement of God's Word show us this Supper's meaning: "This do in remembrance of me." Here is its meaning in one brief sentence: "This do in remembrance of me." But someone asks: "Do we not come to this table to commune with one another?" Such sentiment is widespread and has done incalculable harm.

THE INSPIRATION OF IDEALS

Jesus does not say, "Do this in remembrance of certain loved ones, or to show fellowship for them," but, "Do this in remembrance of me." It is the only thing He ever asked His people to do whereby they might remember Him. Oh, shall we deny Him this simple request?

It is not a question of Christian fellowship. There are other times and places for the tender and beautiful manifestation of Christian fellowship, but this is not the time nor the place to be thinking of that. I believe in the heartfelt, joyous fellowship of all God's children. Though I believe that great multitudes of my Father's children have never scripturally been baptized, yet I love and esteem them as earnest, noble Christians. But, far be from me all such thoughts when I gather at this table to remember my Lord. "This do in remembrance of me."

There is this other Scripture that should always be read in this connection. "Whosoever shall eat this bread, and drink this cup of the Lord, unworthily, shall be guilty of the body and blood of the Lord. But let a man examine himself, and so let him eat of that bread and drink of that cup. For he that eateth and drinketh unworthily eateth and drinketh damnation [i. e., condemnation] to himself, not discerning the Lord's body. For this cause many are weak and sickly among you, and many sleep." (1 Cor. 11:27-30) What Christian has not felt unspeakable trembling as he read that awful sentence? "He that eateth and drinketh unworthily, eateth and drinketh damnation [i. e., condemnation] to himself." What does it mean? The answer is found in the latter clause of the same verse: "Not discerning the Lord's body."

There is but one motive and thought to concern us as we come to this table. To come to it with any other than to "discern the Lord's body" is to harm the soul and to sin against Christ. It is a question touching your motive in coming. It is not a question of your unworthiness. Certainly you are unworthy, and you are also unworthy of all the

The Supper of Our Lord

countless blessings of salvation. But, in coming to this table, for what do you come? It is to remember Jesus. It is to discern His body. All this talk about gathering around this table to show fellowship for mother, wife, child, neighbor, is not only senseless twaddle, but it is a sin against God and men. Oh, my Saviour, shall our thought in coming to Thy table be about dear mother, or wife, or child, and shall these earthly forms displace the broken and bleeding form of Jesus, who gave Himself unto death for us? God forbid! No wonder it is said of those who thus come: "For this cause many are weak and sickly among you, and many sleep." Oh, my fellow Christians, see to it, do see to it, that in coming to this table, but one thing is to engage the powers of your minds and hearts, and that is that you "discern the Lord's body." And know, once for all, that any other coming is mockery against the meaning of this ordinance and against Him who gave it.

There is still another Scripture that we should briefly examine: "But let a man examine himself, and so let him eat of that bread and drink of that cup." (1 Cor. 11:28.) This is often quoted by those who insist upon "individuality" and "liberality" in the observance of this ordinance. Let us examine the verse a moment. To whom were the words addressed? They were addressed to a church, the church at Corinth. This same church, as we have before learned, was instructed concerning this Supper, to "Come together in the church ... to come together into one place ... and to tarry one for another," when they thus came together to observe the supper. (1 Cor. 11:18-20-23.) All thought of individualism in the observance of the Supper is thus destroyed.

Then, when this church, collectively, is ready to observe the Supper, the question of self-examination is pressed upon every individual who proposes to participate in its observance. The individual has his place there with his brethren. The church collectively, and not individually, is about this table. They are going to observe the Supper. The officials are ready to give to each the emblems. Now, what is the supreme object of this self-examination? The Scriptures connected with the verse plainly tell us — it is a question of the motive. The self-examination is to be had with this one end in view — not to so eat and drink as to bring condemnation upon himself, but simply and only so as to "discern the Lord's body." Oh, my brethren, I charge you, see to it that yours is the right motive whenever you observe this beautiful ordinance.

The Baptist Position

I have gone over this subject hurriedly, item by item, presenting the Scriptures touching this ordinance. May I say it modestly, my Baptist people, I do solemnly believe, keep this ordinance as it is demanded by the Holy Word. They believe God's Word plainly teaches that men must be born again, and then be scripturally baptized, and then maintain an orderly church membership, in order to be scripturally entitled to observe this ordinance. For these prerequisites my Baptist people unwaveringly stand. They are the only people who have thus stood for this meaningful ordinance. Their fidelity has cost them reproach, and many have been the charges of "narrowness," "discourtesy," and "illiberality" that have been heaped upon them. But did it ever occur to some good Christian, who forgot himself so far as thus hastily to criticise his Baptist brethren, that one of the sublimest exhibitions of fidelity and unselfishness in the history of Christianity is the Baptist position on the Lord's Supper? Against all critics my Baptist people have stood — and for what? They could have baptized many who are today in Pedo-Baptist churches, if they had not unyieldingly con-

The Supper of Our Lord

tended for the scriptural restrictions of this Supper. Our people feel, they believe with all their hearts, that for them to change their course in this matter would be palpable disobedience to their Master's word.

I repeat, this ordinance has received awful treatment, but not by Baptist hands. It has been individually taken out of the church into the streets, to the beds of the sick and dying, but not by Baptist hands. Some withold part of it altogether, but not my people. Some withold it ever from some whom they say they have baptized, but not my people. Some — from their talk I fear there are many — observe this ordinance for expressing their fellowship one for another, but never so by my Baptist people.

In the long ago, a prince led an insurrection against his country, and thereby legally forfeited his right to life. Though fleeing, he was finally captured and brought before the ruler whose authority he had despised. Looking upon him, the ruler asked him what he would give for his liberty, "The half of my estate," he answered. Again he asked him what he would give for the liberty of his children. "The other half of my estate," he quickly answered. And, again, the ruler, looking upon the prisoner's wife, asked him: "And what would you give for her liberty?" Quick as the lightning flash he answered: "Oh, sir, if you will spare her I will give you my life!" Do you not guess the result? So deeply touched was the ruler's heart that he released them all. One day thereafter, when the pardoned prince spoke to his wife of the wonderful look of the ruler, on that momentous day when he set them free, she replied that she did not see him. "How could that be?" the husband asked. "Oh," said the wife, "I had eyes for nothing but the man who was offering to give his life for me."

The Inspiration of Ideals

O Master and Saviour, thou Son of Man and Son of God, with such motives let thy people ever come to Thy table! Let mother, aged, precious mother; and wife, patient, faithful wife; and children, tender and true; and neighbors, beloved and helpful — let the fair visions of all these be displaced, when we come to Thy table, by the glorious vision of Jesus — of Jesus only!

CHAPTER V

Baptists and Religious Liberty

CHAPTER V

Baptists and Religious Liberty*

Southern Baptists count it a high privilege to hold their Annual Convention this year in the national capital, and they count it one of life's highest privileges to be citizens of our one great, united country.

> Grand in her rivers and her rills,
> Grand in her woods and templed hills;
> Grand in the wealth that glory yields,
> Illustrious dead, historic fields;
> Grand in her past, her present grand,
> In sunlit skies, in fruitful land;
> Grand in her strength on land and sea,
> Grand in religious liberty.

It behooves us often to look backward as well as forward. We should be stronger and braver if we thought oftener of the epic days and deeds of our beloved and immortal dead. The occasional backward look would give us poise and patience and courage and fearlessness and faith. The ancient Hebrew teachers and leaders had a genius for looking backward to the days and deeds of their mighty dead. They never wearied of chanting the praises of Abraham and Isaac and Jacob, of Moses and Joshua and Samuel; and thus did they bring to bear upon the living the inspiring memories of the noble actors and deeds of bygone days. Often such a cry as

---

* Address delivered from the steps of the Capitol at Washington, D. C., on the occasion of the meeting of the Southern Baptist Convention, May, 1920.

THE INSPIRATION OF IDEALS

this rang in their ears: "Look unto the rock whence ye were hewn, and to the hole of the pit whence ye were digged. Look unto Abraham, your father, and unto Sarah that bare you; for when he was but one I called him, and I blessed him, and made him many."

The Doctrine of Religious Liberty

We shall do well, both as citizens and as Christians, if we hark back to the chief actors and lessons in the early and epoch-making struggles of this great Western democracy, for the full establishment of civil and religious liberty — back to the days of Washington and Jefferson and Madison, and back to the days of our Baptist fathers, who paid such a great price, through the long generations, that liberty, both religious and civil, might have free course and be glorified everywhere.

Years ago, at a notable dinner in London, that world-famed statesman, John Bright, asked an American statesman, himself a Baptist, the noble Dr. J. L. M. Curry, "What distinct contribution has your America made to the science of government?" To that question Dr. Curry replied: "The doctrine of religious liberty." After a moment's reflection, Mr. Bright made the worthy reply: "It was a tremendous contribution."

Supreme Contribution of New World

Indeed, the supreme contribution of the new world to the old is the contribution of religious liberty. This is the chiefest contribution that America has thus far made to civilization. And historic justice compels us to say that it was pre-eminently a Baptist contribution. The impartial historian, whether in the past, present or future, will ever agree with our American historian, Mr. Bancroft, when he says: "Freedom of conscience, unlimited freedom of mind, was from the first the trophy of the Baptists." And such historian will concur with the noble John Locke who said: "The Baptists were the first propounders of absolute liberty, just and true liberty, equal and impartial liberty." Ringing testimonies like these might be multiplied indefinitely.

Not Toleration, but Right

Baptists have one consistent record concerning liberty throughout all their long and eventful history. They have never been party to oppression of conscience. They have ever been the unwavering champions of liberty, both religious and civil. Their contention now is, and has been, and, please God, must ever be, that it is the natural and fundamental and indefeasible right of every human being to worship God or not, according to the dictates of his conscience, and, as long as he does not infringe upon the rights of others, he is to be held accountable alone to God for all religious beliefs and practices. Our contention is not for mere toleration, but for absolute liberty. There is a wide difference between toleration and liberty. Toleration implies that somebody falsely claims the right to tolerate. Toleration is a concession, while liberty is a right. Toleration is a matter of expediency, while liberty is a matter of principle. Toleration is a gift from man, while liberty is a gift from God. It is the consistent and insistent contention of our Baptist people, always and everywhere, that religion must be forever voluntary and uncoerced, and that it is not the prerogative of any power, whether civil or ecclesiastical, to compel men to conform to any religious creed or form of worship, or to pay taxes for the support of a religious organization to which they do not belong and in whose creed they do not believe. God wants free worshippers and no other kind.

The Inspiration of Ideals

What is the explanation of this consistent and notably praiseworthy record of our plain Baptist people in the realm of religious liberty? The answer is at hand. It is not because Baptists are inherently better than their neighbours — we would make no such arrogant claim. Happy are our Baptist people to live side by side with their neighbours of other Christian faiths and to have fellowship with such neighbours, and to honor such servants of God for their inspiring lives and their noble deeds. From our deepest hearts we pray: "Grace be with all them that love our Lord Jesus Christ in sincerity." The spiritual union of all true believers in Christ is now and ever will be a blessed reality, and such union is deeper and higher and more enduring than any and all forms and rituals and organizations. Whoever believes in Christ as his personal Saviour is our brother in the common salvation, whether he be a member of one communion or of another, or of no communion at all.

How is it, then, that Baptists, more than any other people in the world, have forever been the protagonists of religious liberty, and its compatriot, civil liberty? They did not stumble upon this principle. Their uniform, unyielding and sacrificial advocacy of such principle was not and is not an accident. It is, in a word, because of our essential and fundamental principles. Ideas rule the world. A denomination is moulded by its ruling principles, just as a nation is thus moulded and just as individual life is thus moulded. Our fundamental essential principles have made our Baptist people, of all ages and countries, to be the unyielding protagonists of religious liberty, not only for themselves, but as well for everybody else.

Such fact at once provokes the inquiry: What are these fundamental Baptist principles which compel Baptists in Europe, in America, in some far-off seagirt island, to be forever contending for unrestricted religious liberty? First of all, and explaining all the rest, is the doctrine of absolute Lordship of Jesus Christ. That doctrine is for Baptists the dominant fact in all their Christian experience, the nerve center of all their Christian life, the bedrock of all their church polity, the sheet anchor of all their hopes, the climax and crown of all their rejoicings. They say with Paul: "For to this end Christ both died and rose again, that he might be Lord both of the dead and the living."

From that germinal conception of the absolute Lordship of Christ, all our Baptist principles emerge. Just as yonder oak came from the acorn, so our many-branched Baptist life came from the cardinal principle of the absolute Lordship of Christ. The Christianity of our Baptist people, from Alpha to Omega, lives and moves and has its whole being in the realm of the doctrine of the Lordship of Christ. "One is your Master, even Christ, and all ye are brethren." Christ is the one head of the church. All authority has been committed unto Him, in heaven and on earth, and He must be given the absolute pre-eminence in all things. One clear note is ever to be sounded concerning Him, even this, "Whatsoever He saith unto you, do it."

The Bible Our Rule of Faith and Practice

How shall we find out Christ's will for us? He has revealed it in His Holy Word. The Bible and the Bible alone is the rule of faith and practice for Baptists. To them the one standard by which all creeds and conduct and character must be tried is the Word of God. They ask only one question concerning all religious faith and practice, and that question is, "What saith the Word of God?" Not traditions, nor customs, nor councils, nor confessions, nor ecclesiastical formularies, however venerable and pretentious, guide Baptists, but simply and solely the will of Christ as they find it revealed in the New Testament. The immortal B. H. Carroll has thus stated it for us: "The New Testament is the law of Christianity. All the New Testament is the law of Christianity. The New Testament is all the law of Christianity. The New Testament always will be all the law of Christianity."

Baptists hold that this law of Christianity, the Word of God, is the unchangeable and only law of Christ's reign, and that whatever is not found in the law cannot be bound on the consciences of men, and that this law is a sacred deposit, an inviolable trust, which Christ's friends are commissioned to guard and perpetuate wherever it may lead and whatever may be the cost of such trusteeship.

Exact Opposite of Catholicism

The Baptist message and the Roman Catholic message are the very antipodes of each other. The Roman Catholic message is sacerdotal, sacramentarian and ecclesiastical. In its scheme of salvation it magnifies the church, the priest, and the sacraments. The Baptist message is non-sacerdotal, non-sacramentarian, and non-ecclesiastical. Its teaching is that the one High Priest for sinful humanity has entered into the holy place for all, that the veil is forever rent in twain, that the mercy seat is uncovered and open to all, and that the humblest soul in all the world if only he be penitent, may enter with all boldness and cast himself upon God. The Catholic doctrine of baptismal regeneration and transubstantiation are to the Baptist mind fundamentally subversive of the spiritual realities of the gospel of Christ. Likewise, the Catholic conception of the church, thrusting all its complex and cumbrous machinery between the soul and God, prescribing beliefs, claiming to exercise the power of the keys, and to control the channels of grace — all such lording it over the consciences of men is to the Baptist mind a ghastly tyranny in the realm of the soul and tends to frustrate the grace of God, to destroy freedom of conscience and terribly to hinder the coming of the Kingdom of God.

Papal Infallibility or the New Testament

That was a memorable hour in the Vatican Council, in 1870, when the dogma of papal infallibility was passed by a majority vote. You recall that in the midst of all the tenseness and tumult of that excited assemblage, Cardinal Manning stood on an elevated platform, and in the midst of that assemblage, and holding in his hand the paper just passed, declaring for the infallibility of the Pope, said: "Let all the world go to bits and we will reconstruct it on this paper." A Baptist smiles at such an announcement as that, but not in derision and scorn. Although the Baptist is the very antithesis of his Catholic neighbour in religious conceptions and contentions, yet the Baptist will whole-heartedly contend that his Catholic neighbour shall have his candles and incense and sanctus bell and rosary, and whatever else he wishes in the expression of his worship. A Baptist would rise at midnight to plead for absolute religious liberty for his Catholic neighbour, and for his Jewish neighbour, and for everybody else. But what is the answer of a Baptist to the contention made by the Catholic for papal infallibility? Holding aloft a little book, the name of which is the New Testament, and without any hesitation or doubt, the Baptist shouts his battle cry: "Let all the world go to bits and we will reconstruct it on the New Testament."

Direct Individual Approach to God

When we turn to this New Testament, which is Christ's guidebook and law for His people, we find that supreme emphasis is everywhere put upon the individual. The individual is segregated from family, from church, from state, and from society, from dearest earthly friends or institution, and brought into direct, personal dealings with God. Every one must give account of himself to God. There can be no sponsors or deputies or proxies in such a vital matter. Each one must repent for himself, and believe for himself, and be baptized for himself, and answer to God for himself, both in time and in eternity. One man can no more repent and believe and obey Christ for another than he can take the other's place at God's judgment bar. Neither persons nor institutions, however dear and powerful, may dare to come between the individual soul and God. "There is one mediator between God and men, the man Christ Jesus." Let the state and the church, let the institution, however dear, and the person, however near, stand aside, and let the individual soul make its own direct and immediate response to God. One is our pontiff, and his name is Jesus. The undelegated sovereignty of Christ makes it forever impossible for His saving grace to be manipulated by any system of human mediation whatsoever.

The right of private judgment is the crown jewel of humanity, and for any person or institution to dare to come between the soul and God is a blasphemous impertinence and a defamation of the crown rights of the Son of God.

Out of these two fundamental principles, the supreme authority of the Scriptures and the right of private judgment, have come all the historic protests in Europe and England and America against unscriptural creeds, polity and rites, and against the unwarranted and impertinent assumption of religious authority over men's consciences, whether by church or by state. Baptists regard as an enormity any attempt to force the conscience, or to constrain men, by outward penalties, to this or that form of religious belief. Persecution may make men hypocrites, but it will not make them Christians.

Infant Baptism Unthinkable

It follows, inevitably, that Baptists are unalterably opposed to every form of sponsorial religion. If I have fellow Christians in this presence today who are the protagonists of infant baptism, they will allow me frankly to say, and certainly I would say it in the most fraternal, Christian spirit, that to Baptists infant baptism is unthinkable from every viewpoint. First of all, Baptists do not find the slightest sanction for infant baptism in the Word of God. That fact, to Baptists, makes infant baptism a most serious question for the consideration of the whole Christian world. Nor is that all. As Baptists see it, infant baptism tends to ritualize Christianity and reduce it to lifeless forms. It tends also and inevitably, as Baptists see it, to the secularizing of the church and to the blurring and blotting out of the line of demarcation between the church and the unsaved world.

And since I have thus spoken with unreserved frankness, my honored Pedo-baptist friends in the audience will allow me to say that Baptists solemnly believe that infant baptism, with its implications, has flooded the world and floods it now with untold evils.

They believe also that it perverts the Scriptural symbolism of baptism; that it attempts the impossible task of performing an act of religious obedience by proxy, and that since it forestalls the individual initiative of the child, it carries within it the germ of persecution, and lays the predicate for the union of church and state, and that it is a Romish tradition and a corner stone for the whole system of popery throughout the world.

I will speak yet another frank word for my beloved Baptist people, to our cherished fellow Christians who are not Baptists, and that word is that our Baptist people believe that if all the Protestant denominations would once for all put away infant baptism, and come to the full acceptance and faithful practice of New Testament baptism, the unity of all the non-Catholic Christians in the world quickly would be consummated.

Surely, in the face of these frank statements, our non-Baptist neighbours may apprehend something of the difficulties compelling Baptists when they are asked to enter into official alliances with those who hold such fundamentally different views from those just indicated. We call God to witness that our Baptist people have an unutterable longing for Christian union, and believe Christian union will come, but we are compelled to insist that if this union is to be real and effective, it must be based upon a clear understanding of the Word of God and a complete loyalty to the will of Christ as revealed in his Word.

The Ordinances Are Symbols

Again, to Baptists, the New Testament teaches that salvation through Christ must precede membership in His church, and must precede the observance of the two ordinances in His church, namely, baptism and the Lord's Supper. These ordinances are for the saved and only for the saved. These two ordinances are not sacramental, but symbolic. They are teaching ordinances, portraying in symbol truths of immeasurable and everlasting moment to humanity. To trifle with these symbols, to pervert their forms and at the same time to pervert the truths they are designed to symbolize, is indeed a most serious matter. Without ceasing and without wavering, Baptists are, in conscience, compelled to contend that these two teaching ordinances shall be maintained in the churches just as they were placed there in the wisdom and authority of Christ. To change these two meaningful symbols is to change their Scriptural intent and content, and thus pervert them, and we solemnly believe, to be the carriers of the most deadly heresies. By our loyalty to Christ, which we hold to be the supreme test of our friendship for Him, we must unyieldingly contend for these two ordinances as they were originally given to Christ's churches.

To Baptists, the New Testament also clearly teaches that Christ's church is not only a spiritual body but it is also a pure democracy, all its members being equal, a local congregation, and cannot subject itself to any outside control. Such terms, therefore, as "The American Church," or "The bishop of this city or state," sound strangely incongruous to Baptist ears. In the very nature of the case, also, there must be no union between church and state, because their nature and functions are utterly different. Jesus stated the principle in the two sayings, "My kingdom is not of this world," and "Render unto Caesar the things that are Caesar's, and unto God the things that are God's." Never, anywhere, in any clime, has a true Baptist been willing, for one minute, for the union of church and state, never for a moment.

A Free Church in a Free State

Every state church on the earth is a spiritual tyranny. The utterance of Jesus, "Render unto Caesar the things that are Caesar's, and unto God the things that are God's," is one of the most revolutionary and history-making utterances that ever fell from those lips divine. That utterance, once for all, marked the divorcement of church and state. It marked a new era for the creeds and deeds of men. It was the sunrise gun of a new day, the echoes of which are to go on and on until in every land, whether great or small, the doctrine shall have absolute supremacy everywhere of a free church in a free state.

In behalf of our Baptist people I am compelled to say that forgetfulness of the principles that I have just enumerated, in our judgment, explains many of the religious ills that now afflict the world. All went well with the early churches in their earlier days. They were incomparably triumphant days for the Christian faith. Those early disciples of Jesus, without prestige and worldly power, yet aflame with the love of God and the passion of Christ, went out and shook the pagan

Roman Empire from centre to circumference, in an amazingly brief time.

An Incomparable Apostasy

Presently there came an incomparable apostasy in the realm of religion, which shrouded the world in spiritual night through long hundreds of years. Constantine, the Emperor, saw something in the religion of Christ's people which awakened his interest, and now we see him uniting religion to the state and marching up the marble steps of the Emperor's palace, with the church robed in purple. Then and there was begun the most baneful misalliance that ever fettered and cursed a suffering world. For long centuries, even from Constantine to Pope Gregory VII, the conflict between church and state waxed stronger and stronger, and the encroachments and usurpations became more deadly and devastating. When Christianity first found its way into the city of the Caesars it lived in cellars and alleys, but when Constantine crowned the union of church and state, the church was stamped with the impress of the Roman idea and fanned with the spirit of the Caesars. Soon we see a Pope emerging, who himself became a Caesar, and soon a group of councillors may be seen gathered around this Pope, and the supreme power of the church is assumed by the Pope and his councillors.

The long, blighting record of the medieval ages is simply the working out of that idea. The Pope ere long assumed to be the monarch of the world, making the astounding claim that all kings and potentates were subject unto him. By and by when Pope Gregory VII, better known as Hildebrand, appears, his assumptions are still more astounding. In him the spirit of the Roman church became incarnate and triumphant. He lorded it over parliaments and council chambers, having statesmen to do his bidding, and creating and deposing kings at his will. For example, when the Emperor Henry offended Hildebrand, the latter pronounced against Henry a sentence not only of excommunication but of deposition as Emperor, releasing all Christians from allegiance to him. He made the Emperor do penance by standing in the snow with his bare feet at Canossa, and he wrote his famous letter to William the Conqueror to the effect that the state was subordinate to the church, that the power of the state as compared to the church was as the moon compared to the sun.

This explains the famous saying of Bismarck when Chancellor of Germany, to the German Parliament: "We will never go to Canossa again." Whoever favours the authority of the church over the state favours the way to Canossa.

When, in the fulness of time, Columbus discovered America, the Pope calmly announced that he would divide the New World into two parts, giving one part to the King of Spain and the other to the King of Portugal. And not only did this great consolidated ecclesiasticism assume to lord it over men's earthly treasures, but they lorded it over men's minds, prescribing what men should think and read and write. Nor did such assumption stop with the things of this world, but it laid its hand on the next world, and claimed to have in its possession the keys of the kingdom of heaven and the kingdom of purgatory so that it could shut men out of heaven or lift them out of purgatory, thus surpassing in the sweep of its power and in the pride of its autocracy the boldest and most presumptuous ruler that ever sat on a civil throne.

Absolutism vs Individualism

The student of history cannot fail to observe that through the long years two ideas have been in endless antagonism — the idea of absolutism and the idea of individualism, the idea of autocracy and the idea of democracy. The idea of autocracy is that supreme power is vested in the few, who, in turn, delegate this power to the many. That was the dominant idea of the Roman Empire, and upon that idea the

Caesars built their throne. That idea has found world-wide expression in the realms both civil and ecclesiastical. Often have the two ideas, absolutism versus individualism, autocracy versus democracy, met in battle. Autocracy dared, in the morning of the twentieth century, to crawl out of its ugly lair and to propose to substitute the law of the jungle for the law of human brotherhood. For all time to come the hearts of men will stand aghast upon every thought of this incomparable death drama, and at the same time they will renew the vow that the few shall not presumptuously tyrannize over the many; that the law of human brotherhood and not the law of the jungle shall be given supremacy in all human affairs. And until the principle of democracy, rather than the principle of autocracy, shall be regnant in the realm of religion, our mission shall be commanding and unending.

The Reformation Incomplete

The coming of the sixteenth century was the dawning of a new hope for the world. With that century came the Protestant Reformation. Yonder goes Luther with his theses, which he nails over the old church door in Wittenberg, and the echoes of the mighty deed shake the Papacy, shake Europe, shake the whole world. Luther was joined by Melancthon and Calvin and Zwingli and other mighty leaders. Just at this point emerges one of the most outstanding anomalies of all history. Although Luther and his compeers protested vigorously against the errors of Rome, yet when these mighty men came out of Rome, and mighty men they were, they brought with them some of the grievous errors of Rome. The Protestant Reformation of the Sixteenth century was sadly incomplete — it was a case of arrested development. Although Luther and his compeers grandly sounded out the battle cry of justification by faith alone, yet they retained the doctrine of infant baptism and a state church. They shrank from the logical conclusions of their own theses.

Baptists and Religious Liberty

In Zurich there stands a statue in honour of Zwingli, in which he is represented with a Bible in one hand and a sword in the other. That statue was the symbol of the union between church and state. The same statue might have been reared to Luther and his fellow reformers. Luther and Melancthon fastened a state church upon Germany, and Zwingli fastened it upon Switzerland. Knox and his associates fastened it upon Scotland. Henry VIII bound it upon England, where it remains even till this very hour.

These mighty reformers turned out to be persecutors like the Papacy before them. Luther unloosed the dogs of persecution against the struggling and faithful Anabaptists. Calvin burned Servetus, and to such awful deed Melancthon gave his approval. Louis XIV revoked the Edict of Nantes, shut the doors of all the Protestant churches, and outlawed the Huguenots, Germany put to death that mighty Baptist leader, Balthaser Hubmaier, while Holland killed her noblest statesman, John of Barneveldt, and condemned to life imprisonment her ablest historian, Hugo Grotius, for conscience' sake. In England, John Bunyan was kept in jail for twelve long, weary years because of his religion, and when we cross the mighty ocean separating the Old World and the New, we find the early pages of American history crimsoned with the stories of religious persecutions. The early colonies of America were the forum of the working out of the most epochal battles that earth ever knew for the triumph of religious and civil liberty.

America and Religious and Civil Liberty

Just a brief glance at the struggle in those early colonies must now suffice us. Yonder in Massachusetts, Henry Dunster, the first president of Harvard, was removed from the presidency because he objected to infant baptism. Roger Williams was banished, John Clarke was put in prison, and they publicly whipped Obadiah Holmes on Boston Common. In Connecticut the lands of our Baptist fathers were confiscated and their goods sold to build a meeting house and support a preacher of another denomination. In old Virginia, "mother of states and statesmen," the battle for religious and civil liberty was waged all over her nobly historic territory, and the final triumph recorded there was such as to write imperishable glory upon the name of Virginia until the last syllable of recorded time. Fines and imprisonments and persecutions were everywhere in evidence in Virginia for conscience's sake. If you would see a record incomparably interesting, go read the early statutes in Virginia concerning the Established Church and religion, and trace the epic story of the history-making struggles of that early day. If the historic records are to be accredited, those clergymen of the Established Church in Virginia made terrible inroads in collecting fines in Baptist tobacco in that early day. It is quite evident, however, that they did not get all the tobacco.

On and on was the struggle waged by our Baptist fathers for religious liberty in Virginia, in the Carolinas, in Georgia, in Rhode Island, and Massachusetts, and Connecticut, and elsewhere, with one unyielding contention for unrestricted religious liberty for all men, and with never one wavering note. They dared to be odd, to stand alone, to refuse to conform, though it cost them suffering and even life itself. They dared to defy traditions and customs, and deliberately chose the way of non-conformity, even though in many a case it meant persecutions and punishments. They pleaded and suffered, they offered their protests and remonstrances and memorials; and, thank God, mighty statesmen were won to their contention, Washington and Jefferson and Madison and Patrick Henry, and many others, until at last it was written into our country's Constitution that church and state must in this land be forever separate and free, that neither must ever trespass upon the distinctive functions of the other. It was pre-eminently a Baptist achievement.

Glad are our Baptist people to pay their grateful tribute to their fellow Christians of other religious communions for all their sympathy and help in this sublime achievement. Candor compels me to repeat that much of the sympathy of other religious leaders in that early struggle was on the side of legalized, ecclesiastical privilege. Much of the time were Baptists pitiably lonely in their age-long struggle. We would now and always make our most grateful acknowledgement to any and all who came to the side of our Baptist fathers, whether early or late, in this destiny-determining struggle. But I take it that every informed man on the subject, whatever his religious faith, will be willing to pay tribute to our Baptist people as being the chief instrumentality in God's hands in winning the battle in America for religious liberty. Do you recall Tennyson's poem, in which he sets out the history of the seed of freedom? Catch its philosophy:

> Once in a golden hour,
>   I cast to earth a seed,
> Up there came a flower,
>   The people said, a weed.
>
> To and fro they went,
>   Through my garden bower,
> And muttering discontent,
>   Cursed me and my flower.
>
> Then it grew so tall,
>   It wore a crown of light,
> But thieves from o'er the wall,
>   Stole the seed by night.
>
> Sowed it far and wide,
>   By every town and tower,
> Till all the people cried,
>   "Splendid is the flower."
>
> Read my little fable:
>   He who runs may read,
> Most can grow the flowers now,
>   For all have got the seed.

THE INSPIRATION OF IDEALS

Very well, we are very happy for all our fellow religionists of every denomination and creed to have this splendid flower of religious liberty, but you will allow us to remind you that you got the seed in our Baptist garden. We are very happy for you to have it; now let us all make the best of it and the most of it.

The Present Call

And now, my fellow Christians, and fellow citizens, what is the present call to us in connection with the priceless principle of religious liberty? That principle, with all the history and heritage accompanying it, imposes upon us obligations to the last degree meaningful and responsible. Let us today and forever be highly resolved that the principle of religious liberty shall, please God, be preserved inviolate through all our days and the days of those who come after us. Liberty has both its perils and its obligations. We are to see to it that our attitude toward liberty, both religious and civil, both as Christians and as citizens, is an attitude consistent and constructive and worthy. We are to "Render unto Caesar the things that are Caesar's, and unto God the things that are God's" We are members of the two realms, the civil and the religious, and are faithfully to render unto each all that each should receive at our hands; we are to be alertly watchful, day and night, that liberty, both religious and civil, shall be nowhere prostituted and mistreated. Every perversion and misuse of liberty tends by that much to jeopardize both church and state.

There comes now the clarion call to us to be the right kind of citizens. Happily, the record of our Baptist people toward civil government has been a record of unfading honour. Their love and loyalty to country have not been put to shame in any land. In the long list of published Tories in connection with the Revolutionary War there was not one Baptist name.

Liberty Not Abused

It behooves us now and ever to see to it that liberty is not abused. Well may we listen to the call of Paul, that mightiest Christian of the long centuries, as he says: "Brethren, ye have been called unto liberty; only use not liberty for an occasion to the flesh, but by love serve one another." This ringing declaration should be heard and heeded by every class and condition of people throughout all our wide-stretching nation.

It is the word to be heeded by religious teachers, and by editors, and by legislators, and by everybody else. Nowhere is liberty to be used "for an occasion to the flesh." We will take free speech and a free press, with all their excrescences and perils, because of the high meaning of freedom, but we are to set ourselves with all diligence not to use these great privileges in the shaming of liberty. A free press — how often does it pervert its high privilege! Again and again, it may be seen dragging itself through all the sewers of the social order, bringing to light the moral cancers and leprosies of our poor world and glaringly exhibiting them to the gaze even of responsive youth and childhood. The editor's task, whether in the realm of church or state, is an immeasurably responsible one. These editors, side by side with the moral and religious teachers of the country, are so to magnify the ballot box, a free press, free schools, the courts, the majesty of law and reverence for all properly accredited authority that our civilization may not be built on the shifting sands, but on the secure and enduring foundations of righteousness.

Let us remember that lawlessness, wherever found and whatever its form, is as the pestilence that walketh in darkness and the destruction that wasteth at noon day. Let us remember that he who is willing for law to be violated is an offender against the majesty of law as really as he who actually violates law. The spirit of law is the spirit of civilization. Liberty without law is anarchy. Liberty against law is rebellion. Liberty limited by law is the formula of civilization.

The Inspiration of Ideals

Humane and Righteous Laws

Challenging to the highest degree is the call that comes to legislators. They are to see to it continually, in all their legislative efforts, that their supreme concern is for the highest welfare of the people. Laws humane and righteous are to be fashioned and then to be faithfully enforced. Men are playing with fire if they lightly fashion their country's laws and then trifle in their obedience to such laws. Indeed, all citizens, the humblest and the most prominent alike, are called to give their best thought to the maintenance of righteousness everywhere. Much truth is there in the widely quoted saying: "Our country is afflicted with the bad citizenship of good men." The saying points its own clear lesson. "When the righteous are in authority, the people rejoice, but when the wicked bear rule, the people mourn." The people, all the people, are inexorably responsible for the laws, the ideals, and the spirit that are necessary for the making of a great and enduring civilization. Every man of us is to remember that it is righteousness that exalteth a nation, and that it is sin that reproaches and destroys a nation.

God does not raise up a nation to go selfishly strutting and forgetful of the high interests of humanity. National selfishness leads to destruction as truly as does individual selfishness. Nations can no more live to themselves than can individuals. Humanity is bound up together in the big bundle of life. The world is now one big neighbourhood. There are no longer any hermit nations. National isolation is no longer possible in the earth. The markets of the world instantly register every commercial change. An earthquake in Asia is at once registered in Washington City. The people on one side of the world may not dare to be indifferent to the people on the other side. Every man of us is called to be a world citizen, and to think and act in world terms. The nation that insists upon asking that old murderous question of Cain, "Am I my brother's keeper?", the question of the profiteer and the question of the slacker, is a nation marked for decay and doom and death. The parable of the good Samaritan is heaven's law for nations as well as for individuals. Some things are worth dying for, and if they are worth dying for they are worth living for. The poet was right when he sang:

> *Though love repine and reason chafe,*
> *There comes a voice without reply,*
> *'Tis man's perdition to be safe,*
> *When for the truth he ought to die.*

Things Worth Dying For

When this nation went into the world war a little while ago, after her long and patient and fruitless effort to find another way of conserving righteousness, the note was sounded in every nook and corner of our country that some things in this world are worth dying for, and if they are worth dying for they are worth living for. What are some of the things worth dying for? The sanctity of womanhood is worth dying for. The safety of childhood is worth dying for, and when Germany put to death that first helpless Belgian child she was marked for defeat and doom. The integrity of one's country is worth dying for. And, please God, the freedom and honour of the United States of America are worth dying for. If the great things of life are worth dying for, they are surely worth living for. Our great country may not dare to isolate herself from the rest of the world, and selfishly say: "We propose to live and to die to ourselves, leaving all the other nations with their weaknesses and burdens and sufferings to go their ways without our help." This nation cannot pursue any such policy and expect the favour of God. Myriads of voices, both from the living and the dead, summon us to a higher and better way. Happy am I to believe that God has his prophets not only in the pulpits of the churches but also in the school room, in the editor's chair, in the halls of legislation, in the marts of commerce, in the realms of literature. Tennyson was a prophet, when in "Locksley Hall," he sang:

> *For I dipped into the future, far as human eye could see,*
> *Saw the vision of the world, and all the wonder that would be;*
>
> *Saw the heavens filled with commerce, argosies of magic sails,*
> *Pilots of the purple twilight, dropping down with costly bales;*
>
> *Heard the heavens filled with shouting, and there rained a ghastly dew*
> *From the nation's airy navies, grappling in the central blue;*
>
> *Far along the world-wide whisper of the south wind rushing warm,*
> *With the standards of the people plunging through the thunder storm.*
>
> *Till the war drums throbbed no longer, and the battle-flags were furled,*
> *In the Parliament of Man, the Federation of the World.*

A League of Nations

Tennyson believed in a league of nations, and well might he so believe, because God is on his righteous throne, and inflexible are his purposes touching righteousness and peace for a weary, sinning, suffering, dying world. Standing here today on the steps of our Nation's capitol, hard by the chamber of the Senate of the United States, I dare to say as a citizen and as a Christian teacher, that the moral forces of the United States of America, without regard to political parties, will never rest until there is a worthy League of Nations. I dare to express also the unhesitating belief that the unquestioned majorities of both great political parties in this country regard the delay in the working out of a League of Nations as a national and world-wide tragedy.

I can certify the men of all political parties, without any reference to partisan politics, that the same moral and religious forces of this country, because of the inexorable moral issues involved, cannot be silent and will not be silent until there is put forth a League of Nations that will strive with all its might to put an end to the diabolism and measureless horrors of war. I thank God that the stricken man yonder in the White House has pleaded long and is pleading yet that our nation will take her full part with the others for the bringing in of that blessed day when wars shall cease to the ends of the earth.

The recent World War calls to us with a voice surpassingly appealing and responsible. Surely Alfred Noyes voices the true desire for us:

> *Make firm, O God, the peace our dead have won,*
> *For folly shakes the tinsel on its head,*
> *And points us back to darkness and to hell,*
> *Cackling, 'Beware of visions,' while our dead*
> *Still cry, 'It was for visions that we fell.'*
>
> *They never knew the secret game of power,*
> *All that this earth can give they thrust aside,*
> *They crowded all their youth into an hour,*
> *And for fleeting dream of right, they died.*
>
> *Oh, if we fail them in that awful trust,*
> *How should we bear those voices from the dust?*

The Right Kind of Christians

This noble doctrine and heritage of religious liberty calls to us imperiously to be the right kind of Christians. Let us never forget that a democracy, whether civil or religious, has not only its perils, but has also its unescapable obligations. A democracy calls for intelligence. The sure foundations of states must be laid, not in ignorance, but in knowledge. It is of first importance that those who rule shall be properly trained. In a democracy, a government of the people, for the people, and by the people, the people are the rulers, and the people, all the people, are to be informed and trained.

My fellow Christians, we must hark back to our Christian schools, and see to it that these schools are put on worthy and enduring foundations. A democracy needs more than intelligence; it needs Christ. He is the light of the world, nor is there any other sufficient light for the world. He is the solution of the world's complex questions, the one adequate helper for its dire needs, the one only sufficient Saviour for our sinning race. Our schools are afresh to take note of this supreme fact, and they are to be fundamentally and aggressively Christian. Wrong education brought on the recent World War. Such education will always lead to disaster.

Pungent were the recent words of Mr. Lloyd George: "The most formidable foe that we had to fight in Germany was not the arsenals of Krupp, but the schools of Germany." The educational center of the world will no longer be in the Old World, but because of the great War, such center will henceforth be in this New World of America. We must build here institutions of learning that will be shot through and through with the principles and motives of Christ, the one Master over all mankind.

The Christian School

The time has come when, as never before, our beloved denomination should worthily go out to its world task as a teaching denomination. That means that there should be a crusade throughout all our borders for the vitalizing and strengthening of our Christian schools. The only complete education, in the nature of the case, is Christian education, because man is a tripartite being. By the very genius of our government, education by the state cannot be complete. Wisdom has fled from us if we fail to magnify, and magnify now, our Christian schools. These schools go to the foundation of all the life of the people. They are indispensable to the highest efficiency of the churches. Their inspirational influences are of untold value to the schools conducted by the state, to which schools also we must ever give our best support. It matters very much, do you not agree, who shall be the leaders, and what the standards in the affairs of civil government and in the realm of business life? One recalls the pithy saying of Napoleon to Marshal Ney: "An army of deer led by a lion is better than an army of lions led by a deer." Our Christian schools are to train not only our religious leaders but hosts of our leaders in the civil and business realms as well.

The one transcending, inspiring influence in civilization is the Christian religion. By all means, let the teachers and trustees and student bodies of all our Christian schools remember this important fact, that civilization without Christianity is doomed. Let there be no pagan ideals in our Christian schools, and no hesitation or apology for the insistence that the one hope for the individual, the one hope for society, for civilization, is in the Christian religion. If ever the drumbeat of duty sounded clearly, it is calling to us now to strengthen and magnify our Christian schools.

The Task of Evangelism

Preceding and accompanying the task of building our Christian schools, we must keep faithfully and practically in mind the primary task of evangelism, the work of winning souls from sin unto salvation, from Satan unto God. This work takes precedence of all other work in the Christian program. Salvation for sinners is through Jesus Christ alone, nor is there any other name or way under heaven whereby they may be saved. Our churches, our schools, our religious papers, our hospitals, every organization and agency of the churches should be kept aflame with the passion of New Testament evangelism. Our cities and towns and villages and country places are to echo continually with the sermons and songs of the gospel evangel. The people, high and low, rich and poor, the foreigners, all the people are to be faithfully told of Jesus and his great salvation, and entreated to come unto him to be saved by him and to become his fellow workers. The only sufficient solvent for all the questions in America, individual, social, economic, industrial, financial, political, educational, moral, and religious, is to be found in the Saviourhood and Lordship of Jesus Christ.

> *Give us a watchword for the hour,*
> *A thrilling word, a word of power;*
> *A battle cry, a flaming breath,*
> *That calls to conquest or to death;*
> *A word to rouse the church from rest,*
> *To heed its Master's high behest,*
> *The call is given, Ye hosts, arise;*
> *Our watchword is Evangelize!*
>
> *The glad Evangel now proclaim,*
> *Through all the earth in Jesus' name,*
> *This word is ringing through the skies,*
> *Evangelize! Evangelize!*
> *To dying men, a fallen race,*
> *Make known the gift of gospel grace;*
> *The world that now in darkness lies,*
> *Evangelize! Evangelize!*

While thus caring for the homeland, we are at the same time to see to it that our program is co-extensive with Christ's program for the whole world. The whole world is our field, nor may we, with impunity, dare to be indifferent to any section, however remote, not a whit less than that, and with our plans sweeping the whole earth, we are to go forth with believing faith and obedient service, seeking to bring all humanity, both near and far, to the faith and service of him who came to be the propitiation for our sins, and not for ours only, but also for the sins of the whole world.

His commission covers the whole world and reaches to every human being. Souls in China, and India, and Japan, and Europe, and Africa, and the islands of the sea, are as precious to him as souls in the United States. By the love we bear our Saviour, by the love we bear our fellows, by the greatness and preciousness of the trust committed to us, we are bound to take all the world upon our hearts and to consecrate our utmost strength to bring all humanity under the sway of Christ's redeeming love. Let us go to such task, saying with the immortal Wesley, "The world is my parish," and with him may we also be able to say, "And best of all, God is with us."

Let us look again to the strange passion and power of the early Christians. They paid the price for spiritual power. Mark well this record: "And they overcame him by the blood of the Lamb, and by the word of their testimony; and they loved not their lives unto the death." O my fellow Christians, if we are to be in the true succession of the mighty days and deeds of the early Christian era, or of those mighty days and deeds of our Baptist fathers in later days, then selfish ease must be utterly renounced for Christ and his cause, and our every gift and grace and power must be utterly dominated by the dynamic of his cross. Standing here in the shadow of our country's capitol, compassed about as we are with so great a cloud of witnesses, let us today renew our pledge to God, and to one another, that we will give our best to church and state, to God and to humanity, by his grace and power, until we fall on the last sleep.

If in such spirit we give ourselves to all the duties that await us, then we may go our ways, singing more vehemently than our fathers sang them, those lines of Whittier:

> *Our fathers to their graves have gone,*
> *Their strife is passed, their triumphs won;*
> *But greater tasks await the race*
> *Which comes to take their honoured place,*
> *A moral warfare with the crime*
> *And folly of an evil time.*

The Inspiration of Ideals

So let it be, in God's own sight,
We gird us for the coming fight;
And strong in him whose cause is ours,
In conflict with unholy powers,
We grasp the weapons he has given,
The light and truth and love of heaven."

CHAPTER VI

The Greatness of Service

CHAPTER VI

The Greatness of Service*

> "But it shall not be so among you; but whosoever will be great among you, let him be your minister; and whosoever will be chief among you, let him be your servant: even as the Son of man came not to be ministered unto, but to minister, and to give His life a ransom for many." — MATTHEW 20:26-28

THIS scripture is a part of the words spoken by our Lord, as a tender and faithful rebuke against the spirit that He saw manifested among His disciples. It was the spirit of rivalry among them as to who should be the greatest. Again and again the Master had need to rebuke His disciples, for the self-seeking spirit that He beheld among them. Only a little while before this occasion of our text, there was another occasion when they gathered about Him and inquired of Him: "Who is the greatest in the kingdom of heaven?" You remember the method of His reply. He set in the midst of them a little child and said: "Whosoever, therefore, shall humble himself as this little child, the same is the greatest in the kingdom of heaven."

Again is their self-seeking painfully apparent upon that solemn occasion of the Master's institution of the Supper, only a few hours before His betrayal and death. In that

---
* An early message delivered during an anniversary occasion at the Baylor College for Women located at Belton, Texas, which institution is now known as Mary-Hardin Baylor College.

solemn presence He told them of what was soon to befall Him, of the sore conflict He must wage, and the unspeakable shame and sorrow and suffering He must soon endure. Sorrowful as was that occasion, and sad though their hearts were, yet the demon of selfishness vaulted in every one of their bosoms, "and there was also a strife among them, which of them should be accounted the greatest." Oh, isn't it a pitiable revelation of the frailty and selfishness of our poor humanity? From every one of their hearts rushed the question: "Lord, who of us shall have the pre-eminence, the control and direction of affairs when Thou shalt have left us?" You recall His reply in the example of unparalleled humility that He then and there exemplified, in the washing with His own hands of the disciples' feet.

In the passage from Matthew which I read just now, there is presented to us a mother, who, in conjunction with her two sons, petitions the Master that these two sons may sit, the one on His right hand and the other on His left hand, in that kingdom of power and glory about which He had talked and which He had come to establish. You will observe that in each of these three instances Jesus does not directly condemn the spirit of ambition, but rather does He seek to guide aright this desire for position and power, and to point out the basis of all true greatness. Ambition is a natural instinct of mankind. It belongs alike to the cultured and uncultured. It obtains among Christian men as well as those who are not Christians.

And so the aspiration for power is not what our Lord is here condemning, He is pointing out the kind of aspiration that has reference to God's glory and the satisfying of human need, in contradistinction to that ever harmful ambition that looks for place and power merely for the sake of self. Let not true ambition be decried. Rightly directed, it is the greatest stimulus in the world to noble endeavor. The teacher would have poor success if his pupil had no higher ambition than to stay at the foot of the class. No lofty heights were ever scaled by one contented merely to keep along on a plane with the achievements of his comrades. The mother would have poor success in the rearing of her children to honorable manhood and womanhood, if she could inspire within them no concern as to the outcome of their lives. Well is it that the mother's heart is stirred with ambition for her child, for within the mother's grasp and power are elements of opportunity committed to no one else in the world. Happy is it when the mother can pass beyond the thought of mere promotion or distinction, and have as her chief concern that her child shall be worthy of such promotion and distinction.

It is evident from Matthew's narrative that the ambition of the mother for her two sons was largely selfish; and here, as is everywhere true, selfishness causes worry and sorrow and disturbance. Just as soon as the other ten of the apostolic company heard of the request presented to the Master, for the promotion for James and John, indignation filled their hearts, for the simple reason that they desired the same place themselves. The ambition of the two was so self-centered that they disregarded the feelings and ignored all the rights of their comrades. Such always is the course of selfishness, and and always in its wake there comes disturbance and trouble.

Selfishness is the essence of all sin. It is the parent from which comes every sin that makes woe and grief and ruin for our race. Human history, in large part, is but the history of the havoc wrought by selfishness. This it was that blasted Eden and passed death upon all the children of man. It crimsoned the earth with the blood of its first murder. Selfishness is the parent of every temptation. It creates every civil dissension in the community or state. It kindles every war that marks the world with devastation and death. Yea, more, it is the maker of every alienation and grief that have afflicted the children of God. There was immediate trouble in the ranks of the Lord's apostles, when it was descried that selfishness had been getting in its work.

It was directly against the self-seeking spirit the the revolutionary words of our text were uttered by our Lord. In such utterance He declared the truceless, unceasing, uncompromising war evermore to be waged by Christianity against selfishness. Sin always and everywhere is selfishness. Christianity always and everywhere is unselfishness. "The Son of Man came not to be ministered unto, but to minister, and to give His life a ransom for many." These are creative words. They are as foreign to the spirit of the world as day is to night. They are the epitome of the whole motive and mission of Christianity. They declare war to the death against all the selfish opinions and customs of men. At the very threshhold of His Kingdom, Jesus meets every man with the unyielding declaration: "If any man will come after me let him deny himself, and take up his cross and follow me. For whosoever will save his life shall lose it; and whosoever will lose his life for My sake shall find it."

We find here also Christ's revolutionary declaration of what constitutes true greatness. It is always, and in all things, unselfish service for others. Spirit Divine, teach us this one lesson today! It is not the talents one has that make him great, however many and brilliant they may be; it is not the vast amount of study that gives mental enrichment to the mind and life; it is not in shining social qualities; it is not the large accumulation of wealth that secures place and honor; in none of these measured by God's standard, does true greatness reside. But true greatness consists in the use of all the talents one has in unselfish ministry to others. All power is under obligation; it is a debtor to others.

Paul recognized this great vital truth of Christianity, when he said: "I am debtor both to the Greeks and to the barbarians, both to the wise and the unwise." If you have a single gift or talent or element of opportunity, to that degree

THE GREATNESS OF SERVICE

you are in debt to men and to God. All power owes. Financial power is everywhere a debtor. So is it with social power, intellectual power, spiritual power. All power is to be used in ministry to others. Education may be gained and hoarded as truly in the spirit of the miser, as is money often gained and gloated over by its covetous owner. Let the great truth find all our hearts today, that all power, of whatever varying degree and character, is under obligation to God and to men. Obedience to this basal Christian truth leads to happiness and safety. Disobedience to it leads to anarchy and death. Service, then, to others, so far from being degrading, is the patent to the only true nobility.

From first to last of God's revealed Word to men, He teaches us on every page, that the men and women who have been and will be the regnant forces of the world, are those who have rejoiced and will rejoice in the title of "servant." Scan the Divine pages and this is the record of the kingly men of the earth: Abraham, the father of the faithful, is everywhere spoken of as God's servant. Moses, from whose brain came the great principles of law, government and religion, that for all the ages shall dominate the world, is everywhere described as a servant. So it was with David, the sweet singer of Israel. So it was with the prophet Elijah. So it was with the intrepid and faithful Daniel. So with Peter, who subscribes himself "the servant of Jesus Christ." So with the incomparable Paul, who gloried in saying: "Whose I am and whom I serve." But, passing by all these patriarchs, prophets, apostles, behold the Son of God Himself stands in the midst of men with the amazing proposition: "I am among you as One that serveth. I came not to be ministered unto, but to minister, and to give my life as a ransom for many."

This, then, is the truth for us all faithfully to ponder today, that there is no greatness in God's sight, save in the unselfish use of all our powers for the well being of others. Humanity's highest conception of God — what is it? Not His omnipotence, not His omniscience, not His omnipresence, not His eternity, not His incomparable majesty and glory, but our highest conception of Him is when we conceive of Him as opening His hands to dispense His favors upon creation everywhere dependent upon Him. Then it is that our hearts bow with the psalmist in lowliest reverence and love and with him we sing: "The eyes of all wait on Thee. Thou givest them their meat in due season."

It is this conception that gives infinite attraction to Jesus of Nazareth. Not His miracles, not His triumph over the grave, but the laying down of His life in unselfish sacrifice for others — this is the mighty magnet that draws the world to Christ. His resurrection appeals to the mind. His cross is an appeal to the heart; and no one ever truly saw that cross that it did not break his heart. Why? Because it was the world's sublimest incarnation of unselfish love. All the charms of the cross would be dispelled if selfishness could be detected in the Master's life and sacrifice. His was the ideal character; His was the one perfect life among men; but the glory of His life and character is found in his words! "I came not to be ministered unto, but to minister." At all times and in all His relations among men the one purpose of His life was enunciated in the words: "I am among you as one that serveth."

It is also true among men, that man's unselfish service to his brother gains the highest element of admiration and power. He who lives only for himself is everywhere despised. He who gives his life in helpfulness to others is everywhere trusted and loved and followed. It is always true that the men who are ever studying to exalt themselves are the men whom others never wish to exalt. The schemer for self is on the road to suicide, while the wondrous paradox appears that the man whose life is lived in forgetfulness of self is the man whom the multitudes seek and will find and follow.

THE GREATNESS OF SERVICE

That last sentence on the tomb of General Gordon, in St. Paul's cathedral, holds the key to his great life: "Who at all times and everywhere gave his strength to the weak, his substance to the poor, his sympathy to the suffering, and his heart to God." Ah! was it any wonder that the Chinese listened to him as though he were a messenger from the skies, and that the poor besotted African tribes actually believed that he had come from the land above the stars? A life of such sublime self-forgetfulness, in its devotion to the wants of others is a sweet, grand song in the storm and shipwreck of earth.

A few years ago a prominent English earl passed away, and at the news of his death the whole civilized world dropped tears of sympathy and love. For what reasons? Was it because he was a man of talents, and had marked celebrity as a statesman and was rich with worldly wealth? Nay, not so, though all these were his. These tears were shed because the distinguished Englishman recognized the sublime meaning of service to others. He gave his time and talents and money to the multitudes. Thousands of orphan children and little bootblacks were gathered by him into societies for their improvement, and he himself was never so happy as when presiding at their anniversary meetings. Added to this gracious service the earl toiled on for years and years, until at last, through equitable laws, he secured the emancipation of half a million of factory women and children from the killing oppression under which they groaned. No wonder that thousands of children sobbed in the streets when the body of this great benefactor was laid in the grave. He was infinitely greater ministering to these hosts of needy women and children, than was Alexander looking upon a world conquered and crouching at his feet and weeping because there were no more worlds that he might conquer.

Dr. Chalmers was a marvelous man when he lectured to his Divinity students; he was great when, in his matchless eloquence, he spoke to vast audiences throughout the length and

The Inspiration of Ideals

breadth of Scotland; but he was greatest of all, when, in his own city of Edinburgh, he might be seen daily going through alleys and lanes with groups of ragged children clinging to his fingers and coat as he gathered them into training schools for their benefit.

Not long ago there passed away a great statesman of the world — Gladstone — the sage of Hawarden. Grappling with the problems of political economy and government, he was unrivalled. A whole world delights to do him homage. And the greatness of Mr. Gladstone was lodged in the moral might of an unselfish character. What Christian eye is not moist with tears as he reads of the visits of this world-famed statesman to the very poorest of his community, that he might read to them God's Word, and then prayerfully commend them to the peace and power of His grace? Ah, here is he most like his Lord: "Whosoever will be chief among you, let him be your servant." This is the spirit that has caused the wilderness to blossom as the rose. Out of this spirit has come every Christian college and orphanage and beneficent work of the world. And this is the spirit that, in the Divine purpose and providence, shall yet revolutionize a selfish world, and present it to Christ as the trophy of His self-giving sacrifice and love.

Sacrifice is the law of all true progress. Before the attainment of any noble goal there is and ever will be somewhat of a Gethsemane and a Golgotha. It is not an infrequent thing to meet with those who sneer at the vicarious element in the atoning death of Jesus Christ. The cross of Jesus is but an empty shell, if He did not vicariously die to expiate the sins of men. It is through the vicarious element that we are today the heirs of all that is noble and good among men. No life is ever rich, save through the sacrifice of another. The great principles of liberty of thought and liberty of speech are vouchsafed to us today, through the vicarious sufferings and sacrifices of those before us. If the vicarious element in life is to be blotted out, go yonder to Washing-

THE GREATNESS OF SERVICE

ton's monument, in the nation's capital, and tear it down. Tear down every shaft in all the states that mark the resting-place of the nation's sons who fell in her defense. They speak of vicarious sufferings and sacrifices in the securing of all the rich treasures, civil and religious, to which we are heirs today.

The history of all real progress, financially, socially, intellectually, morally, religiously, is the story of toil and sacrifice and suffering. Once the cities of Italy were devastated by plagues that swept the people by myriads into the grave. Is there no relief to be had? Yes, John Howard will sacrifice himself to stay the plagues. He sails on an infected ship from Constantinople to Venice, has himself put into a lazaretto, that he might thus find the clue to the mystery and stay the power of the death-dealing plagues.

Within ten years after Livingstone's death, Africa had made more real progress than in the ten centuries before. This, as all the world knows, was because Livingstone gave all his energies to the destruction of the slave trade. Wearied and afflicted, he toiled on to the last, until he fell in an African jungle to rise no more. Yet with his dying hand he wrote this message to the world: "All I can add in my solitude is, may Heaven's rich blessings come down on every one who would help to heal this open sore of the world." Yes, the vicarious element explains the secret of Livingstone's marvelous life and power.

And so it will be seen that sacrifice is the way of all progress. In all the natural world there is giving, sacrifice, death, in order to increase expansion and growth of life. Equally true is this in the world of the mind. And inexorably true it is spiritually, as the Divine Word proclaims from the first to last: "Except a corn of wheat fall into the ground and die, it abideth alone: but if it die, it bringeth forth much fruit." "Whosoever will save his life shall lose it: but whosoever will lose his life for My sake, the same shall save it."

The Inspiration of Ideals

Moreover, this self-giving devotion and service to others, is our only safety. To live for self is surely to die. Selfishness kills as surely as scalding water poured down the throat or the deadly bullet discharged into the body. No man can live long who would live to himself. It will as effectually consume the life, as rust consumes the iron. Oh, I beg you to know it, dear friends, that selfishness is death to all that is beautiful and useful and good in human life. It puts harshness and discord into the singer's voice. It takes away the intensity and conviction of the orator's lips. Struggle though he may to conceal it, yet its coarseness and deformity and disregard of others, will sooner or later appear in the character and conduct of every possessor. Forget not that there is one way only whereby life may be saved, and that is to lose it in service to others. "The Lord turned the captivity of Job when he prayed for his friends."

Had the widow of Zarephath refused to feed the hungry Elijah, then the handful of meal in the barrel and the little oil in the cruse would have sufficed for only one day for herself and her son. But in self-forgetfulness, she thought upon the needs of the stranger, and cheerfully divided her pittance of food with him, and lo! she was supplied with all necessary food through the long, trying days of the famine. The Chinese tell the suggestive legend: An old-time potter long and earnestly strove to give his vases a certain beautiful tint, but it was all in vain. At last, in desperation, he threw himself into the furnace; and when the pottery was taken out, see! there was the beautiful color upon it. This is a true parable. Earth's most beautiful thing is a noble character, and no character can receive its fairest coloring until self is wholly given up to secure it.

We are so prone to look upon the sin of omission as a trivial one, compared with the sin of commission. And yet Jesus in His marvelous picture of the judgment makes the condemnation of men to turn upon their not doing the things

The Greatness of Service

they ought to have done. He speaks of food for the hungry, clothing for the naked, visiting of the sick, and messages of comfort to the prisoner. He puts Himself into the place of all these, and teaches us that neglect of them is also personal neglect of Him. "Inasmuch as ye did it not to one of the least of these my brethren, ye did it not unto Me." Do we sometimes wish that our lives had been given us, while the Master was on the earth? Is it true that we would have had no other delight than in serving Him in every duty and relation He should have given us? Mrs. Preston meets this same question in one of her beautiful poems:

> "*If I had dwelt — so mused a tender woman,*
>   *All fine emotions stirred*
> *Through pondering o'er that Life, Divine, yet human,*
>   *Told in the Sacred Word —*
> "*If I had dwelt of old, a Jewish maiden,*
>   *In some Judean street*
> *Where Jesus walked, and heard His word so laden*
>   *With comfort strangely sweet;*
> *And seen the face, where utmost pity blended*
>   *With each rebuke of wrong —*
> *I would have left my lattice and descended*
>   *And followed with the throng.*
>
> "*'Foxes have holes' — methinks my heart had broken*
>   *To hear the words so said,*
> *While Christ had not — were sadder words e'er spoken?*
>   *A place to lay His head!*
> *I would have flung abroad my doors before Him*
>   *And in my joy have been*
> *First on the threshold, eager to adore Him,*
>   *And crave His entrance in.*"
>
> *Ah! Would you so? Without a recognition*
>   *You passed him yesterday;*
> *Jostled aside, unhelped, His mute petition,*
>   *And calmly went your way,*
> *With warmth and comfort, garmented and girdled.*
>   *Before your window sill*
> *Sad crowds swept by — and if your blood is curdled,*
>   *You wear your jewels still.*

THE INSPIRATION OF IDEALS

You catch aside your robes lest want should clutch them
In its imploring wild;
Or lest some penitent might touch them,
And you be thus defilled.
Oh! dreamer, dreaming that your faith is keeping
All service free from blot,
Christ daily walks your streets, sick, suffering, weeping,
And you perceive Him not!

"Whosoever shall give to drink unto one of these little ones a cup of cold water only in the name of a disciple, verily I say unto you, he shall in no wise lose his reward." This is the divine precept and example, and it invests every life with a sacredness that we dare not disregard. All our fine-spun theories about our duty to others are to be thrown to the winds, if they do not lead us into ways of ministry like unto our blessed Lord, who ever went about doing good. It was a righteous thing when Cromwell, the lion-hearted reformer, tore down the silver statues that he found, of the twelve apostles, converted them into money, and sent it out in helpfulness to the needy multitudes. No man's heart ever truly loved God whose heart did not also yearn to be helpful to his fellows.

Since unselfish ministry to others is, in God's sight, the synonym for true greatness, since such is His rule of exaltation in the heavenly kingdom, then, my mothers and sisters, I hail you happy, for you shall have the fairest crown in the kingdom of God. Faithful, patient, devoted woman, she shall be first, because her ministry of service is the noblest and best. They talk about this as the age of invention and discovery and natural progress and education of the masses, and such it is. But far beyond all these, this age has been crowned with distinction and glory by woman's ministry in the culture and mission of Christianity. Have you paused to consider the great yet powerful part she plays in the affairs of our great republic today? Three-hundred thousand of the teachers in our public schools are women. Over fifty thousand of

The Greatness of Service

the present year's students in colleges and universities are women. Over two-thirds of the membership of our churches are women. And constantly enlarging influence for good shall be hers as the years pass on.

> *They talk about a woman's sphere,*
> *As though it had a limit;*
> *There's not a place in earth or heaven,*
> *There's not a task to mankind given,*
> *There's not a blessing or a woe,*
> *There's not a whisper, yes or no,*
> *There's not a life, or death, or birth,*
> *That has a feather's weight or worth,*
> *Without a woman in it.*

I do not need to argue in this presence that woman's ministry for the future shall be gracious as in the present and past, through the quiet, unobstrusive, yet incomparable consecration of her graces and talents. We shall not change from the old-fashioned notion, because it grows out of the Divine purpose, that woman's ministry shall be most gracious when least conformed to masculinity. The motto in the home of Shaftesbury was these two words: "Love; serve." It told the story of his philanthropic life. So fully did he give his life in service to the English people, that innumerable thousands were in his funeral cortege, and they carried banners, on which was written: "I was sick and in prison, and ye visited me. I was hungry and naked and ye clothed me and fed me." The spirit of this motto, ever carried out in the quiet unobtrusiveness peculiar to the feminine nature, shall always be woman's throne of power and her crown of glory. Is there any influence to compare with hers in her delicate, soothing ministry to the suffering? Her history in such a sphere, though generally not found in a country's annals, because it cannot be put into words, is the most thrillingly beautiful ministry of all the earth.

Yonder business man, anxious and consumed with cares financial, forgets the ministry of mother and sister and wife,

THE INSPIRATION OF IDEALS

until sickness seizes him in its sudden grasp, and then with quivering lips he begs them to carry him to the loving ministry of home. The college lad is stirred with pride to be away from home, for no longer can it be said that he is tied to his mother's apron strings; but one day, when sickness shall grasp him, with feverish anxiety he will beg to be taken where there is home and mother. Every heart is touched by that tender narrative in the Bible, of the lad stricken in the harvest field at Shunem; and when in awful pain his hands clasp his temples, what natural words were said: "Carry him to his mother." And then how tender the later record: "He sat on her knee until noon and died."

Let desolating war sweep over the land, and before the echo of arms has died away in the combat between contending armies, woman, like an angel of mercy, walks that field of carnage; and as she goes, she takes water and medicines for the fainting and suffering soldiers; and as they suffer and weep and die, she pencils their dying messages to the absent loved ones, and with prayer, and promise from God's Word, points them to the all-compassionate sufferer of Calvary, and the eternal mansions awaiting all who trust Him, beyond earth's suffering and night.

There are some great reformations yet to be wrought in society — customs of long standing, yet nevertheless harmful, and woman only can secure these reforms. Her social responsibilities are measureless; society with its triviality and worldliness and masquerade will not be changed until woman bravely leads in the great reform. God help her to lead in this redemption of much of our social life from wasted time and frivolous pleasures, and evil working indulgencies! But the circle in which woman shall do her truest, noblest, most lasting work, is in the home, as mother, daughter, sister, and wife. O my sisters, here is your throne, and from this throne you may shape the destiny of the world. Disregard of the home life is always the precursor of swift coming doom.

THE GREATNESS OF SERVICE

France went down into the dust very soon after the home was ignored and forgotten. O women, give a sacred home life to your fathers and sons and husbands and brothers, and thereby will you mould and conserve all their future! But know today that you are not fitted for this sublime task until you have bowed at the feet of the Divine Redeemer, and committed unto Him your mind, your heart, your all.

Is there a woman in this presence today who has not yet received the crucified one as her personal Saviour? Oh, receive Him today! Believe on Him now and let love and service for Him have full possession of your heart! Someone has well said that "Man without religion is at best a poor reprobate, a football of destiny; but woman without religion is worse. She is a flame without heat, a rainbow without color, and a flower without perfume."

To these young women before me, I give the earnest exhortation that they take to their hearts the glorious meaning of every life which is forgotten in unselfish thoughtfulness for others. Dorcas, with her needle, will be immortal when Napoleon is heard of no more, forever. Mary, with her alabaster box, will live on and on when Alexander's memory shall have been buried in eternal oblivion. Go, my young sisters, into the waiting world with heads and hearts and hands, intent upon having as the ruling motive of your lives that which was first your Lord's — "not to be ministered unto, but to minister." And when you come to the end of the earthly pilgrimage, may His glory rest upon you, and may each of you receive this plaudit from His blessed lips: "Well done, thou good and faithful servant, enter thou into the joy of thy Lord."

CHAPTER VII

Dr. J. B. Gambrell:
The Great Southern Baptist Commoner

CHAPTER VII

Dr. J. B. Gambrell:
The Great Southern Baptist Commoner*

THE duty that is mine today is surely one of the most difficult ever asked at my hands. If I should be allowed to follow my heart, I would now be sitting there beside the family, instead of standing here to speak some words concerning the remarkable life that has just been translated from the lower to the larger spaces of life above. I knew him for a long time, knew him more intimately than I knew any other preacher in all the world. In the good providence of God I have had the privilege for more than twenty years of being often and most intimately associated with him, this joyful, inspiring companion, this valiant, masterful leader, this humble, noble Christian. I have travelled with him thousands and even tens of thousands of miles. I have conferred with him, times without count, concerning the things inexpressibly dear to both our hearts. We have often knelt together in the quiet place, where no eye could see but the eye of the all-seeing Master, and sought His light and leading for ourselves and for our fellow-workers.

As you are privileged to know some conspicuous men with increasing intimacy they do not grow larger. As you are privileged to know some others, perhaps not many, they do loom larger the more you know them. We are called together

---
* Words spoken at the funeral service, First Baptist Church, Dallas, Texas, June 11, 1921.

The Inspiration of Ideals

today to pay the last offices of respect and love to one of the outstanding men of his generation. The more his fellows saw him and touched his life the more was their admiration called out for his remarkable gifts, both by nature and by grace. It seems incongruous and impossible for one so full of life as was he to come to a silent hour like this. You who knew him well are not surprised to hear that the sunset of his life was the crowning chapter of all his earthly pilgrimage.

During the brief months of his illness I was often with him, and during this past week it was my sacred privilege to be by his bedside daily. When he grew very much worse, a week ago today, I was privileged to tarry for a long time at his bedside, and thus it was my privilege to be with him from day to day until he went away yesterday. Day after day I came away from his bedside wondering how one with such a combination of rare wisdom and wholesome wit, of crowning optimism, of sparkling humour, of conquering faith, of compassionate love for mankind, of lofty vision, of wide-reaching outlook, of commanding purpose and program, could die. Nay, he is not dead, but lives on now in a larger sphere than ever before!

What gratitude is in our hearts that God let him stay with us so long! If he had tarried till the coming August he would have reached his fourscore years in the earthly pilgrimage. You can somewhat understand today, as can I, how Elisha felt when Elijah went away. As Elijah ascended into the heavens, beyond the gaze of Elisha, we can somewhat understand how the young prophet felt when he cried out, "My father, my father! the chariot of Israel and the horsemen thereof." How difficult it is for us to realize that we shall see his face no more in the flesh! Let us rejoice that memory will hold the reflection of his noble face, and hear the echo of his challenging voice, and feel the tonic of his conquering spirit.

Dr. J. B. Gambrell

On an occasion like this we must not allow ourselves to think only of our immeasurable loss, but rather must summon ourselves to turn our thoughts to the highest and worthiest. "I have fought the good fight, I have finished my course, I have kept the faith: henceforth there is laid up for me a crown of righteousness which the Lord, the righteous judge, shall give me at that day: and not to me only, but unto all them also that love his appearing."

We are always deeply interested in the last statements made by people as they go away from the earthly sphere. We are interested to know how they went and what they said when their feet came to that stream separating the two worlds. Very often life's ruling passion is predominant even at death. History furnishes us with countless instances. Even so, Paul's ruling passion came out strongly in the face of death. He spoke these great words about his own departure to Timothy, his son in the gospel. He advised the young man what to do about various matters, especially what to do about the supreme cause of all, Christ's cause. He gave the young man this solemn charge: "Preach the word, be instant in season, out of season; reprove, rebuke, exhort, with long-suffering and doctrine." He added this admonitory warning: "For the time will come when they will not endure sound doctrine, but after their own lusts shall they heap to themselves teachers having itching ears. And they shall turn away their ears from the truth, and shall be turned unto fables." He then exhorted Timothy in these pungent words: "But watch thou in all things, endure afflictions, do the work of an evangelist, make full proof of thy ministry." Then he spoke frankly of his departure from earth, and his reflections thereon, in these words: "For I am now ready to be offered, and the time of my departure is at hand. I have fought a good fight, I have finished my course, I have kept the faith: henceforth there is laid up for me a crown of righteousness which the Lord, the righteous judge, shall give me at that day."

The Inspiration of Ideals

How wonderful for Paul to talk like that and to feel like that when he came to the end! Mark how calmly he viewed death when he met it face to face. He spoke of the supremely vital things, and he looked on to the untried future without a fear.

It is exceedingly interesting to observe how the New Testament speaks of death. It doesn't often use that gloomy word "death." Paul talked of his "departure." That is what death is; just a departure, a change of residence. The Bible speaks of death under the metaphors of "sleep" and "rest." Paul calmly declared that he was ready for his departure, for his eternal change of residence. As he reviewed his earthly life, he said that he had three occasions for personal satisfaction. The first was that he had fought a good fight, or better, "*the* good fight." Paul was a warrior. From that eventful day on the Damascus road, when Jesus met Paul and fundamentally changed his life, until the day when the headsman's axe took Paul's head from his body, Paul was a warrior for the faith of Christ, for the betterment of humanity.

Paul, more than any other New Testament writer, represented the Christian life under the figure of conflict, of contest, of struggle, of battle. It was Paul who wrote, "Fight the good fight of faith." It was Paul who wrote, "This charge I commit unto thee, son Timothy, according to the prophecies which went before on thee, that thou by them mightest war a good warfare." It was Paul who wrote, "Put on the whole armour of God, that ye may be able to stand against the wiles of the devil." It was he who most earnestly warned us concerning the weaknesses of the flesh and the dangers from the many adversaries who lie in wait everywhere to harm and hinder Christians.

Now, as Paul looked back he said, "I have fought the good fight." That is to say, he had fought on the right side; he had fought for the right things; he had given his life for the right ends; he had put his life on the side of a cause which is humanity's hope. He had not fought this fight for self, for wealth, for personal notoriety, but that goodness might triumph over evil, that right might be given precedence over wrong, that humanity, enthralled and lost, might through God's grace be disenthralled and saved. Paul had fought in harmony with God's plan to make a better world. He had therefore not wasted his life, but saved it. He had lived for that cause which is supreme and which, in its every relation, is invested with eternal importance.

Paul said again, "I have finished my course." That is to say, he had kept on the right track. Here is the figure of the ancient athlete as he came to the race course, his every power girded for the running of the race, with the watchers on every side beholding the runner as he sped on toward the goal. Henry Drummond said, "God has a will concerning a man's character, and then He has a will concerning a man's career." From the day when Jesus met Paul on the Damascus road and said to him, "Why persecutest thou me?" the uppermost question ever asked thereafter by Paul was, "Lord, what wilt thou have me to do?" Through Paul's whole life, after his notable conversion, Paul was the mighty defender of Christ, the outstanding champion of the Christian faith, the highest product Christianity has ever produced, the greatest human credential the Christian religion has ever known. Paul literally lived to do Christ's will, to follow wherever He might lead. That was the one consuming passion of his life. "He always wins who sides with God." He always loses who goes against the will of God. Paul sought in all his goings to conform his life to the course mapped out for him by his divine Saviour and Lord.

Still again, as Paul reviewed his past, he said, "I have kept the faith." Paul looked upon Christ's gospel as a supreme entrustment, as an incomparable stewardship. He said, for himself, "I know whom I have believed, and am persuaded that He is able to keep that which I have committed unto Him, against that day." Then he gave this exhortation: "Hold fast the form of sound words, which thou hast heard of me, in faith and love, which is in Jesus Christ." In the very next sentence he urged: "That good thing which was committed unto thee, keep by the Holy Ghost, who dwelleth in us." Always and everywhere Paul was found confessing and defending the Christian faith. Thus did he speak of it: "For I delivered unto you first of all, that which I also received, how that Christ died for our sins, according to the Scriptures, and that he was buried, and that he rose again the third day, according to the Scriptures." Listen again to Paul's noble avowal: "I am not ashamed of the gospel of Christ: for it is the power of God unto salvation to every one that believeth." To the last hour of his earthly day Paul grandly illustrated in his own life his own saying, "It is required in stewards that a man be found faithful."

And now, let us turn away from this brief contemplation of Paul's life and departure and think of him who left us only yesterday. What a soldier for Jesus Christ was J. B. Gambrell from the days of his youth! For something like threescore years he followed Christ. He spoke for Christ, he wrote for Christ, he thought for Christ, he lived to extend and uphold the teachings of Christ. He linked his very life with the mission and message of Christ and went forth as Christ's fellow-worker to aid in bringing in that kingdom which is humanity's one sufficient hope. You and I have never seen a more prodigious toiler than was our great brother who now rests from his labours. Whenever and wherever we saw him his brain and heart and hands were filled with plans for Christ's cause, and he was seeking to make such plans effective everywhere. Like Paul, he kept on the main track. He did not allow his life to be consumed with incidental or secondary consideration. Every man who knew him could not but be persuaded that he literally lived to carry out the will of

Dr. J. B. Gambrell

Christ. He could say with Paul, "To me to live is Christ." And then again as the champion of Christ, as the champion of the vital verities of Christ's gospel, this man stood out against the horizon as an almost incomparably inspiring example for his own and succeeding generations.

Speaking yet more personally, one does not have to be at pains to observe the outstanding characteristics that marked the life of Dr. Gambrell, our valiant leader, and brother, and friend. They were known and read by all who knew him. First of all he, was a genuine man. The first thing about anybody is his character. What one is counts for far more than what he says or does. You could not associate anything petty or little or mean with this noble Christian soul. He was a true man. His mind travelled in a straight line, like the light. There was nothing devious about his habits of thought or speech. Sincerity was about his whole life like a well-fitting garment, and sincerity is the fundamental virtue in life. Life is a ghastly falsehood if one be not sincere. He was a true man, without sham or shoddy, whose motives and character were as transparent as the sunlight.

To him the word duty stood out as the majestic and commanding word of life. He thought of the meaning of that word duty as the word was originally spelled — due-ty. Duty is what one is due. Duty is what one owes. Duty is the sense of obligation. This man had the highest sense of obligation in all the relations of life, in his home life, in his community life, in civic life, in religious life, in all life. Duty was to him the most majestic word in the lexicon of life.

He was a man of profound and positive convictions. I have met many men and conferred with them concerning the deep things of the human heart, but I have never met one whose convictions concerning the verities of character, conduct, and destiny were more pronounced than his. What a glorious believer he was! He believed in God. He believed

The Inspiration of Ideals

in Christ as the one adequate helper for mankind. He believed with all his heart in the divine authenticity and integrity of the Bible. He believed in God's people. He believed, without wavering, in the ultimate and certain triumph of Christ's cause throughout all the earth. He said to me just four days ago: "There is not a cloud on my spiritual horizon; there are no doubtful questions; Christ is humanity's one adequate hope; He is my all-sufficient hope today, and to know and to do His will is the supreme longing of my heart."

What pronounced convictions he had concerning the Christian faith! He could say and did say with John, "I have no greater joy than to hear that my children walk in truth!" He believed that some things are unchangeably true and that others are just as unchangeably false. He had no sort of fellowship with the loose contention that some things are either true or false, according to one's viewpoint. He had no fellowship with such trifling with the truth. To him the pulpit was no place for a spiritual stammerer. He said, with the Psalmist, "I believed, therefore have I spoken." He said, with the apostles, "For we cannot but speak the things which we have seen and heard." It is impossible to estimate the value of a man who believes something with all his heart and holds to it against all odds, and summons his comrades to walk in the path of truth, wherever it may lead and whatever it may cost. "For if the trumpet give an uncertain sound, who shall prepare himself to the battle?"

While he was a man of such positive convictions, he was also a man of the largest charitableness toward men differing from him. He would have risen at the hour of midnight to plead for absolute religious liberty for every human being, whether of this creed or of that or of no creed at all. He did not contend for mere toleration, but rather for absolute liberty of conscience in the things of the soul. There is a vast difference between toleration and liberty. Toleration is a concession, while liberty is a right. Toleration is a matter of expediency, while liberty is a matter of principle. Toleration is a gift from man, while liberty is a gift from God. Our mighty champion of the faith of the New Testament, as he understood it and believed it, would have made any personal sacrifice to have defended the indefeasible right of any religionist or non-religionist, anywhere and everywhere, to have absolute freedom of conscience in matters of the soul. The value of a man who can discriminate like that, and believe like that, and go on his way witnessing as a prophet of the Christian faith, is immeasurable.

He was a man of universal sympathies. Especially did his sympathies whole-heartedly go out to the poor, the ignorant, the needy, the unfortunate. To illustrate: I have been with him many times when we would see the little Negro children at their play or on their way to school, and with great soulfulness he would say, "A blessing on all their little kinky heads." Likewise, I have seen his great heart overflow in behalf of the little Mexican children and his lips would move in prayer that God would be gracious to those little people. He said just the other day: "How can anybody be inconsiderate of a little child? When one thinks of the possibilities wrapped up in a little child, how can anyone be harsh and unkind in his relations to a little child?" This was the natural overflowing of what his heart felt and lived.

On the great seas last summer I found him time and again enlightening and enlivening with some inspiring story some humble worker or traveler on the steamer. Especially did his heroic soul burn like a conflagration whenever he saw or heard of the strong oppressing the weak. He practised Paul's ringing injunction, "We then that are strong ought to bear the infirmities of the weak, and not to please ourselves." To him it was unspeakably despicable that a strong man or a strong race would take advantage of the weak. All

The Inspiration of Ideals

that was but a revelation of his remarkable and glorious character.

He was a man of crowning optimism. He sounded no low notes. One never heard him teasing an audience with miserable jeremiads or with wailing dirges. No matter how dark the clouds on the horizon, he believed, with Paul, that Christ must reign until he hath put all enemies under his feet. He said just a few hours ago, when his feet were already slipping over the brink, "I am as certain that Christ will ultimately reign in all the affairs of men, unto the ends of the earth, as I am that tomorrow will come." He was a man of intrepid, dauntless optimism, because of his unshaken faith in Christ.

What a glorious Christian he was! At the same time, how human he was! He was not a formalist. He didn't parade his piety. His religion was not a method of life. His religion was life itself to him, engrossing him, encompassing him. It was the very atmosphere in which he lived, and until the very last hour that sunny soul, that triumphant spirit shone out, though at times his physical sufferings were intense. An apologetic like that at once answers a thousand cheap scepticisms forever. The best argument for a Christianity is the right kind of a Christian. You and I never saw a more vital Christian than was this man.

In his last brief months he had the exquisite joy of being at home with his loved ones. His tribute to them was such as might evoke the sweetest strains of earth's most gifted poet. And likewise his loved ones counted it a privilege which words cannot describe to do everything possible for his comfort as he battled on to the end.

How he loved this church! He has said so often concerning it: "It is a haven of rest and comfort to me, beyond all words." Out of his overflowingly generous heart he would say: "It is the best church I ever saw; the men and women in it stay by the supreme things for which a church exists; they refuse to be turned aside by inconsequential and secondary things."

Dr. J. B. Gambrell

Never did a pastor have a more inspiring auditor and fellow-helper. Surely we shall all ever keep before us his high ideals for a church and hide his benediction in our deepest hearts.

Sometimes, when his heart was laid bare to some of us, we wished to stand with uncovered heads and unsandalled feet before him as he gave his personal testimony about Christ. Again and again during the last weeks his loved ones heard him quoting Whittier's hymn, "At Last":

When on my day of life the night is falling,
   And in the winds from unsunned spaces blown,
I hear far voices out of darkness calling
   My feet to paths unknown;

Thou, who hast made my home of life so pleasant,
   Leave not its tenant when its walls decay;
O Love Divine, O Helper ever present,
   Be thou my strength and stay!

Be near me when all else is from me drifting,
   Earth, sky, home's pictures, day of shade and shine,
And kindly faces to my own uplifting
   The love which answers mine.

I have but Thee, my Father! let Thy Spirit
   Be with me then to comfort and uphold;
No gate of pearl, no branch of palm I merit,
   Nor street of shining gold.

Suffice it if, my good and ill unreckoned
   And both forgiven through Thy abounding grace,
I find myself by hands familiar beckoned
   Unto my fitting place.

Some humble door among Thy many mansions,
   Some sheltering shade where sin and striving cease,
And flows forever through heaven's green expansions
   The river of Thy peace.

There, from the music round about me stealing,
   I fain would learn the new and holy song;
And find at last, beneath Thy trees of healing,
   The life for which I long.

THE INSPIRATION OF IDEALS

Thank God! he has at last found that perfect life for which he longed in the larger spaces above! It rests our hearts today to think that this prodigious toiler will not be weary any more. Among his last audible words were these: "I am so tired; when shall we get to the end of the journey?" God be thanked, this faithful worker will never be tired again! It rests our hearts to remember that he is now with his loved companion, who preceded him to the yonder-land something like eleven years ago, that wonderful woman, fit companion for this wonderful man. Her death also was a transfiguration. I was also with her when she went away, and I have never heard a grander Christian testimony than was hers. These twain are united now, to be sundered no more forever. They are with their children and with other dear ones whom they loved long since and lost for a little while, but have found them again and are to be with them forever. It rests our hearts to think of this worker and friend, meeting again with many of his long-time friends and fellow-workers in the Father's house above.

For the past quarter of a century Texas has had a notable triumvirate of workers. It has been my blessed privilege to stand beside the bier of each of them and speak some final words, even as I am speaking today. There was B. H. Carroll, that incomparable preacher and Bible teacher. There was R. C. Buckner, that great heart, that man of practical philanthropy, that gentle friend of all mankind. There was J. B. Gambrell, practical preacher, veteran missionary leader, constructive editor and author, college president, teacher of theology, champion of evey good cause both in church and in state. What giants were these three men! Shall we ever see their like again? One's heart is moved beyond words as he thinks of them sitting together, this Saturday afternoon, talking about their fellowship when on earth, and talking, it may be, about how the rest of us are going to "carry on."

Dr. J. B. Gambrell

This is an hour for the faithful rededication of our all to Christ. Long or short as our earthly time may be, let us today be highly resolved henceforth to give our best to the cause of Christ. This is the life which is life indeed. "He that doeth the will of God abideth forever." To this end have we been born again and for this cause do we tarry here in the flesh, to do the will of God. Not a talent should be misused, not an hour should be wasted. One cause, and one cause only, is worth our dying for, worth our living for, worth our utmost and our all, and that cause is the cause of Christ. Today, tomorrow and forever may it be our consuming passion to do the will of God!

What shall I say as a final word, before the grave shall enclose all that is mortal of our departed leader and brother? I would hasten to say that we do not celebrate a defeat today, but a release, a triumph, a home-going, a coronation. "Precious in the sight of the Lord is the death of His saints." "To die is gain." "God buries the workman, but the work goes on." When Savonarola was about to die at the stake he strengthened his brethren with these words: "I am certain that if I must die, I shall be able to aid you in heaven more than I have been able to do on earth. The work of the Lord will ever go forward, and my death will only hasten it." In these words he uttered a large part of the philosophy of history. The mightiest men in the world's affairs today are not those who are yet with us, but those who have been taken from us. "And I heard a voice from heaven saying unto me, Write, Blessed are the dead who die in the Lord from henceforth: yea, saith the Spirit, that they may rest from their labours; and their works do follow them." J. B. Grambrell is not dead, he will never die! He lives on today, this leader and lover of mankind, this stalwart champion of the Christian faith, this faithful friend of God, he lives on, and he will henceforth live on, in a far larger sphere than ever before.

The Inspiration of Ideals

At eventide it was light for him. Now it is the eternal morning for him. He has heard his Master's plaudit, "Well done," and he has entered into his Master's joy. Until the day break and the shadows flee away, may our every memory of him quicken our faithfulness to Him who loved us and gave Himself for us.

CHAPTER VIII

C. H. Spurgeon Centenary

CHAPTER VIII

C. H. Spurgeon Centenary*

YOU will generously allow my first expression from this platform to be quite personal. The invitation extended me to be present on this notable occasion, and to give my humble testimony in connection with it, has touched my heart more deeply than has any other invitation that has ever been extended to me. The all too generous words spoken by the Prime Minister, concerning my presence here, add much to the intensity of my emotions. But I must go on and in frankness say that I am responding now to the invitation, with the most poignant sense of my unfitness to speak in a manner befitting this epochal, world occasion.

If the sense of immeasurable indebtedness to Mr. Spurgeon be any qualification for me to speak, then I have that one qualification for my appearance on this platform. From my earliest recollections, my sense of gratitude to Charles Haddon Spurgeon has been a living thing in my life. His printed sermons found their way across the great ocean, and on and on they travelled, until they came to a little mountain home in the remote country. Week by week, I read those sermons, often reading them over and over again, until they became a part of my inmost life. Nor am I alone in such testimony. Mr. Spurgeon's sermons have been read by more American people, and his picture may be found in more American

---

* An address given by George W. Truett, in the Royal Albert Hall, London, on Wednesday evening, April 25, 1934, in connection with the Spurgeon Centenary Commemoration.

The Inspiration of Ideals

homes, than the sermons and pictures of any other preacher of his century, or any other century.

And still more — his sermons are being eagerly and widely read to this very hour. Thrilling are the stories which tell of the vast influence of his printed sermons. For example, one of America's outstanding preachers told me, just as I was leaving on this hurried journey for England, that the influence which saved him during his university course, from being enmeshed by infidelity, was the reading of Mr. Spurgeon's sermons, at least once a week. One of our noblest university presidents gave a similar testimony. An erstwhile society girl, both worldly and wealthy, was won to Christ by the reading of one of these sermons to her invalid aunt. This girl became the nobly useful helpmeet of one of our most distinguished preachers. Such incidents could be multiplied indefinitely, throughout America. The same story reaches us from all sections of the globe. In homes far removed from the great centers of population; in the camps of cowboys and miners and lumbermen, and widely diversified groups of men, these sermons may yet be found, still wielding, under God's gracious blessing, their converting and lifting power. Just here is a fact that should vitally challenge the practical attention of God's people everywhere. If the vendors of foul literature can find money to print it, and agents to scatter it, surely the friends of Christ, everywhere, should be wisely and unceasingly active in the circulation of life-giving, God-honoring literature.

Let me voice the profoundly sympathetic greetings of the several million Baptists of the United States, both North and South, as expressed by the honored Presidents of the two great Conventions, for this memorable occasion. The honored President of the Federal Council of Churches of America, speaking for millions and millions of American Christians, joins in such greetings. Uncounted millions of Americans

C. H. Spurgeon Centenary

cherish the life and labors of Mr. Spurgeon with measureless gratitude.

These assembled thousands now gathered in this Hall are of one mind. I doubt not that this occasion is one of the most significant and challenging of our generation. You will let me follow my heart and say that all our hearts must surely be touched with deep thankfulness to God that the honored Prime Minister of the British Empire graces this Centenary occasion, not only with his presence, but also with words of such vital testimony for Mr. Spurgeon and Mr. Spurgeon's Saviour as will enhearten us through all the days ahead. This occasion calls to remembrance the tribute paid by Joseph Cook when Wendall Phillips went away: "Whom God crowns, let no man discrown. We cannot crown him; the memory of his great career crowns our civilization."

Mr. Spurgeon's going was an international bereavement. In the United States, our requiem was joined with yours, in countless memorial services held throughout all sections of our country. In such services, the people said what the people of Constantinople said about John Chrysostom: "It were better for the sun to cease his shining than for John Chrysostom to cease his preaching." Throughout all the land, the people said what Elisha said as he looked after the ascending Elijah: "My father, my father, the chariot of Israel and the horsemen thereof!" It is no exaggeration to say that the going of Mr. Spurgeon marked the going of the outstanding preacher of his century. He was God's greatest human gift of the nineteenth century for the furtherance of His kingdom throughout all the earth. And when this Greatheart of the pulpit passed over, one does not doubt that "all the trumpets sounded for him on the other side."

This Centenary occasion, to be duplicated in the weeks just ahead throughout all the world, will happily call the attention of millions again to this markedly providential man. Such Centenary reminder ought to bring a world-wide blessing. We do well, ever and anon, to look backward as well as forward. The ancient Hebrews never wearied of taking the backward look and recounting the virtues of their beloved and mighty dead. Their cry rang out: "Look unto the rock whence ye were hewn; and to the hole of the pit whence ye were digged. Look unto Abraham, your father, and to Sarah who bore you." They never wearied of recalling the mighty days and deeds of Abraham and Moses and Joshua and Samuel and Elijah and David and Solomon, and many others.

The present is inexorably bound up with the past. Pungently has it been said: "A nation ashamed of its ancestry will be despised by its posterity." For hundreds of years after the battle of Thermopylae, the children of Greece repeated the names of their heroes who died there. When they ceased to revere the memory of their mighty dead the star of their republic faded out and their nation was buried in the cemetery of dead republics. If any people allow themselves to forget the glorious heritage bequeathed them by their worthy forebears, then "Ichabod" will be written all over the life and labors of such presumption and ingratitude.

This Centenary Commemoration will provoke a renewed and widespread quest for the source of Mr. Spurgeon's power. Various answers will be given in explanation of his manifold personality. The ultimate answer will be this: "There was a man sent from God, whose name was Charles Haddon Spurgeon." The only satisfactory explanation of Mr. Spurgeon must be in the one word: *God*. Yet, from the human viewpoint, there were various factors which claim our most eager attention.

The story of his godly ancestry and upbringing is to the last degree revealing. Both his father and grandfather were preachers, and his mother was a true Hannah with her little Charles, the oldest child, and with the sixteen other children of her home. The early reading of this lad, while he was yet a lad, is nothing less than marvelous. He devoured vast volumes of Puritan writings. He entered into the ever-inspiring secrets of the myriad-minded Shakespeare, and of the incomparable Bunyan. He read Bunyan's *Pilgrim's Progress* one hundred times, we are told. He kept on the most intimate terms, while yet a child, with the writings of Fox and Doddridge and Baxter, and many others too numerous to be named. His early years were literally saturated with great literature, and most of all, with the literature of the Bible. Could you find this record duplicated anywhere in the wide world? The suggestion is sometimes heard that Mr. Spurgeon was a man without education. Where will you find one whose reading was more inspirational, and whose penetrative intelligence in all his reading was more in evidence?

In any correct appraisement of Mr. Spurgeon, faithful account must be taken of his poignant, spiritual struggles, issuing in his glorious assurance of Christ as his personal Saviour, while attending a little Methodist chapel in Colchester. His sense of God's saving grace was so consciously real that, like Bunyan, he wanted to tell even the crows that flew over the fields. Immediately he began to preach the glorious gospel of God's saving grace to his classmates in humble farm houses, in kitchens, in barns, in the open fields, wherever the people might be gathered together. At the age of sixteen, he assumed the pastorate of a village church, meanwhile pursuing his studies in school, and preaching several times each week. We are told that he preached between six and seven hundred times ere he came to London in his nineteenth year.

His coming to London reads like the very romance of divine Providence, as indeed it was. He could say of it, and the people with him, what Wellington said in one of his memorable dispatches from the field of Waterloo: "The finger of Providence is upon me." Although he came to London during an era of eminent statesmen, scholars, and preachers, yet he soon towered like a mountain peak and was far-famed above them all. Like his Master, he could not be hid. The Victorian Era was an era of mighty and famous names. There were Gladstone and John Bright and Disraeli among the statesmen. There were Browning and Tennyson among the poets. There were Huxley and Darwin among the scientists. There were Dickens and Thackeray among the novelists. There were Watts and Holman Hunt among the artists. There were Alexander Maclaren and Joseph Parker and Canon Liddon and John Clifford, and other names I should like to call, if time allowed, who were the mighty contemporaries of Mr. Spurgeon in the pulpit. And in America were such preachers as Henry Ward Beecher, Phillips Brooks, John A. Broaddus, and B. H. Carroll. It is no exaggeration, nor is it any disparagement of any of these great preachers to say that Mr. Spurgeon then held and still holds the primacy as a preacher. Such is the testimony of statesmen and theologians and writers the world around, and such testimony abides unto this hour.

The question persists — What are the secrets of Mr. Spurgeon's abiding influence? Let us begin with the man. Dr. Robertson Nicoll was right: "Mr. Spurgeon was every inch a man." Manhood in the ministry is of transcendent moment. We are correctly told that knowledge is power, but character is far more so. True manhood is to character what a right foundation is to a building. What a man is in himself is of far greater consequence than anything he says or does. Carlyle well says that the first requirement of a great man is that he must be a true man. Spurgeon was a man of incarnate integrity. He abhorred all forms of hypocrisy and falseness. His mind travelled in a straight line like the light. He was a true man without sham or veneer. If Diogenes who went with his lantern searching for an honest man had met Mr. Spurgeon, he would have shouted: "I have found him!" He possessed a moral courage comparable to that of Elijah and John the Baptist and Luther and Knox and Cromwell. His moral manhood towered in majesty like some glorious mountain. He was one answer to Lyman Beecher's prayer: "God grant that our principal men may be men of principle."

He was one of the most prodigious toilers of his own or of any age. From his boyhood till his homegoing, his life was apostolic in zeal and labors for Christ's cause. He could say with Henry Martyn: "I am born for God only. Christ is nearer to me than father or mother or sister — a nearer relation, a more affectionate friend; and I rejoice to follow Him and to love Him." He could say with David Livingstone: "My Jesus, my King, my life, my all — I again dedicate my whole life to Thee." He could say with Paul: "I am debtor both to the Greeks, and to the barbarians; both to the wise and the unwise. So, as much as in me is, I am ready to preach the gospel to you that are at Rome also." His earthly life was literally burnt out for Christ.

He wrought enough in one short lifetime for a dozen strong men. He fully met Emerson's challenge: "Go put your creed into your deed." Think of the vast number of his printed sermons — over thrity-five hundred! Reading one a day would take ten years! And he was the author of many other books besides his sermons. From this one incessantly busy preacher some two hundred volumes have gone forth to the world, in addition to all his other herculean labors. It is an astounding story of vast and far-reaching achievements. Any one of the several institutions vitally linked with his life would be enough to crown his life with an enviable immortality. Look at his Pastors' College with its hundreds upon hundreds of men witnessing for Christ around the encircling globe. Look at his Orphanage, his Almshouses, his Colportage Association. Preceding any and all of these institutions, look at his vast ministry through the great church, with the lines of its testimony going out to the ends of the earth. Great believers are always great doers. It is true in all realms of life. Witness Moses and Paul and Luther and Wesley and Spurgeon and General Booth, and all the rest. Mr. Spurgeon met our Lord's test of life — the test of worthy service. He gloriously vindicated the gospel of grace by the attestation of good works, whether as preacher, author, or administrator,

He was a man of universal sympathies. Especially did his sympathies wholeheartedly go out to the poor, the needy, the ignorant, the unfortunate. The coming to his Tabernacle of Mr. Ruskin the scholar, or of Mr. Gladstone, the Prime Minister, or of Lord Shaftesbury, or of some far-famed Archbishop, gave him no more pleasure than the coming of the humble carpenter, the cabman, the seamstress, the washerwoman. In such fact, we have one of the most revealing explanations of his far-reaching influence and power. It could be said of him as of his Master: "The common people heard him gladly." With Paul he could say, and did say: "We then that are strong ought to bear the infirmities of the weak, and not to please ourselves." To him, the crowning glory of Christ's gospel is that it is to be preached to the poor.

Before all else, Mr. Spurgeon was a preacher of the glorious gospel of the grace of God. When a friend asked Charles Lamb if he had ever heard Coleridge preach, Lamb replied that he had never heard Coleridge do anything else. So might it be said of Mr. Spurgeon that he could not help preaching, and that with a passion that was often irresistible. One can feel him even to this day, in his printed sermons. The pulpit was his throne, and he occupied it like a king. He could say with Paul: "I magnify mine office." And again: "I thank Christ Jesus our Lord, who hath enabled me, for that he counted me faithful, putting me into the ministry." He declared that he had as clear a sense of his divine call to be a preacher as Paul had. He spoke as a divinely commissioned ambassador of Christ. Is it too much to say that he was the most Pauline preacher the world has heard for centuries? He spoke as a prophet of the Most High God. He possessed, and was possessed by, the great truths of the Bible as was no other preacher of his century. His preaching took hold alike of men with and without culture because it possessed the attribute of timelessness. It appealed always to the elemental and fundamental. He was ever an ambassador standing in Christ's stead to beseech a sinful world to be reconciled to God. He preached a gospel of facts of eternal meaning and of divine authentication.

The word ever upon his lips was the word "grace," which is the very essence of Christ's gospel. It is the one adequate hope of a sinning world. It is the sole comfort of mankind as they face eternity. We are saved by grace; we are established by grace; we are justified by grace; we are taught by grace; we are sanctified by grace; we are enabled to grow because of grace; we are given comfort and triumph in all the tribulations of life because of grace. Our salvation in its totality is of grace. This was Mr. Spurgeon's message, always and everywhere. Such a gospel is timeless and changeless. It reaches to the elemental and fundamental. Sin remains the same, and human nature the same, and the need of a divine Saviour remains the same, through all the passing centuries.

Mr. Spurgeon believed, and believed correctly, that there is no substitute for the Christian pulpit. Not the press with all its triumphs; nor the schools with all their learning; nor the amazing triumphs of science can take the place of Christ's preacher. "For after that in the wisdom of God the world by wisdom knew not God, it pleased God by the foolishness of preaching to save them that believe." Nor will history let us forget that the halcyon days of Christianity have always been the days of great preachers and faithful preaching. It was so in the day of Tertullian and Chrysostom and Augustine and Ambrose. It was so in the days of Luther and Calvin and Latimer and Knox. It was so in the days of Whitefield and Wesley and Robert Hall and Jonathan Edwards. It was so in

The Inspiration of Ideals

the days of Spurgeon. The dry bones of the valley have ever lived and been clothed with flesh and blood when the right kind of man with the right kind of message has stood in the Christian pulpit. The moral and spiritual safety of a nation and of a world is very largely within the keeping of the Christian pulpit. The Thermopylae of Christianity is the pulpit.

Certainly it behooves us to look faithfully to Mr. Spurgeon's method in his pulpit. His language ever was marked by clarity and simplicity. He spoke in pungent, wholesome, home-bred words which the humblest hearers could readily understand. In this he walked in the steps of Bunyan whose spiritual allegory remains forever matchless. Like his Master, he spoke always with the accent of authority. It is conviction that convinces. "There is untold power in him who knows his mission is a thing of God's own willing, though doubts may shroud in cloud the transient hour."

Mr. Spurgeon wisely believed and incarnated his belief that the Christian pulpit is the last place under heaven for stammering and indefiniteness, for guesses and speculations, for evasions and uncertainties. Mr. Spurgeon believed with Horace Bushnell that "there is no nerve in a gospel of speculation." He believed that some things are unchangeably true and that others are just as unchangeably false. He had no sort of fellowship with the nerveless, hazy, intellectual libertinism that plays fast and loose with the eternal verities of Christ's gospel. He said with the Psalmist: "I believed, therefore have I spoken." He said with the apostles: "We cannot but speak the things which we have seen and heard." He said with Paul: "For if the trumpet give an uncertain sound, who shall prepare himself to the battle?"

He held fast by the great themes of divine revelation: the sovereignty of God; the holiness of God; the love of God; the grace of our Lord Jesus Christ; the solemn wonders of the cross; the divine forgiveness of sins; the fellowship of

Christ's sufferings; the power of His resurrection; the blessedness of divine communion; the heavenly places in Christ Jesus; the mystical indwelling of the Holy Ghost; the final abolishment of death; the ageless life; the Father's house; the liberty of the glory of the children of God forever.

A great preacher is never a novelty monger. It is impossible for him to turn away from the vitalities and centralities of God's grace, to be a huckster with the passing sensations of the hour. Some gospels are mere novelties, the passing fancies of restless men, who seek ever for something new. Some gospels are but essays with a moral flavor to them. Some gospels are merely a gilded humanitarianism, seeking to satisfy mankind with fruits altogether superficial and external.

Mr. Spurgeon was a true watchman on the walls of Zion. He spoke ever with the note of conquering, Christian confidence. He sounded no defeatist notes. He did not tease his audiences with wailing dirges and miserable jeremiads. He triumphantly shouted with the Psalmist: "The Lord reigneth; let the earth rejoice; let the multitude of isles be glad thereof." Our supreme hope is not in fleets and armies, not in guns and battleships, not in diplomats and politics, not in kings and presidents, but in God. What kind of a God have we? If we start out with a little God, we shall have a little religion, utterly insufficient to meet the needs of mankind. The idea of God is the ground-plan in religion. If the ground-plan be cramped and meager, so will be the building. Even so, we can never build a big religion on a little God. A great religion depends upon a great God. No matter how dark the clouds upon the horizon, Mr. Spurgeon preached a God who is able to do exceeding abundantly above all that we ask or think.

If we inquire about Mr. Spurgeon's theology, he frankly avowed himself a Calvinist, whatever he may have meant by such avowal. The message of Christ's faithful preacher is the one message that will transform human society; that will cure all social ills; that will readily settle the age-old dispute between labor and capital; that will heal race hatreds, and end war, and abolish national suspicions and antagonisms, and make all men brothers. Therefore social unrest and world upheavals are not the despair of Christ's faithful preacher because such preacher has a remedy, the only adequate remedy for them. If permanent disarmament is ever to come, men must arm with the armor of Christianity. If peace covenants among the nations are not backed up by the faithful teaching and practising of the principles of Christ, they will soon be found to be mere scraps of paper. All of us long with an unutterable longing for the coming of that halcyon day foretold by the prophet when men shall beat their swords into plowshares and convert their spears into pruning-hooks and wars shall be hushed unto the ends of the earth. Let us mark well the prophet's further word that such golden day will come only when men's ways please the Lord. The one agency to get civilization off the rocks and keep it off is the gospel of the Saviourhood and Lordship of Christ.

Before we jocosely sneer at Calvinism, we had better take the pains to trace its vast influence throughout the earth. The currents of history were vitally changed by John Calvin. Well does Professor Kuyper say: "Just ask yourselves what would have become of Europe and America, if in the sixteenth century, the story of Calvinism had not suddenly risen on the horizon of Western Europe. In that case, Spain would have crushed the Netherlands. In England and Scotland, the Stuarts would have carried out their plans. In Switzerland, the spirit of half-heartedness would have gained the day. The whole American continent would have remained subject to Spain. If the power of Spain had not been broken by the heroism of the Calvinistic spirit, the history of Europe and of the world would have been sad and dark."

Calvinism has had more to do in building up a strong national character than has any other system of theology. It enabled John Calvin to convert the little Republic of Geneva into a school of morals for all Europe. It enabled John Knox to stand before Queen Mary unabashed, and to convert the half-civilized Scotland of his day into one of the fairest, noblest lands in all the earth. It braced the heart of William the Silent and made little, half-drowned Holland unconquerable to all the power of Spain. It filled the soul of Oliver Cromwell and made it possible for him to fling from the English throne a king who believed he had a divine right to govern wrongly. It set upon the ruins of monarchy a commonwealth, and broke forever the power of the traditions of despotism on English soil. Well does the immortal Dr. Broaddus say: "The people who sneer at Calvinism might as well sneer at Mont Blanc." Calvinism magnified the sovereignty of God and placed a crown on the head of the individual man, whoever and wherever he might be. It reminded man of his direct and inescapable responsibility to God. It laid hold of man and lifted him above the heads of priest and bishop and archbishop and cardinal and pope and king and president and potentate and told him that he must answer directly to God.

Is it any wonder that Mr. Spurgeon was mightily influenced by Calvinism? But whatever the name of Mr. Spurgeon's theology, it all centered in Christ. It was his never-ceasing note about Christ that gave the great preacher's message universal and abiding power. His sermons are remarkably void of anything peculiar to time, place, circumstance, or condition. His preaching, like the preaching of Jesus, was for all ages, times, and conditions. It is this fact which makes his sermons as profitable in America, or in Europe, or in Africa, or in the Orient, as in England. Take any one of his thousands of printed sermons, read it carefully, and I dare to affirm that the truth of such sermon, mind you — the truth of

The Inspiration of Ideals

it — would have been just as pertinent and appropriate one hundred years ago, as now. It will be just as pertinent and appropriate one hundred years hence, as it is this hour. His preaching is founded on the fundamental facts of man's nature, and it is ever addressed to man's spiritual condition. Just as the whole message of Jesus bears upon the supreme purpose for which He came into the world — that is, to save His people from their sins — even so, the never-ceasing spiritual appeal in Mr. Spurgeon's preaching gives it universality of appeal. It is no wonder that a little boy asked his mother why Mr. Spurgeon kept talking to him.

The appeal of Jesus is universal. It is no wonder that a saintly old Welsh woman contended that Jesus was a Welshman because he always spoke to her in Welsh. The great artists tell the story of the universal Jesus. Tissot painted Him with the face of an Arab. Titian painted Him with the likeness of an Italian. Murillo gave Him the appearance of a child of Spain. Rubens painted Him with the appearance of a peasant of Flanders Field. Yet He is the same in them all, whether in Antioch or in Athens, whether in Tokyo or in London, whether in Moscow or in Washington. He is everywhere the same. A Greek came saying, "Sir, we would see Jesus." A Roman centurion cried out at the cross, "Truly, this was the Son of God." At His birth Orientals came to Him; at His death, Greeks came. At His birth came the men of the East; at His death came the men of the West. And yet He is understood by all, because He is the Universal Saviour. "Jesus Christ the same yesterday, today and forever."

Let it be repeated, whatever Mr. Spurgeon may have called his system of theology, the center of his ministry ever and forever was the grace of God revealed in the Cross. Christ died as our Redeemer. His Cross is the central fact of the universe. The supreme lesson in homiletics is thus stated by Christ: "And I, if I be lifted up from the earth will draw all men unto me." And then is added the revealing sentence:

"This He spake, signifying what death He should die." One delights to think of Christ in all His relations, whether as Prophet, Master, Philanthropist, Miracle-worker, Teacher, Friend. But humanity's indispensable need is the need of the vicarious atoning, redeeming Saviour.

Christianity is distinctly a gospel of redemption. Its purpose is to rescue mankind from the guilt and power of sin. Christ did not die as a Socrates or a Seneca, as a Wellington or a Lee, but as a redeeming Saviour of sinners. He is the Lamb of God, who taketh away the sin of the world. The central and conspicuous fact of the New Testament is the death of Christ. It was that fact that conquered the hearts of Paul and his fellow apostles and sent them out as flaming evangels to the conquest of the world for Christ. And the testimony of our missionaries in every land is that it is the story of Christ's death that opens the hearts of the pagan world and wins them to Christ.

Mr. Spurgeon cried out with Paul: "God forbid that I should glory, save in the Cross of our Lord Jesus Christ." And with him again he could say: "But we preach Christ crucified, unto the Jews a stumbling-block, and unto the Greeks foolishness; but unto them who are called, both Jews and Greeks, Christ the power of God and the wisdom of God." This is the gospel and the only gospel that has infallible and invincible credentials that it is the power of God unto salvation. This gospel has conquered South Sea cannibals, African Hottentots, Indian pariahs, Chinese opium sots, Korean demon worshippers, Confucian scholars, Mohammedan fanatics, Brahmin priests, Buddhist devotees, and men of every type and temperament out of every kindred, tribe, and tongue under the heavens.

I asked them whence their victory came;
They with united breath,
Ascribed their victory to the Lamb,
Their triumph to His death.

The Inspiration of Ideals

Mr. Spurgeon believed with His whole being in the divine authority, the divine sufficiency, and the divine finality of Christ's gospel. He had no fellowship with any suggestion that we are to have a syncretistic salvation composed of fragments of Confucianism, bits of Buddhism, and pieces of Hinduism, and the rest. His soul was fixed in the conviction that such a hash of religions is not to be substituted for the Bread of Life, supplied by Him who said: "I am the Bread of Life, he that cometh to me shall never hunger, and he that believeth on me shall never thirst." The religion of our divine Saviour and Lord, like Aaron's rod, swallows up all other rods. Like Aaron's rod, it is the only rod that buds, for it alone is the power and wisdom of God unto salvation.

The going of Mr. Spurgeon made the largest gap in the ranks of Christ's workers that they have known for generations. Wordworth's sonnet to Milton, in a troubled day for old England, may well be our sonnet today: "Spurgeon! thou shouldest be living at this hour! England hath need of thee! America hath need of thee! The whole world hath need of thee!" The Spurgeon spirit of faithfulness, of hopefulness, of intensity, of compassionate sympathy for needy humanity is the spirit needed for today, and for all the days. A mighty heritage comes to us from one of God's mightiest servants. We should faithfully guard and utilize that heritage. This is God's way for His people. The generations stand together in an unbroken solidarity. Joshua must carry forward the work begun by Moses. Solomon must build the Temple for which David, his father, gathered the materials. "One soweth and another reapeth." And if faithful, "Both he that soweth and he that reapeth may rejoice together."

The supreme thing for which Mr. Spurgeon spoke and wrote and wrought was to point men and women and young people to the Lamb of God that taketh away the sin of the world. In such life-course, he set a most challenging example to his fellow-preachers, everywhere. The vast significance of this Centenary occasion will be lost if we overlook this crowning note in Mr. Spurgeon's life. The first and supreme business of every preacher and of every church is to win sinners to the salvation and service of Christ. The supreme indictment against a preacher's ministry is the absence of the note of rescue, the seeking note. This likewise is the supreme indictment against a church. What better is a church than an ethical club if the seeking note for the lost be absent from such church?

Just here, Mr. Spurgeon calls to his fellow-preachers and to his fellow-Christians, both by noblest precept and example, to be true shepherds of souls — of all souls, of all conditions, of all places, and always. This is ever to be our dominant passion. We must not, dare not be indifferent to the spiritual welfare of any soul, anywhere. One recalls the tragedy of the Titanic disaster, and the death of Captain Gracie, a year after the catastrophe. His last words were: "We must get them all into the life-boats." "We must get them *ALL* into the life-boats." The keen intensity of an hour lasted through all his remaining days. He was not satisfied that some of the passengers were being saved — but his heart-moving cry rang out: "We must get them ALL into the life-boats."

Brethren, let us make this Centenary occasion an hour of unreserved dedication to the highest mission of Christ's people — that of winning souls to Him and for Him. This is Christ's way for His people, and there can be no substitutes for His way. The divine marching orders of our risen Saviour and Lord, the appalling needs of our bludgeoned world, and the vitality and safety of our churches, all beseechingly constrain us thus to walk in Mr. Spurgeon's steps, even as He walked in the steps of Christ. If a worthy crusade for the winning of souls to Christ shall go forth from this historic occasion, being faithfully magnified by Christ's people to the ends of the earth, then shall the whole earth rejoice in God's salvation, and there shall likewise be joy in heaven because of repenting sinners on earth. And best of all, Christ will be with us, for "He shall see of the travail of His soul and be satisfied." If we thus give ourselves to such a crusade, we may make the words of the immortal Wesley our words: "The world is our parish, and best of all God is with us."

To such incomparably blessed mission let us rededicate all our powers, yea, our very lives, and let us do so with Mr. Spurgeon's spirit of unhesitating, unfearing, conquering Christian confidence. We are not in any losing battle, as we follow the Prince of Life, who goes forth conquering and to conquer. "For He must reign, till He hath put all enemies under His feet." "Therefore, my beloved brethren, be ye stedfast, unmovable, always abounding in the work of the Lord, forasmuch as ye know that your labor is not in vain in the Lord."

CHAPTER IX

The Dedication of a Church

CHAPTER IX

The Dedication of a Church*

LET my first expression from this platform be the reading of a psalm that seems to be pre-eminently suitable for this hour.

> *Make a joyful noise unto the Lord,*
> *All ye lands.*
> *Serve the Lord with gladness;*
> *Come before his presence with singing.*
> *Know ye that the Lord, he is God:*
> *It is he that hath made us,*
> *And not we ourselves;*
> *We are his people, and the sheep of his pasture.*
> *Enter into his gates with thanksgiving,*
> *And into his courts with praise:*
> *Be thankful unto him, and bless his name.*
> *For the Lord is good;*
> *His mercy is everlasting;*
> *And his truth endureth to all generations.*

Brother pastor and members of the church family and others gathered here or who may be listening in throughout radio land, let me express my deep gratitude to God for the good providence that allows me to be with you on this very significant and even historic occasion. I would offer the church family and community my most cordial and grateful felicitations upon the erection of this remarkably attractive and manifestly worthy house of worship. An achievement

---

* Delivered on February 2, 1941 in Greenwood, South Carolina, at the dedication of a small but beautiful church building erected by Mr. J. C. Self in memory of his mother.

THE INSPIRATION OF IDEALS

like this marks a distinct epoch in the life of a community. Life certainly ought to be richer and larger and deeper and happier and more useful because of the achievement that calls us together on this dedicatory occasion.

Memorials are often put to the memory of our loved ones in the form of some stone or slab to mark their last resting place without any regard to the practical helpfulness that such memorials may be to others. Today you are dedicating a memorial that is to be a continual blessing to the people and a constant challenge to every life coming within the radius of this memorial to walk more wisely and to live more worthily in the sight of God and to seek to be more useful and serviceable in the sight of man.

We are told of Stanley, the great traveler and later the great Christian, when he was married in Westminster Abbey in London, as he went down the aisle toward the altar where he was to stand for the marriage ceremony, he paused a moment as he came down the aisle and laid a beautiful wreath of white roses on the tomb of his great predecessor, David Livingstone. Emotions, more tender than our words can say, well up in our hearts today as we think of this memorial to be dedicated before the hour is over to the worship of God and as a blessing to the people.

In my city there lives a nation-famed poet, Grace Noll Crowell. She pens two simple stanzas to Christian mothers.

Blessed are they who have for memory a mother whose spirit
White was a flame for righteousness. Who gave them eyes to
See the glory of an everlasting name, the splendor of a
Highway to be trod, straight to the great and loving
    heart of God.

Blessed are they whose mother is today a living presence
Walking by their side, whose love enfolds them as she kneels
To pray, pleading for one to be their strength and guide.
Who have a mother in their desperate need — Ah, truly such as
    they are blessed indeed.

The Dedication of a Church

One often wonders wistfully if our departed loved ones are cognizant of what is taking place here with us in the earthly work and warfare of our lives. We do not know, but we are happy to believe that if our departed loved ones now in the land and life above take notice of what is going on with us down here in the earthly journey, then a gentle, useful, faithful, Christian mother looks upon this scene today with untold joy in her eyes and in her immortal spirit.

Of old, when the people came to make record of an unusual and worthy deed, they said, "This is the day which the Lord hath made. We will rejoice and be glad in it." In casting about for some suitable word to say in connection with this dedicatory service, my mind and heart have taken hold of a tribute paid by Paul long ago to a group of Christians who did a beautiful and worthy deed — Christians of Macedonia, described by Paul in one of his letters. What was their worthy deed?

They heard that far away there were those in distress, fellow Christians, whom they had never seen but whose distress was very acute, and, though these Macedonian Christians were themselves in dire straits because of physical affliction and poverty, yet out of that unusual situation they gathered together a gift and sent it on to help people in distress far away. And Paul paid them a tribute — one of the most beautiful on record in all the Scriptures. And he gave us a revealing explanation of their behaviour. What is it? "But they first gave themselves to the Lord."

We are to give a house presently to our Lord and he searchingly looks into our hearts and says, "But I want you. I want you." "They first gave themselves to the Lord." "The gift without the giver is not good. I seek not yours but you. I want you."

It is not pleasing to Christ for us to offer him some of our money and withhold from him ourselves. He wishes our per-

THE INSPIRATION OF IDEALS

sonality, our manhood, our womanhood, our wills, our brains, our hearts, our deepest loyalty, our lives.

Now there are lessons for us in this old-time tribute that we may well lay to heart on this dedicatory occasion. Let us look for some of those lessons this morning in our quiet meditation together and may the Holy Spirit illumine our understanding and search our hearts, that our meditations may be according to the will of God. And, first of all, let us note what those early Christians, applauded by Paul, did. They gave Christ's cause the first place in their lives. Surely they gave it the right place. They were following in the steps of him who said, "Seek ye first the kingdom of God and his righteousness and all these things (temporalities that you need, food and raiment, the simple necessities of life — all these things) shall be added to you." They gave Christ's cause the first place in their lives. Surely they gave it the right place. You and I are to have an attitude toward Christ's cause in the earth. He has a cause in the earth. He has a kingdom in the earth. He has established his church with the great assurance that the gates of Hell shall not prevail against it. Now, what should be our attitude toward our Lord's cause in the earth? These Christians praised by Paul point the way for us. They gave Christ's cause the first place in their thoughts and loyalties and devotion.

Many a time, the question passes to and fro, "What is the supreme prerequisite to make Christ's cause in the earth victorious?" And answers are given to that searching question. Sometimes very superficial answers are given. For example, one hears the answer sometimes, ofttimes, that the supreme prerequisite to make Christ's cause victorious is that it shall have larger numbers bound up with it.

Never one time does God, in his Book, place the emphasis on numbers. Never one time. It is not quantity that tells in the sight of God, or anywhere else, but quality. It is not how many we count, but how much do we weigh. It is not the duration of our life that spells most of all, but its intensity. The Lord warns us again and again as to the peril that may be in numbers. You may recall that David got into serious trouble long ago by having his men take a census of the people throughout his kingdom. They went up and down the land for months counting the heads of people and while they did so, they took their thoughts and eyes away from God and the outcome of their census-taking was their downfall and defeat — at least temporarily. So, we are warned about the snare that may be in numbers. One soul living at the highest and best means more in the kingdom of God than a vast army living irregular, inconsistent and unworthy lives.

These Christians whom Paul praises set the pace for us when they gave the Lord's cause first place in their lives. So many times we hear the answer that the great need to make Christ's cause victorious is that it shall have more money and that answer is wider of the mark than the first. Never one time does God put the primary emphasis on money. He tells us, "The cattle on the thousand hills are mine. The silver and gold are all mine. If I want it and need it, I can command it." He warns us with warnings that bite and burn of the peril that can be in money. He reminds us that the love of money is the root of every kind of evil and that we are to watch against its dominating and blinding passion, all of us, whether our property be little or much.

And yet, I go on to say, as a moral and religious teacher, that I have no sympathy at all with the anarchistic outcry sometimes heard against property. I dare to say, as a moral and religious teacher, that men who can amass property ought to do so. To be sure, by the right methods, always, and to be sure, for the dedication of such property to the right uses, always.

Men have their talents, God-given, and men are to employ their talents with an eye to the will and honor of God. Then they may go on and on in their achievements and witness and warfare in the earthly journey. "Ill fares the land, to hastening ills a prey, if wealth accumulates and men decay."

Then we hear the cry sometimes that the great need to make Christianity victorious is to have beautiful architecture and wonderful organization and much is to be said for beautiful architecture and a worthy organization. A church family ought to have an organization far flung and scriptural and applicable in the reach of it to all the people about and a place of worship ought to be made attractive and beautiful to a marked degree, and yet never once did our Lord put the primary emphasis on organization, machinery, design, architecture, or form.

What is the supreme need to make Christ's cause victorious anywhere and everywhere? It is that we give Christ's cause the primacy in our lives, the first place in our lives, the preeminence in our lives. Paul tells us that whether you eat or drink or whatesover you do — do all for the glory of God. Go to your work, shop, farm, bank, store, doctor's office or law office, to the editor's desk or to the teacher's calling — go to your task, whatever may be appointed for you in the plan and providence of God, and there labor for the glory of God and the blessing of your fellow men.

We sometimes hear a remark about the sacred and the secular in life. There are no secularities for the properly ordered life. None at all. Whether we eat or drink, whether we do this or that, we are to do it all for the glory of God.

Years ago, I was preaching for ten days in the great Third Baptist Church of St. Louis. Mr. Brown, a member of that church, was one of the leading shoe men of America. Some of you older men knew him, no doubt, and had dealings with him. He had thousands of employees and was one of the most devoted and useful church men I ever knew. He came and sat on the second pew morning and night for the ten days I was there and one day as we walked away together, I said to Mr. Brown: "If you should put your dominant life

The Dedication of a Church

passion in one sentence, what would it be?" He said, "Now, if you had been to my office, as I have invited you to be, you would know, for it is there in my office on a little cardboard of six words — this dominant life's passion that sweeps me on." And I said: "Well, I'm going right on to your office now, for I want to see for myself what you account as your dominant life passion."

Presently we reached his office and there was his life's passion standing on a cardboard on his desk. Six words. GOD FIRST — FAMILY SECOND — SHOES THIRD. That is exactly the right way for one to live. God first. Certainly, He is first. "If a man doesn't love me more than he loves father or mother," says Jesus, "he cannot be my disciple." God first, and then family. God before family. God. Maker, Creator, Preserver, Upholder, Benefactor. "God First — Family second — Shoes Third." Business third. This calling or that or the other, wherever in God's providence you're placed, that's it. That's the right view. The right interpretation. God's interpretation for our lives.

But we want to look a little more closely at this tribute paid by Paul to those Macedonian Christians who did a beautiful, noble thing. How did they come to do it? What was the animating motive behind it? What was the challenging cause that constrained them? Paul tells us. First — FIRST. They first gave themselves to the Lord, and then they did this beautiful, worthy, gracious, helpful deed. We cannot please our Lord if we withhold ourselves from him.

One calls to mind that widely quoted story of a small boy from the streets, a newsboy, who crept into one of our city churches and was converted. He wanted to do God's will and he sought out the preacher; and the outcome was that very soon the little fellow, ten or eleven years of age, presented himself as a candidate for baptism and church membership and was so received.

175

The Inspiration of Ideals

Soon the minister preached on the great program of Christ. That is, the business of Christ's people to carry the news of Christ throughout all the earth. "We are to go into the world and preach the gospel to every creature, whatever the difficulty; whatever giant cities are to be conquered; whatever the difficulty, we are to pay the price and go to earth's remotest bounds and tell every human being that the Son of God — the only begotten Son of the Eternal Father, came down to earth and lived a little while and then climbed the lonely cross and died thereon, for the just and the unjust, that he might bring us to God. We are to tell the world, the whole world, that great story."

The lad heard that. He'd never heard anything like it in his life. The minister said, "We are to go in person, or if we can't go in person, we are to send men and women to go for us and we are to hold up their hands. We are to support them. We are to maintain them. When they go down into a well, we are to hold the rope. They are our substitutes and we are to support them."

Then the preacher made a powerful appeal to the people to give money for the support of Foreign Missions. And the officers came along with their baskets, gathering up the offerings of the people for their "World Missionary Offering," and the little boy, all disconcerted, didn't know what to do. He had no money to give. When the officer reached him, the little fellow touched the basket and said, "Put it lower." And then the officer put it lower. The little fellow said, "Put it on the floor." And to humor the little fellow, the officer put the basket on the floor and the little fellow stepped into it and said, "I give myself. I have no money to give." That's the heart of it! "I give myself."

These early Christians gave themselves. They gave themselves and the mightiest preacher of all the ages, the incomparable Paul, takes time and space and wonderful words

The Dedication of a Church

to describe that glorious, praiseworthy, humanity-helping deed of generosity.

Here I am — two thousand years after that occurrence — talking about it on this dedicatory occasion, far removed from the ancient times and those ancient conditions. Those early Christians gave themselves. Here is the crux of the great matter of vitally and victoriously serving our Lord. Paul and Barnabas, we are told, hazarded their lives for the name of Jesus. I have seen, in recent years, men and women in the far east and throughout Europe doing identically the same thing — hazarding their lives for the name of Jesus, and wherever that occurs, the kingdom of God goes forward by leaps and bounds.

I remember far in the interior of China, several years ago, where every member of a church died for Christ. They were people won by missionaries. And the barbarians came along with their purpose to exterminate Christianity and the name of Christ from the very thoughts and memories of people. When they came to that church, they said: "You must step on this metal, which has on it the cross; you must trample it under your feet, showing your contempt for Christ and the cross. And, if you do not, your head will be chopped from your shoulders."

Every member of the church died rather than deny Christ. They had one boy eleven years of age in the church and the murderers had a little spark of humanity left. Just a tiny spark. They said to the boy, "Boy, you are a little fellow. We don't want to kill you. Just step on this one time and then you may go free." And the little fellow lifted his eyes toward heaven and said, with a great sob, "Lord Jesus, you died for me. I am willing now to die for you." And he said to the men, "Chop my head off. I am not going to deny Christ." And they chopped off his head.

What happened? In that community for five hundred miles, when you talk about Christ, their faces are serious and

The Inspiration of Ideals

they say, "Yes, he had some friends back there who were devoted to him and loved him so that the last one of them laid down their lives for Christ." The blood of those Christian martyrs became the seed of the kingdom of God over a wide area of Inland China. We are told why the early Christians triumphed, in one sentence: "They overcame Satan by the blood of the lamb and by the word of their testimony and they loved not their lives, even unto death."

For thirty-odd years I have been holding annual camp meetings for the brave, brawny men of the plains. Mighty men. Great fathers, honest as sunlight for the most part. I have been going there and have seen hundreds and hundreds of them converted and added to the churches. I went out there years ago and one day I preached to the men on this text: "Ye are not your own. Ye have been bought with a price. Therefore, glorify God in your body and spirit which are God's." The burden of my message was: "Ye have been bought. You've been redeemed. Christ died in your stead. Poured out his blood unto death for you to keep you from condemnation eternal. Now, by the three-fold plan of creation and redemption and preservation, you belong to Christ."

When the service was over, one of the great cattle men — perhaps he had twenty thousand head of cattle on his great ranch — locked his arm through mine and said, "Would you mind waiting a little today for lunch? I have something very serious to say to you." And I said, "Certainly, I will tarry." He said, "I want to talk with you alone."

And we went up a gorge in the mountains about a mile and a quarter. He didn't say another word until we got to our destination. His great chest rose and fell as if beneath it there were some seething furnace — and there was. He turned and said, "I want you to pray a dedicatory prayer for me." I said, "What do you wish to dedicate?" He said: "I want to dedicate my ranch. I don't know much about Christianity. You've taught me what little I know since you have

The Dedication of a Church

been coming out here, but I have faced the situation today. You are right that we belong to Christ. He created us. He died for us. He preserves us. We live and move and have our being in him. You are exactly right. I have faced it today. You kneel down here and tell him that I dedicate my ranch to him and I will seek to run it for his glory from now on. I will seek to make it go. I will give all the energy and devotion I can put into it; but it shall be from now on for the glory of God." And then he said: "When you are through, you wait a minute and let me pray if I can. I have something to tell the Lord you can't tell him."

I offered my prayer, telling the Lord that this man bade me tell him so-and-so. And the big cattle man, kneeling by me, sobbed and said, "Yes, Master." They all call Jesus "Master." Every cattle man says "Jesus, Master." "Yes, Master. I mean what the preacher says. Yes, Master. Yes, Master, I mean just what he is saying." And when I got through my prayer, I waited and the big cattle man put his face to the ground as if to bite it in humiliation and sobbed and sobbed and when he waited a minute, I got over by him and laid my arm on his shoulder and said, 'Now just tell the Master what is in your mind and heart." He began with sobs and said, "Master, from this time on, I will be your steward. I will be your trustee. I will seek to carry out your will as the main thing in my life. But, Master, Master, I want to give you one thing the preacher couldn't give you. I want to give you my wild boy. His mother and I have lost all control over him. He's as wild as the deer of these mountains. He has formed habits that break our hearts. I want to give you my wild boy. Take him and for the glory of your great name, save my boy and let him count for the glory of God in the life that's before him."

That was his prayer. We walked back to the camp, speaking not one word on our return. There are times when silence is golden. And the day wore away to nightfall and

The Inspiration of Ideals

the men sounded the trumpets calling us together and some two thousand of the people came and worshipped together. I stood up to preach and I hadn't preached fifteen minutes until there was a commotion on the outskirts of that great throng. A young man, some twenty-one or two years of age was standing at the rear of the audience. He was evidently under strong emotion for I saw tears coursing down his cheeks. Then he started down the aisle leading to the platform where I was standing and continuing to preach in spite of the commotion his movements were causing in the audience. I thought he was coming to say something to me. But not so. He came all the way down the aisle and turned to one side towards a post against which was leaning an elderly man — the same man who had prayed with me on the mountainside at noon that day. Hundreds of people were now standing. When the young man was within twenty-five or thirty feet of his father, he called out so that all heard him say: "Daddy, I can't wait until that preacher has finished his sermon. I have made my surrender to Jesus."

What mattered the rest of the sermon! There was joy in a father's heart, and in the hearts of the people, and also among the angels in heaven.

Oh, men, my brothers and ye gentle women, my sisters, when men give Christ the primacy in their lives — the first place — the dominant place — his rightful place — they may call upon him. Then they may plead his promises. Then ask for great things and ask in victorious, conquering faith.

How much are we giving of ourselves to Christ? Here is a church family and pastor on this historic and very happy occasion. In a few moments we present a house of beautiful structure — a poem in stone — present it to our Lord with a background of emotion too tender for words. How are we going to give him this house?" He said, "I will take the house, but I want you first. I want you first. I want you first." How are we going to give this house now, in a few moments, to Christ? "I want you. I seek not yours, but you. I want you first." It is the unchanging call of our divine Saviour and Lord. "I want you first."

Fancy, if you will; try to imagine that if Jesus came in that door, visibly, stood here on this platform and said, "Let me have a word with the people." Some day we shall see him. All of us. Every eye shall see him. "And they that cherish him one day shall see him." What if he came like that and said, "Let me have a minute or two with the audience before this dedicatory occasion takes its final form." And what if he said, "Today I've come to ask if I may have you from this time on. You say you have your faults and imperfections. I know it better than you and I came on purpose to help men and women. I did'nt come to call righteous people, but sinners to repentance. I came to seek and to save people who needed seeking and saving. I want you, and I want you from today."

What would be your answer? One of two centers dominates every life: self or Christ. The self-centered life is doomed. The self-centered life is marked in the end for disaster. The self-centered anything is doomed. The self-centered nation is doomed. And great nations now are trembling in the balances and are not far from destruction because of self-centeredness or wrong motives. The self-centered organization is doomed. The self-centered man or woman is doomed.

But there is another center, and if we follow the other center, whatever comes — up or down, sick or well, rich or poor — whatever comes, it is victory if we have that other center as the dominating center of our lives — and that center is Christ. "He always wins who sides with Christ." To him no cause is lost.

Which center shall we have for today? George McDonald of Scotland pens for us this idea in one of his most frequently read poems:

THE INSPIRATION OF IDEALS

I said, 'Let me walk in the fields.'
He said, 'No, walk in the town.'

I said, 'There're no flowers there.'
He said, 'No flowers, but a crown.'

I said, 'But the skies are black.
There's nothing but noise and din.'

And He wept as He sent me back.
'There is more,' He said. 'There is sin.'

'I said, 'But the air is thick
And fogs are veiling the sun.'

And He said, 'But hearts are sick
And souls in the dark undone.'

'I said, 'I shall miss the light
And friends will miss me, they say.'

But He said, 'Choose tonight
If I am to miss you or they.'

I pleaded for time to be given.
He said, 'Is it hard to decide?

'It will not seem hard in heaven
To have followed the steps of your Guide.'

Then I cast one look at the fields
And set my face to the town.

He said, 'My child, do you yield?
Will you leave the flowers for the crown?'

Then into His hand went mine.
And into my heart came He.

And I walked in a light divine,
The path I had feared to see.

The Dedication of a Church

Oh, men and women, how beautiful and how glorious if as we give this house in dedicatory prayer, we give ourselves without reserve, without hesitation, with undisguised and wholehearted purpose. From today let Christ have us, our wills, our loyalties, our loves, our lives, our all. "Love so amazing, so divine, demands my soul, my life, my all." Let us give it today.

CHAPTER X

Civic Righteousness

CHAPTER X

Civic Righteousness*

MORE than nineteen centuries ago, James, pastor of the Jerusalem church, wrote an arresting sentence which states a principle of wide application. He wrote: "To him that knoweth to do good and doeth it not, to him it is sin." This means that the sin of omission is just as serious and really a sin as the sin of commission. That is to say, that the sin of not doing what one knows he ought to do is as sinful as doing what he knows he ought not to do. As a matter of fact Jesus put more emphasis upon the sins of omission than upon the sins of commission.

All too often, truth that we know is sadly inoperative in our lives. It was through the sin of omission that the fall came. It is through the sin of omission that all sin comes, for the sin of omission paves the way directly for the sin of commission. When in the garden the first pair failed to think about righteousness, they committed the sin that wrought their fall and the fall of the race.

Omission always precedes commission, and the commission of sin always succeeds the omission of right thinking about sin. No lesson taught by our Lord finds stronger words than this. Indeed, as I have remarked, the burden of our Saviour's teaching seems to have been upon the sin of omission. By

---

* This address was delivered in the midst of a hotly contested municipal election in Dallas, Texas. Moral issues and principles of civic righteousness were at stake. It reveals how this preacher avoided personal and partisan politics while proclaiming basic truths of righteousness for the guidance of citizens.

parables, by illustrations, and by precepts our Lord sought to enforce the great lessons of the gravity and the heinousness and the undoing of the sin of omission. One must not only refrain from wrong-doing — many think that is the ultimatum, many think that is sufficient; but our Lord plainly teaches that one must positively do that which is right.

I was in the death chamber of a citizen recently. I said: "How is it with you with respect to the world to come?" After a moment he said: "I think it will be all right, for I do not think I have done much wrong."

"But," I said, "my friend, have you done right?"

It is not a question of not doing wrong, but the positive question of doing right, doing the right commanded of God that we should do. Just there Jesus gave argument and precept and parable and illustration throughout his public ministry.

See Jesus as he came to the fig tree without fruit, looked upon it, and cursed it that self-same day — the only thing he ever cursed here upon the earth. The fig tree was guilty of the sin of omission, and for that it was cursed. Hear Jesus' parable of the talents. To one man was given five, to another two, and to another one. The five-talented man doubled his capital; the second man doubled his; but the man with one talent hid his talent in the earth and kept it for the return of his master. Then when the master came back he pronounced his condemnation severely and overwhelmingly upon the man that had hid his lord's talent. The man guilty of the sin of omission, the man who went off and did not operate, did not act, was barren and useless, upon him was pronounced the gravest curse, casting him into outer darkness.

One great lesson — there are many others — in the story of the good Samaritan is that the Priest and the Levite were guilty of the sin of omission. They passed down the Jericho road and saw a man wounded and suffering and they passed

CIVIC RIGHTEOUSNESS

by. They did not go and kick the wounded man, they did not harm him in any way. Their sin was that they failed to do for him what they ought to have done.

In the twenty-fifth chapter of Matthew where Jesus gives his most graphic picture of the final judgment, we find a mighty denunciation of the sin of omission. In that great day the Son of man shall come in his glory, and all the angels with him, and before him shall be gathered all the nations: and he shall separate them one from another, as the shepherd separates the sheep from the goats. Then the unrighteous shall gather round him saying, "Lord, when saw we thee hungry, or athirst, or a stranger, or naked, or sick, or in prison, and did not minister unto thee?" Then shall he answer them, saying, "Verily I say unto you, Inasmuch as ye did it not unto one of these least, ye did it not unto me. And these shall go away into eternal punishment: but the righteous into eternal life."

Let us recall an incident out of the Old Testament story of a small town called Meroz. It occurred in the days of Israel's battles against her enemies, and the trumpet sounded forth calling every man to battle for Israel. The one community which heeded not the call was Meroz. The men of Meroz stayed at home to look after their crops and take their ease while the others went forth to battle. In time the victory was won and the warriors returned with the great acclaim of their country, the spoils of war, and the approval of God. But in the midst of that great celebration God's angel cursed Meroz bitterly because Meroz did not come to the help of the Lord. Because Meroz did not, therefore was Meroz cursed. Meroz was blotted from the map long ago, but Meroz stands in history and literature as a symbol of the useless, the unprofitable, the barren. Meroz was doomed for doing nothing.

What was the reason Meroz did not go forth? It was not evident that Meroz was in league with the enemy; there was no intimation that Meroz was out of harmony with her country; there was no suggestion that Meroz was treasonable, giving out the secrets of her fellows. Full many a time a man does not do his duty because he is cowardly. Alas! that it should ever be so. And yet, Meroz may have stayed away from the field of battle with all its hardship and peril and wounds and death because of cowardice. Sometimes men do just that when great issues are at stake, when great principles are in the balance. Full many a time men stay away from the field of battle for no other reason than cowardice. That may have been the reason with Meroz.

Or it may have been that Meroz did not go to battle purely because of self-indulgenece. It is easier to stay at home than it is to go to battle. It is easier to swing in our hammocks and lounge at ease than to go into conflict. Meroz may have let loose the reins of self-indulgence and simply stayed at home. But whatever the cause, Meroz went down in overwhelming and eternal doom under the curse God gave her because her sin was the sin of not doing what she knew she ought to do.

All of this illustrates one of the greatest principles of the Word of God: "To him that knoweth to do good and doeth it not, to him it is sin." Now this principle finds the very widest application. It goes without argument that the extent of a man's responsibility is the extent of a man's ability. Responsibility is always measured by ability. What a man can be and what a man can do is the measure of his responsibility for being and for doing. How often this is true in this strenuous day in which we are living. And this principle is true in every relation of life. This principle is true in the Church, it is true in the home, it is true in the state, it is true everywhere.

I have named three great institutions which are divine — the home, the church, and the state. God ordained them all. We are confined too narrowly in our conception of the ordinances of God. Not only has God ordained the church as a divine institution, but he has also ordained the home, and likewise he has ordained the state.

If a Christian man shall think to live without the church, if a Christian man shall think not to take his place in the church, then shall his life be ignoble, for he is against the plan of God. If a man cares little for the home, then he loses much of life's nobility and happiness. If a man ignore the state he defaults in a God-given duty.

It is time for this application to be specially made with regard to the state. "To him that knoweth to do good and doeth it not, to him it is sin." The greatest of all the apostles said the powers that be are ordained of God. Paul was referring to civil powers, to the powers of human government, to men who direct and administer the affairs of state. Few things today are more disheartening than the attitude of good men toward the affairs of civil government. All about us we have men who are splendid men in their homes. They provide well; they guard well; they live unselfishly, and home is a gracious place. And yet, such men, full many a time, seem wholly recreant with regard to their duty to the state. All about us we see good men, men who are devoted — and noble in their devotion — to their churches. They love the ordinances, the discipline, the principles, the fellowship; they provide for their churches, they defend them, they maintain them by their sympathy and gifts and prayers. It is distressingly true that some of these same men are recreant when it comes to their duty to the affairs of civil government. Civil government is ordained of God as well as the church and men may not with impunity ignore or disregard their responsibility. Alas! full many a time good men are lukewarm, if not utterly neutral toward the affairs of state.

If we had right ideas about civil government then I tell you no Christian man would be careless with reference to any office that is to be filled in the affairs of state. What would come to pass in our churches if our members were altogether careless about the church officers? What would come to pass in our churches if the great rank and file of thoughtful men in the church should wholly ignore the choice of a pastor or allow other important officers to be chosen without due consideration and forethought and prayer? It is easy to imagine the sad consequences. And as men are obligated to give the noblest sort of consideration to the affairs of their church to the end that the officers may be such officers as they ought to be, so in like manner all citizens are obligated to God to give their noblest consideration to the affairs of civil government, to the end that every officer elevated to a position of responsibility should be the man that he ought to be. If this truth were laid to heart as it should be, then there would be a change in civil administration, there would be a dignifying of civil affairs, and there would be a glorifying of the powers of state such as we have never seen.

A great man stated recently a vital truth when he said that this state is fearfully afflicted with the bad citizenship of good men. Good men ought not to stay away from the polls; good men ought not to be indifferent toward the officers that are to be elected; good men ought not to shirk their responsibility in the leadership of affairs of civil government. There needs to be a renaissance of municipal patriotism in the state as well as in holy allegiance to our churches. Woe betide the country when her best men, her highest, cleanest, and noblest men, fail to do their full duty by the affairs of municipal patriotism and civic righteousness.

Jesus during his earthly ministry gave honor to civil government. See him in his relation to men exhibiting the loftiest and most unselfish patriotism, weeping over the proudest city of the Jews — Jerusalem. That is the exhibition of a great heart mightily filled with sanctified patriotism. And long before Jesus a Jewish patriot had cried: "If I forget thee, O

Jerusalem, let my tongue cleave to the roof of my mouth; let my right hand forget her cunning."

Municipal patriotism is one of the crying demands of every state in this great world of ours, fast being dominated by the cities. It is a great thing when men love their city. It is a great thing when the citizens take pride in their city. It is a great thing when men wince when their city is being criticised. But when a city does not wince, when she does not blush at wrong things that find endorsement and run rampant in her life, then decay has begun.

Not only is it important that every citizen should have the loftiest municipal patriotism, that every citizen should cherish the good name of his own city, but it is important that every good citizen should take his part in the affairs of his own city. That city is wonderfully fortunate which has public officials whose hearts seek to promote the city's honor. That city is wonderfully fortunate when she has citizens keenly jealous for the honor and enforcement of law. But a city is headed toward the rocks if her citizens forget to give proper emphasis to the enforcement of all law and of all right. What if a city has men with narrow vision guiding the reins of government? What if a city has men with low ideals sitting in her places of rule and authority? What if a city has officers that fail to do their duty? It is your fault and it is mine, and it is the fault of every good citizen who desires righteousness and order in the affairs of state. Oh, we need not sit under the willows and hang our harps upon the bushes and cry our eyes out if our city has men in authority of low ideals who do not care to magnify such authority. The citizens themselves are at fault, and the citizens themselves are responsible.

A brewer said recently: "The church people can beat us if they will ever get together, and we know it. But our hope is that when they make one effort they will get tired, while we will work on 365 days in the year." He spoke an awful and lementable truth. The good men in a city can change public

THE INSPIRATION OF IDEALS

sentiment. One man standing impregnable in his convictions can bring a city largely to his feet. Governor Folk did that in Missouri with one of the greatest cities on the American continent when he said: "You gentlemen will obey the Sunday law as well as the other laws." Let the good men in any community band together for law and order, and they can bring in a train of public sentiment that will overcome that which is evil by that which is good.

This principle finds its application in civil affairs as well as in religious affairs. It is your fault and mine if the affairs of government are poorly administered. It is your fault and mine if God's Day is ignored and his Word despised. Public sentiment can do what it likes. Public sentiment can bring to pass any result that it chooses. Years ago when Mr. Ingersoll, the colossal infidel, was in the heydey of his brilliancy and strength, he wanted to rent a great hall in Canada where he could assail the Christian faith. But nowhere in that great land could he find a hall. Canada said: "You may have no God down in the United States, but we have one in Canada, and not a hall that we have can be hired by any man to blaspheme God's holy name." That is public sentiment.

Oh, what a time is this for the enforcement and the dignifying of the majesty of law! Oh, what a time is this for righteous citizens to band themselves together in one great phalanx with one aim and one consecration and then things unspeakably gracious may be brought to pass in every such community. Oh, how you and I long for our city to have the right tone! I know down in my heart what the Psalmist meant when he cried out: "O Jerusalem, let my tongue cleave to the roof of my mouth; and my right hand fall paralyzed at my side if I forget thee." That is the highest patriotism, and every right thinking citizen should feel that with respect to his city's life. Oh, I tell you, my brethren, it is not municipal patriotism when a city's laws are debauched, when a city swings wide open every gate on the Lord's day purely for revenue. That is building a city with blood; that is defying the will of God; and that is inviting destruction.

It is your business and it is mine to remember that we have a duty to our civil government as well as to our churches. We must put ourselves on the side of right where there is no apology, where there is no embarrassment. Nor is that enough. We must become men who feel so deeply for our city's life, and honor, and purity, and cleanliness that we will make other people feel our influence. We must ourselves live at our highest and noblest, for righteous lives count more than anything else. A good man in a city is worth more than a public park; a good man in a city is like a light shining out over the storm-tossed sea for the people who need to be brought safely to shore.

Alas! that the truth uttered so long ago by James should frequently find application in the realm of religious duties. The man who is a Christian at heart and knows that he ought to take his place in the church with God's people but does it not, to him it is sin. The secret disciple also who does not openly confess Christ Jesus as Saviour and Lord, to him it is sin. Forget not that Jesus said: "He that is not with me is against me."

Oh, men and women who know your duties, your obligations, your responsibilities in the home, the church, and the state, I beseech you not to be remiss in the faithful performance of every duty which these three divine institutions have a God-given right to expect from you. Thus, and only thus, may we hope for domestic, spiritual, and civic righteousness to be established in our beloved land.